D0215404

UNSCIENTIFIC PSYCHOLOGY

NATIONAL UNIVERSITY
LIBRARY   LOS ANGELES

UNSCIENTIFIC PSYCHOLOGY

A Cultural–Performatory Approach to Understanding Human Life

FRED NEWMAN **and** LOIS HOLZMAN

PRAEGER

**Westport, Connecticut
London**

Library of Congress Cataloging-in-Publication Data

Newman, Fred.
    Unscientific psychology : a cultural–performatory approach to
understanding human life / Fred Newman and Lois Holzman.
      p. cm.
    Includes bibliographical references and index.
    ISBN 0–275–95412–9 (alk. paper)
    1. Psychology—Philosophy. I. Holzman, Lois, 1946– .
II. Title.
BF38.N45 1996
150—dc20   96–2801

British Library Cataloguing in Publication Data is available.

Copyright © 1996 by Fred Newman and Lois Holzman

All rights reserved. No portion of this book may be
reproduced, by any process or technique, without the
express written consent of the publisher.

Library of Congress Catalog Card Number: 96–2801
ISBN: 0–275–95412–9

First published in 1996

Praeger Publishers, 88 Post Road West, Westport, CT 06881
An imprint of Greenwood Publishing Group, Inc.

Printed in the United States of America

The paper used in this book complies with the
Permanent Paper Standard issued by the National
Information Standards Organization (Z39.48–1984).

10 9 8 7 6 5 4 3 2 1

Copyright Acknowledgments

The authors and publisher gratefully acknowledge permission to use excerpts from the following:

The Birth of the Clinic by Michel Foucault. Copyright © 1973 by Michel Foucault. Reprinted by permission of Pantheon Books, a division of Random House, Inc. and by permission of Tavistock/Routledge.

The Collected Works of L. S. Vygotsky, Vol. I by L. S. Vygotsky. New York: Plenum, 1987. Reprinted by Permission of Plenum Publishing Corp.

Constructing the Subject by Kurt Danziger. Copyright © Cambridge University Press 1990. Reprinted with the permission of Cambridge University Press.

Deconstructing Developmental Psychology by E. Burman. London: Routledge, 1994. Reprinted by permission of Routledge.

Remarks on the Philosophy of Psychology, Vol. I by L. Wittgenstein. Copyright © 1980 by Basil Blackwell. All rights reserved. Not previously published in German. Reprinted by permission of The University of Chicago Press and by permission of Blackwell Publishers.

This book is dedicated to our teachers:
Lenora Fulani, Kenneth Gergen, Lev Vygotsky, Ludwig
Wittgenstein, and all of our many colleagues, students,
and friends in our developing community.

Contents

Preface

For many years we published very little. After all, first and foremost, we are practitioners, activists. For the last few years (and the next few years) many books written together and separately have been in circulation. But we remain, most fundamentally, activists. Our earliest joint writing effort, in 1979, was a monograph called *The Practice of Method*. The title was meant to distinguish our work from the more orthodox left "method of practice." Practice is not our method. Rather, method is what we continuously practice. To us, method is not something *applied* to something. In our view, it is, to paraphrase Marx, an activity "for itself" as opposed to "in itself." In Vygotsky's language, method is a "tool and result" as opposed to a "tool for result."

Our practical–critical activity over the past two decades has been developmental beyond our wildest dreams. Our community, which is not defined geographically, numbers in the tens of thousands and is growing daily. We sometimes jokingly refer to our development community as not so much a 60s-style "university without walls" as postmodernist "walls without a university." Many, many people "outside" our community wish to know more about what we are doing. And we have grown slightly more confident that we can tell our story without totally distorting it. But, again, we are primarily practitioners and activists. Accordingly, we hope that you, the reader, will practice our books more than just read them. How? Let this and our other works help you. In the end, we believe, no book is worth writing unless it changes at least some people's "form of life." It has ours. We will be delighted if it does yours.

Acknowledgments

In addition to our intellectual mentors, we would like to thank our coworkers on this project, those without whom the creation of this book in its final form would not have been possible: Phyllis Goldberg for her invaluable copyediting and editing; Kim Svoboda for her tireless typing and retyping of the many, constantly evolving versions of the manuscript; Kate Gardner, Chris Helm, Kim Sabo, and Karen Steinberg, our research team who helped us pull it all together.

We would also like to thank the many friends, colleagues, and students for encouragement and support for and during the writing of this book. These include, among others, the participants in Newman's The Performance of Philosophy seminars and in Holzman's Empire State College study groups.

Finally, this book could not have been written without the two decades of hard work of our colleagues at the East Side Institute for Short Term Psychotherapy, the East Side Center for Social Therapy, the Barbara Taylor School, and the Castillo Cultural Center, whose continuous creative production of developmental tools-and-results gave us something to say.

UNSCIENTIFIC PSYCHOLOGY

1

Introduction

You can fight, hope and even believe without believing scientifically.
—*Ludwig Wittgenstein*

PHILOSOPHY, SCIENCE, AND PSYCHOLOGY

If, as seems reasonable to assume, you are now reading something, must there be *something* that you are reading? If what you are reading is an introduction, must it be an introduction to *something?* These seemingly abstract and philosophical questions and others in their "family" are to a large extent the quite practical subject matter of this book. What turns on them, in our opinion, is nothing less than whether human beings—personally and as a species—will continue to grow and develop. This book is not an analysis or critique of current trends in pop psychology or an exposé of unscientific psychological practices being carried out in clinics, schools, universities, and research laboratories. Likewise, it neither praises recent moves to bring psychology closer methodologically and substantively to other sciences (such as neurology, biochemistry, genetics, and cognitive science), nor pleads for psychology to become more scientific. If the book does "contain a message" (as opposed to merely being a provocation), it is this: scientific psychology has contributed significantly to the cultural, political, and moral morass we find ourselves in as the twenty-first century dawns.

As the modern study of what philosophers and psychologists call the subjective, psychology, born (as was science) of Western philosophy, outwardly shunned its mother almost immediately (all the while incorporating most of her belief system and pathology) and began to shape itself in the "healthy" image of modern science, the sibling it most idolized, and to commodify itself in the manner of capitalism, the father it ultimately revered. But such posturing has not advanced human growth at either the personal or the species level. We believe that the humane development of our species requires the ongoing creation of what philosopher Ludwig Wittgenstein called new forms of life (as opposed to new forms of alienation), particularly but not exclusively new forms of subjective life. Such activity, as we see it, will not (cannot) be scientific for the simple reason that science normatively precludes it. What it can be is a cultural approach to understanding that is relational, radically democratic, and noninterpretive—a distinctly unscientific psychology; indeed, not a psychology at all but a qualitatively new kind of play, a continuous uncommodified performance of subjectivity.

In *Lev Vygotsky: Revolutionary Scientist* (1993), we repeatedly raised the question, What are revolutionary psychologists to do? This work is, in a sense, a sequel to that book, in which we provided a mostly theoretical discussion of Lev Vygotsky's contribution to creating the kind of revolutionary science activity needed to reinitiate human development. We presented our reading of Vygotsky as an affirmation of the philosophical and political power of the fundamental socialness of human beings. Here we expand that discussion, locating Vygotsky as a "pre-postmodernist" who serves as a bridge between the stifling (pseudo)scientific psychology of modernism and the possibilities presented by its current postmodernization. In telling the story of how psychology was born of philosophy and constructed (commodified) itself in the image of science and capitalism, we also draw attention to what makes building a new, unscientific psychology such an arduous task.

Our story begins (only in stories are there beginnings!) in ancient Greece, for it is here that we find the ancestors of the gods of modern science and scientific psychology—Truth, the Particular and the Individual, Systemization, Explanation, and Interpretation, to name a few of the most powerful. Part I, "Some Stories of Philosophy," is a series of narratives about philosophy's life and death, a kind of postmodern introduction to (actually an obituary of) philosophy. Philosophy (the ancient Greeks) defined what thinking is. (Among other things, it insisted that thinking is definable.) It solidified duality as both an ontological characteristic of life on earth (and beyond) and an epistemological characteristic of understanding. In addition, it gave rise to systems of thought that contain their own particular dualities and that, although born in the West, have come (for better or worse) to rule the world: religion, politics, science and technology, and psychology.

Among these children/stories of philosophy, it is psychology—the most conceptually impoverished—that became in the late twentieth century the most politically powerful. For it was psychology that took upon itself the task of transforming millennia of philosophical musings about the twin human capacities of abstraction and self-consciousness into systematic and scientific investigation. Disguising itself as science, psychology insinuated itself into modern society as the voice of reason (and the reason for voice and other uniquely human traits). Part II, "Psychology's Unheard-of Story," shows how this new discipline succeeded in perpetuating many of the ancient myths and in creating new ones of its own, how it constructed new investigative practices and knowledge claims, and how it created a market for itself, often with unabashed opportunism. The myth that is psychology—it has discovered nothing (for, we would insist, there is nothing to discover!), but shamelessly invented its subject matter—is identifiable with three of its more destructive pieces of pseudoscience: the myth of the individual, the myth of mental illness, and the myth of development. Taken together, they effectively form the myth of psychology.

As the commodification of subjectivity/cognition, scientific psychology became, during the twentieth century, the dominant product of market demands during an era of super- or metacommodification. However, few details of Western economic history, although critical to our stories, are provided; to do so, we felt, would have been to write a different book. Ours is primarily a story of the corruption of intellectual production.

Throughout our narrative, we weave postmodern insights and analyses that have inspired us. While we do not agree with all of them, we find cause for optimism in the voluminous social constructionist, deconstructionist, activity-theoretic/cultural psychology, feminist, and psychological philosophy literature of the present day. The interest some contemporary psychologists are showing in Ludwig Wittgenstein's antifoundationalism is, in our opinion, particularly significant. What seems clear is that systematic philosophy's nearly 2500-year metaphysical reign (and, perhaps, modern science's 350-year reign as *the* singular absolute paradigm of understanding) is coming to an end. What will the world be like without it? The current postmodernization of psychology—an unprecedented rejection of science as a superpower and *scientism* as its ideology—suggests that history might continue far more developmentally unfettered by moribund philosophy, absolutist science, and scientific psychology.

ACTIVITY SPEAKS LOUDER THAN STORIES

The German essayist and critic Walter Benjamin has said that "mankind, which in Homer's time was an object of contemplation for the Olympian gods, now is one for itself. Its self-alienation has reached such a degree that it can experience its own destruction as an aesthetic pleasure of the first order." The recent turn away from the modernist view of knowledge, understanding, and meaning as absolute, truth-referential objects and toward further analysis of conceptual frameworks has brought *storytelling* out of the humanities and onto center stage in social science thinking. Stories, narratives, metaphor, and myth are some of the postmodern "stuff" of knowing and understanding. Truth, reason, logic, and argument, members of the family of conceptions long associated in Western thought with knowledge, understanding, and meaning, are, it is being said, becoming relics of a bygone era. They form the methodological foundations of modern science and technology as essential elements in what has become, over hundreds of years, the paradigmatic modernist explanatory epistemology. But explanation as *the*—or even *a*—way of knowing is currently being challenged in what has been termed (we think accurately) an "epistemological revolution" (for example, McNamee, 1993).

The influential American psychologist Jerome Bruner describes it as a turn away from a *paradigmatic posture*—where what is sought are explanations (general laws, categories, and absolute deductive or inductive truth)—to a *narrative posture* (1984, see also, Bruner, 1993). From the narrative posture, knowing and understanding are interpretive, not explanatory. Meaning resides neither "out there" in the objects it supposedly denotes nor "in our minds," but in our conversations, in our discourse, in the language we create and use. We are a meaning-making, not merely an information-processing, species. We live and make sense through the socially constructed narratives (stories) we create (generate, construct).

This is not to say that storytelling and narrative are newly discovered human phenomena, nor that their significance in the formation of cultural and personal identity had not been noted previously. What is relatively new, however, is the recognition that stories and storytelling are *psychologically* important and interesting, especially for developmental psychologists and psychotherapists. Of particular interest to us is the role of narrative and the narrative posture in the mounting critique of modern social science ideology and methodology.

In our view, a constructionist and narrative perspective of human understanding is a valuable step away from modernist scientific absolutism. Moreover, replacing the dominant metaphor for understanding—seeing and sight—with the metaphor of voice (the medium of conversation) has exposed the gendered nature of Western thought (and thought about thought). We ourselves have been inspired by and have made use of the important work produced by this young tradition. At the same time, we think that it has not made a complete break with a modernist worldview, and that a move beyond stories—to what we call *revolutionary, relational activity*—is not only necessary but possible.

You might wonder, then, why we refer to what we are doing in the pages that follow as telling stories—specifically, some "stories of philosophy" and "psychology's unheard-of story." On the one hand, we are making the narrative–constructionist point that these are only possible stories: what we have to say is neither history (the history of philosophy or the history of psychology) nor truth. But as contemporary pop culture repeatedly shows us (even as postmodern thought has not yet done so), while stories may have no claim to the truth they still have an impact on all of us to varying degrees. In this sense (and no doubt in others), some stories are better than others.

On the other hand, we want to highlight the point that the notions of story, narrative, and even interpretation itself are not outside, but part of the very tradition we are trying to explicate critically. As we see it, the narrative posture is a critical posture. Narrative and storytelling are valuable critical tools for exposing the methodological and ideological biases of modern social science. They are, and they produce, a reform of the dominant paradigm. But they are not, in our opinion, *practical–critical, revolutionary, or development tools and results* (in Lev Vygotsky's sense). This difference, which is central to our own work, will, we hope, become clear as we proceed.

The narrative posture is, among other things, a tradition subtextually preoccupied (if not intentionally) with truth. Many narrative–constructionist theoreticians and practitioners attempt and sometimes claim to have abandoned truth via the method of interpretation. For example, in contrast to traditional psychotherapeutic practice in which the therapist replaces the client's "story" with "the truth" (that is, the core, the essence, the deeper real meaning), narrative–constructionist therapy has no preconceived notion of what is true. As Lynn Hoffman, a prominent psychotherapist in this tradition, puts it: "Postmodern therapists do not believe in essences. Knowledge, being socially arrived at, changes and renews itself in each moment of interaction. There are no prior meanings hiding in stories or texts. A therapist with this view will expect a new and hopefully more useful narrative to surface during the conversation, but will see this narrative as spontaneous rather than planned. The conversation, not the therapist, is the author" (Hoffman, 1993, p. 18).

Regardless of whether or not therapists and others appeal explicitly to some notion of truth (as, for example, Anderson and Goolishian do when they refer to clients' "narrative truths, the coherent truths in their storied lives," 1993, p. 30), it seems to us that a preoccupation with truth is at the core of the narrative posture. The concept of truth is embedded in the meanings of fiction, narrative, story, and interpretation. They are, ultimately, truth-referential. An interpretation is a proposition that is true *under certain circumstances;* that is, given a certain interpretation, one takes something to be true.

Gergen and Kaye (1993) make a similar point in urging that we must go beyond narrative reconstruction if we are to create a therapeutic approach that is not based in truth. Seeing narrative as the system of understanding within which and through which a person lives her or his life, they say, expresses a "commitment to narrative" that is problematic: "To be committed to a given story of self, to adopt it as 'now true for me,' is vastly to limit one's possibilities of relating. To believe that one is *successful* is thus as debilitating in its own way as believing that one is a *failure*. Both are only stories after all" (Gergen and Kaye, 1993, p. 179). Seeing some stories as more true than others hardly eliminates truth; it merely pushes it back to another level. The commitment to narrative is, ultimately, a commitment to truth.

Gergen and Kaye also take issue with how therapists understand the value of coconstructing narrative in therapy. According to the usual accountings, it provides clients either with a new way to see the world or with a structure for action. To Gergen and Kaye, these views reinforce an overly static, individualistic, and nondevelopmental understanding of human beings, narrative, and therapy. They offer a more relational alternative. Drawing on Wittgenstein's concepts of *language-games* and *form of life*, they suggest that narrative gains meaning and has utility within a particular language-game that is embedded in "broader forms of life" (Gergen and Kaye, 1993, p. 177). A story, within their interpretation of Wittgenstein, is a "situated action in itself, a performance with illocutionary effects" (p. 178). The meaning and effect are relational; their value is pragmatic, deriving from their location as a move in a particular form of relationship, or game.

We are in agreement with Gergen and Kaye's critique. We share their desire to push beyond narrative reconstruction. While sympathetic to the thrust of their analysis, however, we nevertheless find it in need of friendly *completion* (in Vygotsky's sense). Going beyond narrative reconstruction requires, in our view, going beyond the narrative posture. It means going beyond creating new stories to creating new forms of life. (Stories are, after all, about life.) It means going beyond the equation of meaning with use—what, to us, is an all too common overly pragmatic understanding of Wittgenstein's notion of language and language-games. We are among those (Newman and Holzman, 1993; Shotter, 1991, 1993a; Shotter and Newman, 1995; van der Merwe and Voestermans, 1995) who have pointed out that while certain of his formulations clearly point to a meaning–use equation, others suggest that the value of language-games is that they allow language to be seen as activity, as a form of life (for example, §23 in *Philosophical Investigations*: "The term 'language-game' is meant to bring into prominence the fact that the *speaking* of language is part of an activity, or of a form of life" [Wittgenstein, 1953]).

Our reading of Wittgenstein is more activity-theoretic than pragmatic. We see his "form of life-ism" (not to mention the form of his life) as an attempt to create a mode of comprehension that is not only not relative to truth or reality but not relative to anything at all precisely because it is relational, and life-as-lived relationality requires such radical monism.

By activity-theoretic, we are referring to the tradition known as *activity theory* within contemporary culturally oriented cognitive, educational, and developmental psychology. What Marx in his early writings identified as "revolutionary, practical–critical activity" (1973) was advanced into psychology by Vygotsky (1978, 1987, 1993). For Vygotsky learning, development, and more specific psychological processes within this continuously transforming dialectical unity are social–cultural–historical activities—not properties of individuals, not internal, mental processes. To our way of thinking, the Vygotskian notion of activity is a far better candidate than the story for making a break with the dualistic and cognitive philosophical–psychological paradigm. A story, after all, entails something other than the story in order for it to be a story. Stories require a stepping back and, thereby, an "aboutness" which is separate from the story. In this way, regardless of whether they are socially constructed and reconstructed or not, they perpetuate a model in which growth and development are seen to come from understanding. Activity is, in contrast, creatively emergent, not relative to anything other than itself; it is fully self-reflexive. It is the social–historical form of life in which understanding is inseparable from development.

From our developmental, relational, activity-theoretic perspective, the "aboutness" of stories presents two problems. First, there is the concern with idealism. If there are nothing but stories, if narrative is or creates reality, as many who take a narrative posture suggest (for example, the authors in McNamee and Gergen, 1993), then how—within the narrative framework—is a story to be distinguished from everything (anything) else? Doesn't whatever is outside the narrative or narrated reality have to be inside it?

Many narrative–constructionist therapists and others attempt to resolve this paradox by appealing to the concept of *the self*. Narrative realities are really personal realities (there is no other kind). People construct their identities or sense of self through stories. As we have already noted, this is generally understood to be the utility of narrative reconstruction—to construct a better story/self/identity so as to live a better life.

The linking of narrative to self and identity formation can also be seen in developmental research, where children's ability to understand and tell stories at a very young age is said to be essential to the emergence of self (that is, to the differentiation of self from other). The self–other dualism is not unique to studies of narrative, however. It is the framework for most current developmental studies (stories) of language and discourse in general. Infants and babies are described as "transcending their private world" or "co-creating intersubjectivity" as they dialogue with the significant adults in their environment. Dialogue is a vehicle through which infants and babies are able to attain higher levels of "relatedness" (see, for example,

Dore, 1985; Stern, 1985, 1990; Trevarthen and Hubley, 1978; Wertsch, 1985a, 1991). Language is seen as a tool used to create the self and to share personal knowledge. The emergence of a sense of narrated self in the very young child through the coconstruction of narratives is a significant developmental milestone—the beginning of "the autobiographical history that ultimately evolves into the life story a patient may first present to a therapist" (Stern, 1985, p. 174).

It is this powerful role of narrative in creating the self that poses for us a second problem with narrative's "aboutness." For we agree that storytelling, as it has evolved over thousands of years in Western culture, is constructive of the self; that it is "about" the very self it is constructing is precisely what is problematic from a developmental, emergent, practice of method perspective. Far from being relational, identity and self (even, or especially, "the social self" and "the relational self" that are now being written about) are antirelational. The self and the narratives through which it is constructed are a dominant feature of modern and postmodern alienation. They express a commitment to an individuated ontology; eliminating the hidden self does not eliminate the self–other duality. The sense of otherness (what is "outside" the narrative, what is "other than" the story) entailed in the notion of narrative is, we believe, identity-based, not relation-based. To put this matter another way, self, like alienation (and, more generally, dualism), is effectively used, in our culture, to resolve the *paradoxicality* of human life. An activity-theoretic approach is more concerned to give expression to this self-referential paradoxicality than to resolve it coherently (scientifically). For us, a relation-based view of understanding demands the practical acceptance of paradoxicality.

Our longstanding concern is that human beings be able to create new forms of life, to create development. We believe that to do so we must practically–critically engage alienation. The self—alienation's author and protagonist—must be deconstructed, not reconstructed. For this task we must, necessarily, move beyond the narrative posture. In its tendency to reify the story, the narrative posture obscures the *narrative activity* (just as, for Wittgenstein, our ordinary use of language obscures the fact that "only in the stream of thought and life do words have meaning," 1967, §173). The story is separated from the process (the relational activity) that produces it, and becomes an instrumental and critical tool for the reconstruction of self and societal adaptation without engaging historical adaptation (that is, alienation). As we see it, a development tool is not instrumental. It is, following Vygotsky, "prerequisite and product, simultaneously the tool and the result" (1978, p. 65). Narrative activity is developmental insofar as it is a tool-and-result of creating new forms of life (not a tool for the result/purpose of making better stories). What gets generated from this relational activity, that is, from cocreating the dialectical unity of stories told and untold, of the said and the unsaid, is more activity, more history. It is a nonreified storytelling—an invitation to relational completion by the continuous activity of creating new forms of life—that we have struggled to create.

Part III, "The Practice of Method: A New Epistemology for an Unscientific Psychology," considers some of what we have created. We discuss the "ecologically valid" environment (community) that we and our thousands of associates have developed over a quarter of a century, the linking of Vygotsky and Wittgenstein as both "tool-and-result" of this "practice of method" community and the emergence of social therapy—an explicitly unscientific and unphilosophical cultural alternative to scientific, truth-dominated, clinical psychology. Vygotsky's and Wittgenstein's views on meaning and language (making) permeate our stories, our unscientific psychology, and our community. Indeed, though we make little explicit reference to linguistics and philosophy of language, we see this entire book as a discussion of language. In the final analysis Vygotsky helps us to "do in" psychology (make it vanish) precisely as Wittgenstein "did in" philosophy (made it vanish). Ultimately we complete Vygotsky by rejecting his project of creating a sociocultural, scientific psychology, abandoning psychology altogether in favor of an unscientific cultural (performatory) approach to the practical–critical understanding of human life.

The psychological community will, we suspect, be aghast at our conclusions, although not because they necessarily disagree with all or even much of what we say. At the 1995 meetings of the American Psychological Association in New York City, thousands of practitioners listened in basic agreement to postmodernist, critical–theoretic discussions of psychological issues. But in public and private conversations they were quick to note that giving up the pseudoscientific rhetoric of clinical psychology would cost them credibility and dollars via third-party payments. "Science-talk" is the coin of the clinical realm. It might not cure, many clinicians will agree, but it does procure. We clinicians may laugh at *DSM-IV* in the privacy of our own meetings and, moreover, make little or no use of it in our efforts to help our clients rid themselves of emotional pain. But we articulate just enough "science-speak" to fill out the forms printed by the bureaucracy to stay validated and paid in this age of managed care. Obviously, this is not true for all clinicians. Yet among those who profess to be outraged will be many who are simply performing as good old American cash-value pragmatists. And what choice do they have?

If the psychological community will be provoked into (a partially mock) outrage, the scientific community, we predict, will react in its usual arrogant above-it-all way. In one of the more pompous books that we have read in recent years, *Higher Superstition: The Academic Left and Its Quarrels with Science* (1994), Paul Gross and Norman Levitt "take on" the academic left community (postmodernists, feminists, neo-Marxists, social constructionists, followers of Derrida, Foucault, and so on) for its ignorance of hard science. The book is a remarkably ill-argued (by any, including scientific, standards) anecdotal history of recent writings by the postmodernist crowd which points out the many scientific "gaffes" (the authors' word) that permeate critiques of science. Some of what they say is accurate. But for Gross and Levitt to employ un-self-consciously the *criteria of science* (its epistemology and methodology) to critique writings designed primarily to discredit the criteria of science is about as arrogantly unscientific as one (or in this case, two) can get. Science, while more and more on the defensive in recent years, is like that. It insists that its method be used to determine the validity of anything and everything—including its own method. When the nineteenth- and twentieth-century metaphysicians and, before them, the church Fathers did this, the scientists (much younger then) and the philosophers of science (their spokespersons) protested bitterly.

But this is not the worst of Gross and Levitt's defense of science. Conspicuously absent from the author index (and the book) is Lev Vygotsky. Ludwig Wittgenstein is mentioned only once, and that in a short and innocuous listing of important Western philosophers. It is not their virtual absence from the book but what it reveals that is significant. Gross and Levitt do not, for the most part, consider the failure of the (hard) scientific community to critique in any serious way the so-called social sciences. Vain (and pragmatic) to their paradigmatic core, the hard sciences have (with some few exceptions) looked on smugly as psychology (for example) prostituted serious scientific method in an effort to look like (and pay like) physics. Indeed, the breeding ground of a good deal of the postmodern critique of science is this authoritarian politic of paradigm control as practiced by the scientific establishment.

Our work (like Stephen DeBerry's valuable study of consciousness and quantum physics, *The Externalization of Consciousness and the Psychopathology of Everyday Life)* is not particularly a critique of "hard science" and its accompanying technology. Rather, it is a critique of the hegemony of the modernist scientific and epistemological paradigm as applied to the understanding of human life and relationships. Beyond critique, it is an effort to display a cultural approach to such understanding which consciously rejects the modernist scientific paradigm (by way of denying the validity of modernism, scientism, and paradigmism). Gross and Levitt's failure to consider the role of social science (and the hard sciences' unwillingness to critique it, which is the political posture of the academic right) makes their critique of the academic left a disingenuous and unscientific political polemic. There is little the left can take credit for these days. But the academic left can properly be pleased by its ongoing efforts to critique and dismantle the antidevelopmental, pseudoscientific, and dehumanizing social science of psychology. Gross and Levitt's political tract would be far better directed at the capitulation by the hard science community. The "weak link," that is, the so-called social sciences, have even gotten physics in trouble. Such is the consequence of not dealing with impostors just because they are of pragmatic help to you.

Often on the lecture circuit we are asked, "But what will happen to science if your unscientific approach prevails?" Our first answer is "Nothing." Science as a method for studying (and controlling) nature has an extraordinary track record and will, no doubt, continue to evolve—hopefully in the full service of all of humankind. It is the gross overstatement of scientific method (its transformation into a metaphysics or religion and, most particularly, its mistaken application to the study and the living of human life) that we hope to alter. Our second answer is "We don't know." For the development and general employment of an unscientific, cultural approach to the study and understanding of human life will, no doubt, impact profoundly on all of life, including the activity of hard science, which is, after all, a critical cultural posit of a Western-dominated world (see, for example, Lerner 1991). No, Gross and Levitt and others like them need not defend science against our work. For it is the tyranny and patriarchy of the modernist epistemology that we challenge. If hard science overidentifies with it, then hard science must pay the price of such a political act, much as the soft and silly scientific psychology is now doing. For while the left has failed shockingly in the field of political revolution here in the twentieth century, it has done very well indeed in the area of cultural revolution. *Unscientific Psychology* and our other work are proudly a part of that culturally revolutionary postmodern tradition.

Part I

SOME STORIES OF PHILOSOPHY

The emergence of philosophy in the West is, in our opinion, quite properly associated with the Greeks and, most particularly, with Plato and his student/critic Aristotle. While we in no way adhere to what we believe is the transparently biased position that either explicitly or implicitly identifies the ancient Greeks and ancient Greece as somehow superior to other cultures, we do think the self-conscious concern with abstraction (and the abstract concern with self-consciousness) which is the very "essence" of Greek philosophy is, for better or worse, a recognizable development of the human species. Why it happened in Greece is neither an uninteresting nor an unimportant question. It is simply not our question. *That* it happened in Greece seems to us undeniable. Indeed, seeing it fundamentally as one of many particular extended moments of species development undercuts

---

My modest knowledge of the history of ancient philosophy comes mainly from two former teachers of mine at Stanford University: the distinguished scholars John Goheen and John Mothershead. Obviously, they bear no responsibility whatsoever for what I have done with their marvelous lectures some thirty-five years later.

The logical and mathematical formulations contained herein are imprecise, although, of course, not intentionally so. I have both studied and taught logic at the university level. Yet I have never thought of myself as having any "depth" at all in this area. Nonetheless, the ideas of the great thinkers in mathematics and logic have indirectly influenced my thinking about related subject matter in this and other writings that Lois Holzman and I have done, separately and together. As such, it always seems important to share these ideas honestly (although perhaps inaccurately) with our readers.

In the final analysis, she and I take full responsibility for our stories.—F. N.

claims of moral or intellectual superiority. That human beings first stand erect in central Africa or northern Asia and build extraordinary civilizations in northern Africa, India, China, and the Americas no more accords superiority to black, brown, yellow, or red people than does self-conscious abstraction make white people better than anyone else.

That said, in becoming the author/parent of Western religion (scholasticized Christianity), politics (the socially contracted state), science and technology (the mathematicization and objectification of nature), and psychology (the Cartesian, and ultimately Kantian, mediation of mind and body), Western philosophy has ruled the world for the past 2500 years. In spite of dramatic transformations over the millennia, such core conceptions as truth, reality, certainty, cause, particularity, and self and other have shaped the way we human beings think, talk, and even dream about thinking, speaking, dreaming, and the infinity of other things we do and experience. Now, however, the ideological continuity—the calcified conceptual framework—is cracking. The enormously rich and developmental era of systematic philosophy is, to our way of thinking, drawing to a close. Philosophy, we believe, is dead. If and when the great-great-grandchildren of those who are reading this book now should look back, we predict that what will appear to them as the singularly significant event of this, the twentieth century, is likely to be not the death of communism, but the death of philosophy.

Western religion, politics, science and technology, and psychology are philosophy's principal children/stories—extraordinary epic narratives which in themselves and in connection with one another have ideologically overdetermined much of human history and life for millennia. But in our own time philosophy, the mother and author of them all, has herself finally succumbed. In Part II we will present what we think is persuasive evidence that philosophy, which in its final years suffered from self-inflicted wounds, was eventually destroyed by psychology—the deadly and dull child not only of philosophy but of science. With philosophy dead, will further development(s) be possible? And what of the children/stories she created? Do they continue to transform—and, if so, how? Postmodernism is not, as Francis Fukuyama argues, "the end of history" (Fukuyama, 1989). It is, in our view, the continuation of history without philosophy.

2

Between the *Iliad* and the *Odyssey*

In *The Origin of Consciousness in the Breakdown of the Bicameral Mind*, Julian Jaynes (1976) speculates that a quite remarkable human species development took place in ancient times somewhere "between" the *Iliad* and the *Odyssey*. These great epic poems have commonly been attributed to someone named Homer who was supposed to have completed them by around 800 B.C. However, many scholars have thought for some time that there may never have been such a single historical person. Both works may in fact be products of an oral storytelling tradition, with hundreds (or perhaps thousands) of years between the two. From this point of view they are better understood as compilations of tales told in various locations, all pretty much within the boundaries of what we now call ancient Greece; that is, they are artifacts of historical and anthropological significance as well as works of literary art. As such, not only the substance of these tales but their very form reveals something of human species development. Jaynes contends, in fact, that the difference between the *Iliad* and the *Odyssey* is not merely "in the story" but in how the stories are told.

If the two works are indeed the expression of many voices rather than just one (Homer's), they may more reasonably be viewed as evidence of a historical, developmental, cultural transformation of the human activity of storytelling in particular and human communicating in general. This is how Jaynes sees them. He urges us to consider a significant change in their voice(s). In the *Iliad*, he suggests, we have storytelling without self-conscious, creative human agency; that is, the narrator is merely the instrument for conveying what he or she has been told by others, from without or—more significantly—by another voice within. In the *Odyssey*, by contrast, the narrator's voice is at once that of the teller and the creator of the story. From this evidence Jaynes argues for a "breakdown" of the "bicameral mind" (one part of which speaks of what it has been told by the other), and the birth of self-consciousness—an awareness (leaving aside whether it is valid or not) of oneself as the unified, "unicameral" author of one's words.

These, at least, are our speculations on Jaynes's speculations. They are of interest to us because they set the stage for our somewhat less speculative thinking about the social–cultural–historical construction of human consciousness from the pre-Socratics to the late-twentieth-century "theory of mind" speculators. If nothing else, Jaynes's provocative science-fictionalized anthropology about Greek thinking and speaking lends support to a developmental framework for viewing the Greek experience. It helps us to consider philosophy and its evolution in Greece as the ideological consolidation of an extended moment in species development. The essence of that extended moment and its consolidation appear to have much to do with two interrelated, uniquely human activities/states of being: self-consciousness and abstracting.

THE PRE-SOCRATICS

In the story that is Western philosophy, it all begins with the "fragments" that remain from the pre-Socratics. Socrates (?470 B.C.–?399 B.C.) is, of course, the Christ figure of philosophy: ethically pure, falsely accused of corrupting young minds, dying as a consequence of betrayal (and hemlock); all of philosophical history is understood as coming either before Him or after Him.

In standard introductions to Western philosophy, the first pre-Socratic character we meet is usually Thales. His appearance on the scene is dated around 585 B.C., the time at which he is said to have predicted a solar eclipse. With little actual evidence, even by the criteria typically used to interpret "fragments," we are taught that Thales said everything was made of water. If our teacher has any pedagogic skills at all, Thales' claim is scrutinized not so much for its truth value as for its form or, perhaps, its meaning.

What is meant by saying that everything (as opposed, for example, to something in particular) is made of something (some one thing)? What does *is made of* mean? What is the sociocultural environment or occasion for asking what something (no less everything) is made of? It is one thing to ask, or know, how something is made. But what, if anything, does that have to do with seeking to know what that something is made of? And what of the universality of Thales' claim? *What is everything*? Is it only physical things? Is everything a list of all (physical and/or mental) things? What is the source of the notion that everything could be (or should be, or might be, or is) made of a single thing? And what kind of thing might that be? What kind of thing is water, for example? Indeed, what is water? Is it anything other than what everything is made of? Is water made of water? If not, what is water made of? Etc., etc., etc.

If one is still disposed these days toward a "containment" metaphor, it could be said that all (or at least the very essence) of philosophy (or, at a minimum, philosophical questioning) is "contained in" Thales' fragment. The other pre-Socratics, such as Anaximander, Anaximenes, Pythagoras, Xenophanes, Heraclitus, Parmenides, and Empedocles, as well as those contemporaries of Socrates who are "pre-Socratic" by convention (among them Anaxagoras, Zeno, Melissus, Leucippus, Democritus, and Protagoras), attempt to answer some of the preceding philosophical questions and, in so doing, raise still others. In a less academic context, we have sometimes referred to this activity as asking big questions about little things (for example, Newman, 1996). After all, "everything" is a qualitatively little, ordinary, concrete thing(s), while "What is it made of?" is a qualitatively big question. In any case, the philosophical mode (if not yet systematic philosophy proper)—the self-conscious examination of abstraction and its inverse—is, it seems, well established by the time Socrates begins to stroll the streets of Athens as an itinerant teacher.

Socrates takes the next critical developmental step of questioning the activity of questioning itself. He thereby brings together these new human activities/states of abstracting and self-consciousness. Socrates moves beyond the question "What is everything made of?" and the various answers that his predecessors had come up with (water; air; a primordial ooze; numbers; atoms; the elements earth, water, air, and fire; change; permanence) to an examination of method—most particularly the method by which we might consider answering such questions. How, Socrates dialectically and dialogically inquires, can we ask big questions about little things or, alternatively, self-consciously abstract questions about concrete matters? How is it that the mind engages in this rather remarkable activity? Indeed, is that really what we are doing? If so, how is it possible? (If we take Jaynes's thesis seriously, remember that this was a relatively new activity at this time in human history.)

It is this self-reflexive "spin" that establishes both the what and the how of philosophy. In fact, it is probably Socrates, and surely Plato (?427 B.C.–?347 B.C.), the author of the dialogues that have come down to us as the teachings of Socrates, who can be said to have thereby created/discovered/systemized the subjects that comprise philosophy—methodology, epistemology, and ontology. (Cosmology and its question "Where does it all come from?" predate the Greeks, although in the *Timaeus* Plato produces a cosmology to support his epistemology and ontology.) Thus philosophy, in the context of a major species development, gives birth to itself as the distinctly Western metastory. Eventually, over the course of the next 2500 years, it will parent/author the "Great Books of Western Civilization": Western religion, politics, science and technology, and psychology. Psychology, in particular, will take as its self-defined task the exploration of these ancient questions, although with great conflictedness. (The American philosopher William James, a pioneering father of psychology, perhaps best exemplifies both the crossover from philosophy to psychology and the fledgling discipline's conflictedness.) As we shall see in Chapter 4, there have been relatively long periods in psychology's short life when the study of consciousness was all but disallowed.

PHILOSOPHY AS METHODOLOGY, EPISTEMOLOGY, AND ONTOLOGY

Plato's responses to and thoughts about the pre-Socratic questions and fragmented answers, given in the Socratic dialogues, in effect created philosophy. Plato's significance lies not so much in his having given the world a particular philosophy (the idealistic worldview we today describe as Platonic), but in his creation of *worldviewism* as the paradigmatic expression of the then newly acquired human capacity for and/or propensity toward self-conscious abstraction.[1] His insistence that there must be a view or an accounting of the world (that is, a philosophy) seems to imply that there must be a world, a view(er), and a method for somehow bringing the two—the world and the view(er)—together: hence, ontology (the reality of the world), epistemology (knowledge of the world), and methodology (the means of joining reality and knowledge). This shockingly simplistic characterization of the historical development of Greek thought is, of course, far too neat and, if you will, systematic. Yet one (that is, we Westerners) should not complain too vociferously, since neatness and systemization are no small part of our Greek ideological heritage.

As a species, we have learned from the Greeks to think and speak (and write) in ways that "make sense" even if they have little or nothing to do with what goes on historically, practically, moment-to-momentarily. Self-consciousness and abstraction, after all, are not so much the products of alienation as two of its critical developmental preconditions. Since the Greeks, alienation has come more and more to dominate Western civilization (until, under Western capitalist economics and ideology, it becomes itself the social–psychological precondition for comprehending—the lenses through which we see—a fully commodified reality). Alienation is inseparable from the neat, systematic worldviewism that is philosophy and her children/stories (Western religion, politics, science and technology, and psychology). Philosophy (lifeless as an academic discipline, but living on in our everyday constructed experience and understanding of our world and lives) is as much a part of our way of life as the free market—and, let us add, equally misunderstood.

But while the free market economy easily bested so-called centralized and controlled (planned) communist economics in this, the twentieth, century, its ideological companion-piece philosophy (systematic world-viewism) has all but become anachronistic. The posturing of the economic victors notwithstanding, what we have to look forward to is not so much a New World Order as a No World Order. For this, we may all, in our opinion, be thankful (although deeply concerned). But we are getting way ahead of our story. Back to the Greeks.

PHILOSOPHY AND PERCEPTUALITY

Arguably, at least from Plato's point of view, Heraclitus and Parmenides were the most important of the pre-Socratics. It is they who seem to have shifted the philosophical question from "What is everything made of?" to the even less concrete and less material "What is the nature of everything?" or "What is the principle to which everything conforms?" The Heraclitean–Parmenidean shift further magnifies self-conscious abstracting by introducing perception and illusion into the evolving philosophical mix.

According to Heraclitus (?540 B.C.–?475 B.C.), perception reveals to us that everything is in a constant state of flux; that is, it is ever-changing. Furthermore, he argues, this fact of nature (or nature of fact) is troublesome in that it makes knowledge (not to mention stepping into the same river twice) impossible. Our favorite Heraclitean, Cratylus, took this point of view so seriously that, so the story goes, he did not utter a single word for some thirty years because he felt he could not possibly say something true; by the time he got it out everything would have changed. Presumably, he overlooked the possibility of either saying in the present tense or without tense what is normally said in the future tense and then waiting for the world to catch up. (In modern science this activity is called "predicting.") Supposedly, one day thirty or so years later Cratylus began to speak again. We have always hoped that he did so when he realized that his silence was, after all, as much a statement (and, therefore, as subject to falsification) as anything he might say aloud. In any event, Heraclitus (the Dark, or the Obscure, as he was called) lamented the ever-changing state of the world as revealed to us by perception. Or so the story goes.

Parmenides (?515 B.C.–?after 450 B.C.), on the other hand, faced with the same problem, said something like "So much the worse for perception." In fact, Parmenides insisted, nothing changes at all; there is only permanence. He and Zeno, his countryman and disciple, "proved" that change and motion were merely perceptual illusions. It was Zeno, you may recall, who pointed out that contrary to what perception indicates, it is impossible to get from here to there in a finite amount of time because to do so we must cover half the distance between here and there, and then half of that distance, and so on ad infinitum. But since any distance (like the line) is infinitely divisible, it cannot be traversed in a finite amount of time. The perception that we do traverse it must therefore be an illusion, given that it is logically impossible: no motion, no change. In effect, Parmenides agreed with Heraclitus that to know something it must be permanent. But unlike Heraclitus, he thought that there is something which is permanent, namely permanence, which is everything.

Thales' theory about water seems remarkably innocent when looked at from this Heraclitean–Parmenidean point not all that far down the philosophical road. Abstraction had come a long way in a short time. Speaking in Socrates' voice, Plato—a skillful debater and a most creative thinker (or, to put it another, Wittgensteinian way, a sophisticated player of the abstraction language-game)—responded to Heraclitus and Parmenides with one of the first and best tricks a moderator in a debate between two intelligent yet opposing points of view has: he affirmed them both. In doing so, what Plato takes from the Heraclitean–Parmenidean dispute is their agreement on the central role of perceptuality (most particularly sight) in the creation of a worldview. The picture of man (women being both unseeing and unseen in Greek thought and life) as epistemological perceiver and the world as ontologically perceived entails a fundamentally dualistic worldview that, together with varying forms of mediating between the duals, has dominated Western thought as ideology ever since. The point we are making is that the centrality of dualism to philosophy is not merely positional or accidental. It is definitional, essential, structurally necessary, for Plato and, therefore, for philosophy—and, therefore, for modernist Western intellectualizing, which is descended from philosophy.

FROM DUALISM TO INDIVIDUATED IDENTITY

Dualism, systematic worldviewism, models for interpretive understanding (what, in contemporary terms, is called paradigmism) dominate Western thought for the next 2500 years. Philosophy's ideological children/stories—religion, politics, science and technology, and psychology—all display in a priori systematic fashion the self-conscious abstracting and accompanying alienation that Jaynes surmises emerged as a human characteristic in that ancient period of Greek life between the *Iliad* and the *Odyssey*. Each is constructed with its own "special" dualisms that stem from and reinforce the separation of human being from the world. God and man; man and society; observer and observed; and mind and body come to define religion, politics, science and technology, and psychology, respectively.

Despite periodic "revolts against dualism," the divided (that is, alienated) form of life—the Platonistically systemized, perception-based, dualized (albeit mediated) worldview of things—has characterized Western culture and ideology through the ages up to and including our own.

Philosophy and its companion-piece, dualism, are not merely one among many ways of thinking. Refined by Aristotelian logic, together they comprise what thinking, or reasoning, or systematically comprehending, *is*. For Plato, for philosophy, and for nearly all ensuing Western ideology, dualistic abstractive knowing and perceiving are inextricably connected. It is no accident that the expressions "I see" and "I know" are virtually synonymous; Western thought is firmly rooted in the visual and in metaphors of seeing and sight. With postmodern "hindsight," some feminist philosophers and psychologists, noting how pervasive the employment of the visual is to account for knowledge, have suggested that the visual metaphor is essentially phallocentric. In an essay exploring the complexities of investigating whether an epistemology modeled on vision is male-biased, Evelyn Keller and Christine Grontkowski (1983) tell us there have been other metaphors in use. Ironically, Heraclitus used the Greek verbal form that originally meant "to know by hearing" for "to know."

In what have come to be known as his middle dialogues (and, to a lesser extent, elsewhere), Plato formulates a theory of knowledge which is attentive to both the Heraclitean concern with impermanence (constant change) and the Parmenidean preoccupation with the necessity for an unchanging object of knowledge. Recognizing that our earthly perceptions are ever subject to doubt—because the objects of perception are essentially shadowy and potentially illusory—Plato postulates another, qualitatively different, kind of perception: the inner remembering or recalling (consciousness) of a realm of reality characterized by permanent ideals which the individual eternal soul experienced directly in a life prior to this earthly one. Earthly, material objects are the shadowy instantiations or reflections of the ideals; the soul itself is only embodied during life on earth.

The dialectical–dialogical method of philosophical inquiry known as the *Socratic method* is the process by which we move from the shadows on the cave wall to the blinding light of truth that shines outside the mouth of the cave. We (rather, the ethical man, the philosopher) see (not hear or touch or feel) the truth and are thus attuned to the harmony of the world and full of thought about what is real. It would be difficult to overstate the significance of this particular story of philosophy, the story of the cave, for Western culture. From then on, the inner "seeing" of perception and the outer "seeing" of knowledge are permanently linked. The concepts of doubt and certainty, synthesized by Plato and solidified as perceptually based, become one of the most critical dualities in Western ideology in the 2500-year-old epoch and epics dominated by systematic philosophy.

A further consequence of the perceptualism on which abstractive Western dualism is predicated and by which it is defined is individuation. *Who* sees is the individual. Undoubtedly, the history of the last few thousand years would have been very different indeed if what became hegemonic had been a theory of knowledge in which the fundamental phenomenon was not perception but something else—for example, work. (Imagine what things would be like if Plato had been Marx!) For in contrast to seeing, work is typically a shared relational activity of human beings which is necessarily joint, collective, social. As it turned out, however, Plato (who, in fact, was Plato!) would transform the inquiry begun by philosophy's pre-Socratic founding fathers into a theory based on the experience of the *individual viewer*, thereby introducing a new character (a new persona) into the human drama. This Platonized, individuated, abstracting, inner and outer episte-mological viewer (accompanied by the ontologically necessary objects to be viewed) walked onto the stage of history (in Jaynes's scenario, sometime between the *Iliad* and the *Odyssey*). It is he who comes to dominate, although transformed in significant ways, the next 2500 years of Western ideology as manifest in the epic, modernist stories that are religion, politics, science and technology, and psychology.

The emergence of modern science and technology some 350 years ago, like the emergence of self-consciousness and abstraction themselves, was perhaps rooted in another crucial developmental moment (or submoment) in the life of our species. With it, the seeing "I" reached its apotheosis as the paradigmatic human being. This idealized individual is the more or less passive subject of premodern religion, of the modern state, and, since the second half of the nineteenth century, of psychology. This new "science" was created to study and to treat the normality and the ills which that self-conscious individual manifests and from which she and he suffer. But psychology itself, like the rest of philosophy's progeny, is a story—a myth. Born in the dotage of philosophy, psychology is as well the misbegotten child of science. As such it is a second-generation myth—the mythic prod-uct of an incestuous relationship between mother and child. It has success-fully laid claim to the truth about subjectivity, and in doing so it has achieved an influence throughout most of the twentieth century that is in some ways unparalleled in human history. In our time it is the psycholo-gized form of the seeing "I" of science which most and best expresses the dualistic, perceptualistic, abstractive worldviewism of a now defunct phi-losophy. But we are getting ahead of our story again. Back, once more, to the Greeks.

SCHOLASTICISM: THE PREMODERN STORY

In its historical origins, Christianity is, in our opinion, an Eastern mysti-cal religion. Christ and his monotheistic Old Testament predecessors were, among other things, mystics. The miracle is no accidental element of the Christ story; it is essential. However it may have happened, materially and historically speaking, the influence of Eastern, mystical irrational thought on and in the pre-Socratics and Plato seems clear. As Christianity became a "Roman world–wide" religion in the first millennium A.D., it was the more mystical, irrational, Platonized (via Plotinus) dualistic features of Greek thought that helped shape it. The various popular introductions to Western religion and philosophical thought point out that Platonism (particularly its more other-worldly mystical features) and Eastern thought (for example, Manichaenism via St. Augustine) dominated the emerging story and practice of early Christianity. Apparently, Aristotle's demystifying writings were "missing" for centuries.

Then, semipopular culture tells us, something called "the Dark Ages" comes along to grip Western pre-premodern civilization (a centuries-long era notorious for its irrationality, superstition, poverty, and plague). Whereupon in the thirteenth century, Aristotle, the ancient Greek, reappears (that is, his writings do) to "reinvent" Christianity as a worldview, thereby setting the stage for and prefiguring the modern era, and the telling of the modern epic stories: politics, science and technology, and psychology. The story of the Greeks' and, most particularly, Aristotle's influence on premodern Western thought is complex and filled with uncertainties. However, that the ideas of Aristotle and those of the thirteenth century Thomas Aquinas somehow came together (also in complex ways) in the form of scholasticism is about as certain as (premodern) intellectual history gets.

Aristotle (384 B.C.–322 B.C.), a student of Plato (and a teacher of Alexander the Great), brings "down to earth" (that is, rationalizes) the mystical dualism of Plato's worlds—the world of forms perceived only by the philosopher–kings through the dialectical–dialogical method of philosophical inquiry, and the world of substance falsely perceived by ordinary people using their physical senses, in particular, sight. Aristotle suggests that earthly objects (particulars) of perception embody both the formal and the substantial. The form of chairness, for example, shapes the substance of wood to "make" a wooden chair. The chair is a thing in the world that has been "brought forth" from the real, the truth, the "divine." The same reality that shapes things, Aristotle says, shapes our consciousness of them. Consciousness of chair is made of a different substance (mind) from the chair itself. The form of chairness shapes the substance of mind to "make" a consciousness of chair. Understanding for Aristotle is not a correspondence of our perceptions with objects, as it is for modern man. It is, rather, a harmony of the individual with reality and of things with reality and, because of that, of individual with thing.

In uniting form and substance in the particular, Aristotle transforms man into a rational, unified (albeit still dualized) perceiver/conceiver of worldly objects which are themselves conceptually unified duals of form and matter. He places man—ordinary man—at the center of the conceptualized universe, just as Ptolemy (100–170 A.D.) made earth the center of the physical universe. The Aristotelian demystification of Plato's mystical dualism prepares the way for the further, modern scientific advancement of rationality that is to come after the few centuries during which Christian scholasticism dominated the world.

Aristotle's anthropocentric (although still dualized) worldview required a principle of motion. That is, there needed to be a way of accounting for things moving in the varied, complex, seemingly continual ways that they do, a way that was coherent with the new worldview dedicated to "the rational man." (Here, as elsewhere, our use of "man" and "Man" is deliberate and meant to highlight the manner in which Plato, Aristotle, and most of their followers believed that only men, and not women, were rational, as detailed in, for example, Nancy Tuana's *Woman and the History of Philosophy*, 1992.) In his accounting, Aristotle analogized from rational man to everything worldly; it was the distinctly intentional human characteristic of purposeful action that underlay the Aristotelian principle of motion. Thus, Aristotle completed his rationalistic worldview by introducing teleology, the philosopher's term for things moving in accordance with their purpose. Accepting the primitive materialistic notion of Empedocles (which was popular, we are told, in the first half of the fifth century B.C.) that all physical objects are simply various mixtures of the four basic elements Earth, Water, Air, and Fire (each object shaped by its particular form), Aristotle postulated a cosmological system of spheres which included natural beyond-this-world resting places for each element. Every object (particular) moves purposefully toward its natural resting place (with the dominant substantive element—Earth, Water, Air, or Fire—of a particular object determining its basic motion). They do this in a world which constantly seeks (even if it never fully achieves) a return to its own natural state of rest.

It is no overstatement to suggest that Aristotle "discovers" the thing (that is, the concrete particular) and, as well, the logic of the thing (both of which remain with us to this day). The particular—the form/substance object of human perception/conception—increasingly became the object of study as scholastic premodernism turned to modernism.

Some critical features of Greek–Aristotelian thought are totally abandoned in the transition from premodern scholasticism to the modern epics of politics, science and technology, and psychology, as when Galileo and the other founders of modern thought (that is, modern science) would mount a fundamental challenge to the Aristotelian, scholastic theory that rest is the natural state of things. But the particular as the embodiment of Greek dualism (and, thereby, systematic philosophy) has proved far more difficult to uproot. In our view, particularity, along with the family of concepts (including identity, for example) of which it is a member, is the ultimate ideologized product of that ancient Greek historical moment (on which Jaynes speculates) when self-conscious abstracting appeared in the human species. Indeed, so fundamental is the dynamic conception of the particular (and containment) to Western thought that, 2000 years after Aristotle, no less of an anti-Aristotelian (antiphilosopher) than Karl Marx would imply that particular commodities contain the whole of capitalism's productive system in much the same way that the Greek philosopher spoke of the acorn's containing the oak.

It is only now, in the late twentieth century, that Aristotelian particularity and the laws of identity which govern it are being challenged in any serious way. (Earlier arguments, such as those centering on realism versus nominalism, although sophisticated, remained framed in quasi-Platonic notions of universality.) The postphilosophical, postsystematic, postrational period just now getting under way is, at root, as much an engagement of the core conceptions of the ancient worldview as of the modern. We applaud this element of postmodernism in the conviction that nothing less than such a fundamental challenge is required if our species is to move developmentally beyond systematic, self-conscious abstraction—the 2500-year-old species development which has dominated human history through the ideological and social hegemony of Western European civilization.

It was Thomas Aquinas (1225–1274), the Italian-born philosopher canonized in 1323, who established Catholic doctrine on the basis of Aristotelian thought; in 1309 it became the official doctrine of the highly influential Dominican order. Aristotle's theories of "natural rest" and teleology, already more than 1500 years old, would remain the guiding principles of Western prescientific, premodern thinking for at least another 350 years. Those who first dared to challenge it by asserting that the natural state of things was not to be at rest, but in motion, were denounced not only for their heresy but, interestingly, for their (from the Catholic and Aristotelian view) irrationality. For the assertion that the natural state of things is in motion was untenable and sacrilegious: if it is true, then the scholastic's rationalistic God, the prime mover and the first cause, has nothing to do; in a purposeless universe constantly in motion, there is no rational need for God. Thus it was that in 1633 Galileo, the chief apostate in the eyes of the church, was compelled to recant publicly his view that the earth moves around the sun. ("And yet it moves," tradition has him mumbling defiantly, but discreetly, to himself.) The church, of course, was right in pointing out that Galileo's view was irrational. From the vantage point of the scholastic notion of rationality, the Galilean "new science" was hopelessly irrational. What turned out to be at issue was a new meaning of rationality. First and foremost, that is precisely what modern science is.

THE SCIENCE STORY

There is an interesting irony in this chapter of the story of "rational man." On the face of it, premodern anthropocentric teleology and geocentrism might seem to be the ultimate expressions of "human-centrism"; what could place human beings in a more central location than believing that everything, including inanimate objects, has human traits and believing that the earth is the center of the solar system? But it is with denying purposeful behavior to inanimate objects and denying the centrality of the earth that man truly becomes the "center of attention"—man becomes unique. Modernism redefines rationality and human beings in relation to both nature and God. Man becomes modern man, "rational man"—the extraordinary creation of God who is fundamentally different from nature and yet capable of understanding (and controlling) nature through empirics and mathematicization. God's omnipotence remains intact, cosmologically speaking—after all, He did start everything up! But his omniscience, epistemologically speaking, is challenged by the humanist/scientist, the human being who proves capable of comprehending a world of continuous and endless motion. It is this reconceptualization of rationality and its various accompaniments and accomplishments, such as the comprehension of relationality, a calculus of movement, a much improved technological capacity to see, and, even more importantly, the ability to formulate the "deeper" laws of motion in mathematical terms (ultimately, some say, Zeno's paradox was resolved only with the creation of the Liebnizian/Newtonian calculus), that are the conceptual essence of the emerging science story.

The transition from the ancient to the modern epoch is a continuous and complex interplay of change and continuity. Teleology is completely abandoned in the "new science" (since a principle accounting for motion is obviously unnecessary in a world which is naturally—that is, ontologically—in motion as opposed to being naturally at rest). Rationality is redefined. Man, separated from "the divine," becomes self-defining. Knowledge, now uniquely human, becomes connected to power and control over nature rather than being divine, an expression of a state of harmony with reality (see Faulconer and Williams, 1990). Yet along with these significant changes, elements of the core remain. Aristotelian logic and the critical notion of particularity are maintained; it is through particularity, and the logic and psychology of identity and self which accompany it, that Greek philosophy remains effectively unchallenged in modern science and beyond—that is, until the present day.

From the birth of modern science, the human being (as we have noted, typically called "man") as observer/perceiver/conceptualizer, whose knowledge of the world is made possible in the twin activities of observing it empirically from a distance and mathematically understanding its deeper laws (abstractive natural philosophical thought), will come to be embodied in the person of the scientist as the paradigmatic, ideal knower. Thus begins the mathematicization/empiricization of the world—the ideological transformation of the universe from one in which men, like all things, are primarily and directly the subjects of God's unseen hand to one governed by rules which men alone can make and know and thereby establish their species' control over it. Modern science will come to set aside Aristotelian physics, but Aristotelian logic—a logic of static particulars, not a logic of relations or change—remains dominant well into the twentieth century. It is only then that the discovery and acceptance of relational or functional logic (the predicate calculus and mathematical logic as its formal expressions) transform rationality once again. And it sets the stage, conceptually speaking, for postmodernism.

Mathematicization (the quantitative rule-governedness of nature) is, in our view, even more fundamental than empiricism for the extraordinary development of modern science, a story about the conquest of nature and/or the instrument by which nature is rendered conquerable. After all, it was mathematicization that told us what to look at and for. Modern science is not simply about new observations. Nor is it even a new way of comprehending reality which is simply superior to Aristotelian, scholastic Catholic dogma. Rather, with its advent the meaning of comprehension itself changes, as does the nature of those who comprehend. Epistemology becomes hegemonic over ontology. The early Greek dualists, including Aristotle, might well have said, "I am (a rational human being); therefore I (have the capacity to) think." But it wasn't until the beginning of the age of humanism and science that Descartes (1596–1650) could make the epistemology-first claim, *Cogito ergo sum* ("I think, therefore I am"). Henceforward, reality will no longer be viewed in essentially ontological terms, with man and his planet at the center of things where they had been placed by God. Now reality is fundamentally epistemological, with man an all-knowing outsider (a viewer, a perceiver, a technological intervener) whose very existence and identity are contingent on his knowing, his epistemic capabilities. Bishop Butler neatly puts the ontological question to rest with his famous utterance "Everything is what it is and not another thing." What remains for modernism is to consider the epistemological question, "How do we know what is?"

Not coincidentally, with the breakdown of the premodern religious teleology of scholasticism, the divine right of kings begins to give way to the so-called social contract as the organizing principle of the new politics—still another major story of Western civilization. A new concept of state comes into existence, based on the "natural" rights of individuals, who are no longer quite so attached (by God's hand) to the land but move (in accordance with the needs of early capitalism and the nascent bourgeoisie) from town to town and from job to job. The "state of nature" and "social contract" stories (two of the more blatantly ideological and ludicrous tales in all of Western folklore) gain currency through Hobbes (1588–1679), who succeeds in creating a piece of political science fiction or anthropology which "justifies" and "rationalizes" the evolution of monarchist bourgeois democracy in England.

Even the most hard-core observer of the day discovered and mathematicized concepts more than simply finding new facts. It was Copernicus

(1473–1543), a Polish clergyman–mathematician–astronomer (he also occasionally had to practice medicine to support himself), who reintroduced the notion (first put forward about 1800 years earlier by Aristarchus, a contemporary of Euclid) that the earth and the other planets revolve around the sun—a theory that was regarded as blasphemous not only by the Catholic church but by what had become its "official opposition," the Protestant followers of Martin Luther. But the so-called Copernican revolution was not based on a simple new noticing of the heavens. It was rooted in a notion of mathematical simplicity which deemed the heliocentric view simpler than the complex epicycles which the geocentric view required in accounting for the movements of heavenly bodies.

Copernicus' views were, then, essentially conceptual. So were those of Galileo (1564–1642), who argued that motion is the normal state of things, and Isaac Newton (1642–1727), the English astronomer who (falling apples notwithstanding) first set down the laws of motion and force that would become the basis of modern physics and, thereby, the bedrock of modern scientific thought. Throughout the sixteenth and seventeenth centuries, advances in science, and particularly mathematicization, informed the growth of sophisticated military and navigational technology. New means and machines of war and discovery, in turn, produced further scientific and technological advances.

To summarize, modern science, emerging in the middle of the second Christian millennium as the dominant worldview, rapidly took over the world. Epistemological man reigned. Philosophy, on the one hand (the progressive epistemological side), successfully modernizes itself. On the other hand (the conservative ontological side), philosophy retains its ideological influence on science through the Aristotelian logic of particularity and identity. Neither the remarkable first and early second millennium debates (about, among other things, the number of angels that could dance on the head of a pin) which took place between "realists" and "nominalists," nor the evolution of modern science in the next two centuries as a radically new worldview based on the mathematicization of the laws of physical motion (and the accompanying empirics and technology) that constituted nature, attempted to uproot particularity and identity. That the Aristotelian logic which is based on them remains the form of thought will go fundamentally unchallenged until relatively late in modernism's day. What did change with the advent of modern science and modern philosophy were the view of the natural world (the ontology was made scientific), the view of its perceiver (the modern epistemological man), and the view of how the two interact (the deductive–causal methodology)—and the relative importance of each. But the challenge to logic, the fundamental form of thought, is not fully undertaken until centuries later, when the effort to reduce mathematics to logic runs into serious trouble.

THE LOGIC OF PARTICULARITY AND IDENTITY

The attempt to discover how humans think—not an effort to describe, psychologically speaking, the way in which cognition happens, but a more normative analysis of the "form of thinking," that is, the essence of "correct thinking"—produced Aristotle's greatest and longest-lasting contribution, his logic. Once again the brilliant demystifier of Plato seemingly transforms the other-worldly metaphysical conception of "containment" into a more mundane and earthly syllogistic, deductive logic: the Platonic *This red chair instantiates or is contained in the idea or form of redness* becomes via Aristotle *All red chairs are red; this is a red chair; therefore, this chair is red.* Thus, the well-known (to introduction to logic students) syllogism *All men are mortal; Socrates is a man; therefore, Socrates is mortal* becomes the normative paradigm of thought, a way of attributing characteristics to an individuated particular based not on direct observation but on thought alone or, if you will, "pure thought" or logic. To be sure, we may have to discover by observation and/or induction whether all men are mortal and/or whether Socrates is a man. But if we know these two claims to be true, we can attribute mortality to Socrates by something other than direct observation; we can logically infer (deduce) his mortality from the two earlier premises. Logic tells us, then, what one thing must be when something else is. As such, it defines proper thinking, not empirically but normatively.

The Aristotelian definition of deduction, it is worth noting, is basically classificatory: if all of the things in a class A are also in a class B, then if a is in A it is also in B. This principle of thought is transformed and ultimately takes on the form that general laws and explanations have in modern science, that is, a causal–deductive form. If there is a mathematically expressible and/or empirically verifiable connection between A-type events and B-type events, and if a is an A-type event, then ("then," of course, is the key word) we may be assured (independently of any verification) that a is also a B-type event. And so, even as modern science becomes increasingly preoccupied with physical motion (physical change) and the mathematical laws which govern it, the form of reasoning about them remains fundamentally classificatory, deductive, and static. It is a logic of particularity, identity, and deductability—the particular elements contained in a grouping A, a grouping B, and the particular a also contained in the grouping A implies or allows us to deduce that a is in B. It is not a logic which considers the relational notion of "contained in" qua relationality. Rather, it defines normative thinking (particularity, identity, and predication) in terms of a static and classificatory notion of containment. To be sure, Aristotle demystifies the Platonic notion of containment—but only by an appeal to an extraordinarily intuitive picture of "is a member" ("is contained in"). Some 2000 years later, when efforts were first being made to represent logic mathematically, using set theory, such a notion of containment would turn out to be permeated with troublesome contradiction.

Thus from the outset modern science, that most remarkable and pragmatically valuable construct/story of Western man, embodies a critical contradiction inherited from Greek philosophy and passed on through Aristotle's logic of particularity. In no way did this deter Western science and technology from their stunning accomplishments or from being disseminated to the farthest corners of the world. In this it strikingly resembles capitalism, the economic system and ideology. Indeed, the presence of contradiction (Karl Marx notwithstanding) has not stopped either of them yet. But in the late-nineteenth and early-twentieth centuries, as Western science moves to replace philosophy (in some instances, with the enthusiastic cooperation of philosophy itself) as the meta-author, foundation, and definition of all human understanding, the paradox begins to reveal itself more and more. In seeking to systemize and formalize all elements of itself (particularly mathematics, logic, and psychology), philosophy comes to discover the deeper paradox of particularity/identity on which modern science rests.

But we have run way ahead of our story once again. Back to modern philosophy, and the circumstances under which she produced her final stories/children: the epic psychology; and the short story of the late logical positivism, philosophy's ultimate (and suicidal) attempt to justify the elevation of science to the level of an all-encompassing understanding of understanding.

NOTE

1. Arguably, Pythagorean mathematical mysticism was another candidate (story). But while mathematics (developed in the East in the context of Arabic culture) eventually played a most critical role in the advance of modern science and technology, mysticism (otherwise known as irrationalism) never completely dominated premodern and modern worldviewism (otherwise known as rationalism) in Western civilization. It is commodified/particularized Aristotelian rationalism which has been ideologically hegemonic for over 1500 years, even as Western modes of production (not at all unrelated) have come to control the world economy.

3

The Glorification of Experience: Modern Philosophy, Psychology, and Logic

Modern philosophy, with its almost complete focus on issues of epistemology, both shapes and is shaped by a rapidly emerging modern science. The change in focus from the "other-worldly" religiously defined man to the "more earthly" self-defining knowing man motivates and requires a deeper epistemic analysis of knowing. The popular story of modern Western philosophy all too neatly divides matters into Continental rationalism and British empiricism. Rationalism's "Big Three," Descartes, Spinoza (1632–1677), and Leibniz (1646–1716), are typically matched up against the British empiricists Locke (1632–1704), Berkeley (1685–1753), and Hume (1711–1776). This simplistic classification typically identifies rationalism as the study of knowing from the vantage point of the rational, or mental, input, and empiricism as the study of knowing from the vantage point of the empirically perceptual input. It goes without saying that rationalists and empiricists alike were concerned with both, since scientific (even early scientific) knowing obviously involves both. Long before Kant (1724–1804) "joined" the rational and the perceptual "sides" of scientific knowing, it was well understood by modernism's fathers that they "went together." The modern man, the scientific man, the epistemological man, the knowing man, the self-defining man demands a deeper understanding of human experience.

It is the search for *certainty in experience*—in this world and in this life—by modern science which links the superficially divergent labors of modern Western philosophy's two major schools, rationalism and empiricism. Descartes, "the first of the rationalists," searches for the "indubitable" (the unquestionable experience) in the act of thinking itself; it is this, he asserts, that ensures the certainty (the existence) of the thinker. On the basis of this fundamental truth (*Cogito ergo sum*), he reconstructs all that is known so as to embody the necessary certitude required of scientific experience and knowledge.

Meanwhile Hume, "the last of the empiricists," searches for truth and/or certainty of experience in the discovery of the most basic ontological elements of perception (what Bertrand Russell later calls *sense data*). Hume hopes to find within the complex gestalt of perceptual experience a particular, a unit which cannot be denied, an irreducible element from which complex perceptions and ideas and thoughts based on perception (that is, all else) are built but which is itself somehow true in its "sensible immediacy."

Immanuel Kant ultimately challenges both views on the grounds that rationalism does not sufficiently take into account the *experience of the world*, while empiricism does not sufficiently take into account the *experience of the viewer*. Experience, says Kant, is even more fundamental than mind or matter. Kantian experientialism (with its emphasis on cognition) will come to lay the modern philosophical foundation (although not the modern scientific basis) for the birth of psychology.

FROM KANT TO MARX: THE HEIGHT OF PHILOSOPHICAL MODERNISM TO THE BAREST BEGINNINGS OF POSTMODERNISM

The introduction to Kant's *Critique of Pure Reason* begins with the following words:

> There can be no doubt that all our knowledge begins with experience. For how should our faculty of knowledge be awakened into action did not objects affecting our senses partly of themselves produce representations, partly arouse the activity of our understanding to compare these representations, and, by combining or separating them, work up the raw material of the sensible impressions into that knowledge of objects which is entitled experience? In the order of time, therefore, we have no knowledge antecedent to experience, and with experience all knowledge begins.
>
> But though all our knowledge begins with experience, it does not follow that it all arises out of experience. For it may well be that even our empirical knowledge is made up of what we receive through impressions and of what our own faculty of knowledge (sensible impressions serving merely as the occasion) supplies from itself. If our faculty of knowledge makes any such addition, it may be that we are not in a position to distinguish it from the raw material, until with long practice of attention we have become skilled in separating it. (1965, from the 2nd edition, published in 1787, pp. 41–42)

In this way, Kant effectively formulates the modernist paradigm and the modern problem of knowledge and the study of how we obtain it. What we know (and therefore what we learn, since knowledge is, presumably, the product of learning) is a complex combination or synthesis of "what we receive through impressions" and our minds. Experience, Kant tells us, is almost certainly the starting point of knowing. But experience itself is never pure or raw (as suggested by Hume and some of his empiricist followers). Neither is experience the cause of knowledge. Rather, Kant goes on to say, an analysis of experience reveals truths that are not simply based on ("come after") experience a posteriori but are a priori conditions of experience itself. Yet these a priori truths are not true merely by definition (what is termed *analytic*); they are special truths about the world (what is termed *synthetic*). They categorically define our "faculty of knowledge," our "minds" (at least our cognitive minds). Kant's insight—it is only with "the long practice of attention" that we are able to separate out the raw material of experience from the totality of experience—would become the raison d'être of much of twentieth-century psychology's myth making, in particular, its myths about cognition.

Was the Kantian paradigm a simple combinatorial model in which the "faculty of knowledge" makes an addition, or was it more constructivist than combinational, with the faculty of knowledge *operating on* experience? Did Kant advance a new understanding of subjectivity? Did he establish subjective certainty? Did he rid Western ideology of inner–outer duality? Is the Kantian "experiencing individual" qualitatively more active than its pre-modern and Cartesian perceiving and thinking predecessors? We are of the opinion that, as provocative as his insight was, Kant also essentially retains Aristotelian formal logic. He, rather than Hegel, may well have been the originator of the modern dialectic, but the Kantian paradigm is not ultimately a serious challenge to philosophy's dualism. The Kantian categories of experience are an attempt to bring together the dualistically divided knower and what there is to be known. Kant's notion of human activity, however, remains Aristotelian in its logic, passive, mentalistic, metaphysical, and quasi-vitalistic (as when he says, "Objects . . . partly arouse the activity of our understanding"). Kant provides a taxonomy of certainty with his construction of the four-valued notion of analyticity, syntheticity, a priori, and a posteriori to distinguish degrees of certainty in its various forms. Modern philosophy, science, and psychology are profoundly shaped by Kant's critique. All that is true. Yet he does not challenge the pursuit of certainty per se. The Aristotelian logic of particularity, identity, and the Greek conception of systematic certainty (truth) remain intact. No. Kant never gets beyond experience and the logic of particularity. To be sure, he crystallizes the modernist preoccupation *with* experience. But it is Marx, not Kant, who breaks with modernist philosophy to introduce *activ-*

ity-based thought as an alternative to experience-based thought and begins a fundamental challenge to Aristotelian logic.

In his earlier, methodological, philosophical writings, Marx presents the fundamentals of dialectical historical materialism. In one of the clearest and briefest formulations of his new methodology, Marx states what a premise is in the interpretation-free science/philosophy he was attempting to develop. He says, "This method of approach [dialectical historical materialism] is not devoid of premises. It starts out from the real premises and does not abandon them for a moment. Its premises are men, not in any fantastic isolation and rigidity, but in their actual, empirically perceptible process of development under definite conditions" (Marx and Engels, 1973, pp. 47–8).

Virtually all of Western philosophy (including Aristotelian logic) is challenged by Marx's insistence that the starting point of science and history is life-as-lived, not interpretations or abstractions extrapolated from life, that premises are real people in their "process of development under definite conditions." The story of Western philosophy, from Plato and Aristotle onward, has always included an ahistorical dualistic conception of premises as separate from (though somehow contained in) what follows from them. Marx's historical and methodological monism (present mainly in his early writings) is one of his most important contributions to a postmodern activity-theoretic epistemology.

Marx's notion of activity (that is, of "revolutionary, practical–critical activity," 1973, p. 121) has a historical character which synthesizes the knower and the known well beyond Kant's modernist, experientialist effort. While it was Hegel who began the process of historifying Kant (identified by the contemporary American pragmatist Richard Rorty [1982] as "the least historicist of philosophers"), Marx subjects Kant's rationalistic–experientialistic synthesis (arguably, by using Hegel's idealistic monism) to a radical historical materialist activity-theoretic monism. Opposing Kant, Marx insists that a human being is not to be understood primarily as a perceiver/conceiver—a cognizer—but as an active producer. A theory of knowledge which does not recognize the fundamentality of labor and laboring, that is, of human creative productivity, says Marx, is ultimately more an aesthetic than a human psychology.

Against Hegel's idealistic, metaphysical (albeit historicist) version of Kant, Marx offers a materialistic, monistic, labor-based, activity-theoretic, dialectical historicality. It is not the intellectual or cognitive act (the experience) of the person that must be analyzed to understand understanding, says Marx, but the more ordinary, hour to hour, minute to minute relational acts (indeed, the continuous collective activity) of human production. It is human practice, in all its banality, Marx insists, not experience, which is the starting point.[1]

Yet even Marx's method of practice is not a sufficiently thoroughgoing rejection of Aristotelian logic and particularistic idealism. Premises may indeed be real people and not abstractions, but how—in what relational activity—was that discovered? Marx's method leaves such questions unanswered (and, it appears, unasked). Surely, it cannot be that what is discovered is identical with the act (or activity) of discovering it. What is discovery? Marx's method, while it qualitatively transforms the object of discovery, does not self-reflexively engage what the discovery of discovery (including his own discovery) is. He does not replace Descartes's method of doubt with a method of affirmation or discovery, that is, with a dialectical theory of learning. In clinging to the notion of starting point (for him, "real people"), he has not fully abandoned truth and certainty altogether. To answer these questions and accomplish these tasks, we go (via Vygotsky) beyond Marx's still modernist, still rationalist method of practice to the postmodern practice of method (Holzman and Newman, 1979; Newman and Holzman, 1993).

It is this activity-theoretic rejection of systematic philosophy and its children/stories—the relation-based process by which the sustained and continuous activity of human development occurs—that is a major concern of Chapter 9. While we might agree that experience is the *occasion* of all knowing and therefore of the most basic kind of knowing (in Kant's terminology, the knowing of the a priori synthetic), experience, for us, is not an abstraction, a starting point, as it was for Kant. Nor are human beings premises and, therefore, self-defined particulars (another name for a starting point), as they were for Marx. Rather, our view is that the continuous *work activity of experiencing* is the occasion for continuously discovering what we know as the historical precondition for the experience itself. Experience is a developmental, productive activity, the labor of knowing and growing. And what experience (most particularly, the experience of human life, including the experience of experiencing) yields is not permanent abstractions, such as categories of knowledge or, indeed, even categories of experience (space, time, cause, substance, or anything else). Experience generates ongoing, continuous learning of the preconditions for experiencing as a social productive activity.

Using this postmodern (Marxian- and Vygotskian-inspired) epistemological antiparadigm, all knowing and, therefore, all learning is (to use Kant's language once again) a continuously transforming a priori synthetic. We must challenge the direction (the flow) of time itself to understand understanding activistically. What we know is what we had to know (had to have known) in order to have had the developmental relational experience of constructive discovery. From our postmodern deconstructionist/reconstructionist sociohistorical location, what we are able to see and, therefore, deny in both Kant and Marx is the notion of particularity in all its guises: starting points, selves, categories, experiences, origins, premises, presuppositions, assumptions, and so on. There is always an origin, a starting point, that can be imposed on discourse, just as there is always an explanation, an interpretation, or a description that can be imposed on life events. But it is not necessary. The postmodern rejection of systematic philosophy entails the exposure of the depth and breadth of the fallacy of originism (see, for example, John Morss's [1992] valuable essay "Making Waves").

Our claim that all knowledge is a kind of relational a priori synthetic— that is, that there is no fixed "faculty of knowledge," no categories antecedent (in any meaningful causal sense) to learning, but rather that knowledge (learning) is a discovery of "what was already there"—has, of course, been prefigured in Western philosophical thought from Plato's *Meno* to C. I. Lewis's *Mind and the World Order* to Chomsky's *Syntactic Structures*, with a million other stops in between. But the three of them (and, in our view, all the others) invariably suffer from the "sin of originality" in their insistence that there is always a particular beginning, whether absolute or relative. Thus "what was already there" is defined in terms of a dualistic notion of origin. From our radically relational activity-theoretic point of view (where point of view, of course, is as much relational activity as everything else), developmental relational activity (discovery) is continuous (unless, and, of course, it is coercively halted by the status quo).

In the absence of what, to use postmodernist terminology, is a deconstruction–reconstruction of Western ideology and methodology, the kind of learning that has dominated Western philosophized culture for thousands of years is an instrumentalist acquisition of knowledge. Indeed, this has been critical to our species' mastery of nature and ascendance to animal hegemony. Such learning has been accompanied, lawfully, by the nondevelopmental and essentially "religious" practice and study of human life. As we approach the twenty-first century, growing numbers of people are coming to see, with understandable fear and perhaps panic, that our species might well be living in a moral and developmental Dark Age, overdetermined by prehistoric religious myths of both the clerical and secular variety, but with a high technology that has simultaneously conquered and destroyed nature. We (the authors) believe that what has brought us (human beings) here will not take us (our species) further. The varied crises of scientific psychology (a secular religious worldview) have as much to do with its subject matter (human life) and with philosophy and science as with the discipline itself. But as usual we are getting way ahead of our story.

SCIENCE'S EFFORT TO FORMALIZE AND UNIVERSALIZE

By the late-nineteenth and early-twentieth century, modern science had fully adopted and adapted as its credo the notion of systematic truth it inherited from philosophy. The Einsteinian worldview made explicit the belief that science (unlike philosophy) would ultimately find a true answer to every question, an explanation for or a prediction of everything. It might even find a single fundamental law (a starting point, an origin) from which all truth could be deductively and/or inductively inferred. This belief expressed the confidence of the scientist–rulers, their political sponsors, and the world's masses, who were understandably in awe of technologic miracles. It was in such a climate that the unanswered earthly riddles of logicality and human subjectivity were vigorously engaged. How could something so certain as mathematics derive from something so uncertain as the human mind?

If mathematics, one apparent source of modern science's certitude, could itself be justified by an appeal to logic (that is, systemized by the normative "form of thought") and if the mysteries of the mind could be scientifically analyzed, we should have gone a long way toward enthroning science and modernism as the ultimate universal system. During the late-nineteenth and early-twentieth centuries, there were inspired efforts to do both. Indeed, the ultimate crusade of the then-humanist child, science and technology, was to overthrow her Greek mother, philosophy, and philosophy's first child, religion.

Thus it was that the extraordinary human growth engendered by that species development which (as Jaynes speculates so interestingly) may have occurred sometime between the *Iliad* and the *Odyssey*—a development which gave rise to Greek philosophy, which would become the mother/author of Western religion, politics, science and technology, and psychology—finally reached its limits. Ironically, it was in pursuing to their extremes the logic and the psychology of that early developmental moment in the name of creating an ultimate starting point, an ultimate system of truth, that the paradoxes of both science and philosophy were fully exposed. It would be the work of the modernists-moving-beyond-modernism, especially, in our opinion, Ludwig Wittgenstein (in logic) and Lev Vygotsky (in psychology), which laid the foundation for what would eventually become unsystematic, relation-based, non-truth-referential development—in a word, postmodernism.

RELATIVITY, QUANTA, AND THE UNCERTAINTY PRINCIPLE

Even as the efforts to "scientize" psychology and to "logicize" mathematics bounded ahead (typically, and, even to the present day, oblivious of each other), physics (the jewel in the crown of modern science) saw advances within the accepted paradigm that raised eyebrows. Various empirical studies based on new technology urged that subjective factors must be more seriously taken into account in any objective analysis of physical phenomena. In particular, subatomic physical activity close at hand and astronomical activity at a great distance both demanded (or at least seemed to demand) a reconceptualization of the basic space/time-defined entities of orthodox Newtonian physics. As long as the viewer (the measurer) and her or his subjective role were kept out of the picture, neither subatomic movement nor astronomical movement could be fully understood.

It was not merely a matter of controlling for accidental personal factors such as fatigue. Rather (to put it simplistically), the rate of speed at which the viewer was moving was as much an "objective" (or a subjective/objective) factor as the rate of speed at which the viewed object was moving, when the "object" viewed moved at a rate approaching the speed of light. Similarly (and also simplistically), some subatomic particles (motions) seemed to move so fast that one could not safely identify a particular particle using simple particular and identity-based space–time coordinates. Doing so (or attempting to do so) would produce seeming logical contradictions, such as the conclusion that some thing "went" from point A to point B in "no time at all." Alternative, more process-based ways of understanding (for example, relativity, uncertainty, quantum leaps) which recast modern/contemporary physics were discovered.

Nevertheless, orthodox physicists and traditional methodologists argued then and still do, we think correctly, that the Newtonian paradigm was not fundamentally challenged by these new process discoveries. Indeed, it was the Newtonian picture (and, of course, extraordinary advances in technology, such as high-powered telescopes and microscopes) that led us to these strange new worlds. Moreover, the exceedingly odd behavior of these previously unknown things *was* still comprehensible in terms of Aristotelian logic and Newtonian laws of modern physics. No. Discoveries in modern physics do not themselves undermine the paradigm. Yet they do contribute (validly or invalidly) to the overall postmodern attack. In spite of this, as the sixteenth-century religious orthodoxy had with Galileo, the modern scientific orthodoxy turns on the latter-day heretics, the postmodernists. The modern orthodoxy insists (see, for example, Gross and Levitt, 1994) that most of those (largely nonscientists) who use discoveries in physics to deny, in quasi-postmodern fashion, the basic paradigm of physics simply misunderstand physics. The members of the scientific orthodoxy are, of course, quite right in many senses. Most importantly, like their predecessors among the church fathers, they define what is right; it is, after all, their science.

The issue, then and now, turns on whether a new conception of understanding itself (not merely a new paradigm for physics, but a new, nonparadigmatic epistemology) is emerging. That, of course, is a social issue that goes well beyond the limits of physics and the institutions of the physical sciences. We are no longer somewhere between the *Iliad* and the *Odyssey*. We are, quite possibly, "between" one form of human life—the form of alienation (see Chapter 9)—and another.

RELATIONAL OR FUNCTIONAL LOGIC

Sometime during the nineteenth century (although there are earlier examples), the quaint Kantian view of mathematics as a constellation of "deep" truths that correspond to quantitative features of reality—that is, as being true by virtue of stating very general characteristics of the physical world—came under more careful scrutiny by mathematicians and philosophers alike. The invention of a new, non-Euclidean geometry by Riemann (1826–1866), for example, raised the issue of whether Euclidean geometry owed its apparent certitude to having captured the empirically verifiable nature of space. Or was something else going on?

The challenge to Kantian taxonomy, which identified mathematics as *synthetic*, compelled many to consider whether mathematics might instead be *analytic* or true by definition. If that should turn out to be the case, they asked, then how are we to explain the seemingly special (that is, accurate) relationship between how the world is and the mathematical accounting of it by science?

Perhaps, it was suggested, the definitions that make up mathematics are not exactly arbitrary. While not based on features of physical reality, they might well be based on features of the normative mode of reasoning, that is, on logic. This reevaluation of mathematics as definitional, and as more closely related to logic than to fact, produced major new developments in both logic and mathematics. It also brought the two of them much closer together.

In this context Gottlob Frege and others sought to functionalize or mathematicize the Kantian view of understanding and cognition. To them, Kant's mixing, in experience, of empirically verifiable perceptions (such as that perceptual experience is always causally ordered) and synthetic a priori categories of experience itself (such as the causal category) cries out for an understanding of "mixing" which moves beyond the logic of Aristotelian categories.

If "7 + 5 = 12" is true by definition rather than because it corresponds to how the world is, then what must be defined (what must definition be) to comprehend its analyticity? While the numbers (in this case "7," "5," and "12") are no doubt definitionally important as particulars, the relational operations (in this case "+" and "=") become at least as important to consider definitionally because, among other obvious things, there are (at least intuitively) far fewer operations than numbers. To discover the essence of numbers in and of themselves and then derive mathematical truths from them is to invoke or at least suggest a kind of Pythagorean mysticism. Thus on this new view, "7 + 5 = 12" is not to be seen as definitionally true by virtue of the deep or essentialistic definitions of "7," "5," and "12." Rather, it is necessary to understand how the "+" operation and the "=" operation function (almost mechanically speaking) on triads of positive integers to produce truths of arithmetic. There is a function $f(x)$ where f is some appropriately employed use (operation) of "+"-ing and "="-ing and x is an ordered (first integer + second integer = the third integer) n-adic (in this case triadic) selection of positive integers (for example: <7, 5, 12> or <7 , 4, 12>) such that $f(x)$ = true in one case, x = <7 , 5, 12>, and false in the other, x = <7 , 4, 12>. The understanding of particularity (in this case the numbers) in terms of the operations that transform them, and not as being somehow intuitively fundamental or basic, was central to the process of mathematicizing logic. This, in turn, suggested that a program to reduce all mathematics to logic might well be successful.

This effort culminated in the appearance of the monumental three-volume *Principia Mathematica* by Bertrand Russell and Alfred Whitehead in 1910 and 1913. Logic itself, as we have pointed out, was already being mathematicized (relationalized and functionalized). The *Principia* promised to show how mathematics could be reduced to a logic which included not only the Aristotelian apparatus but some of the newer conceptual elements derived from its nineteenth-century mathematicization.[2]

The most significant piece of "new" logic (logical equipment) introduced by Russell and Whitehead in the *Principia* to aid in the project of reducing mathematics to logic was the set. The set, or the grouping, is a collection of particulars of any kind; that is, it is an abstraction defined in terms of its members. Yet some, more mathematically relevant, sets have an infinite number of members; an example is the set of all positive integers (often symbolized as {1, 2, 3, . . . }). Such sets can therefore be described in terms of the necessary and sufficient conditions for group or set membership, rather than by enumeration or shorthand (what philosophers call ostensive definitions). For example, the set of even numbers is often described as the set of all positive integers divisible by 2 without remainder (symbolized as {2, 4, 6, 8, . . . }).

To most of those concerned (and surely to Russell and Whitehead), the abstract set and the particular in terms of which it was defined seemed, intuitively speaking, clear as a bell—an intuition that was undoubtedly based, among other things, on our culture's Greek (especially Aristotelian) heritage. But it turned out that embedded in the notion of the set was a self-referential paradox whose discovery would lead to the unraveling of the substance/form particular handed down from Greek philosophy and logic.

What is the so-called self-referential paradox in set-theoretic form? Simply this. Consider the set R, an infinite set, identified by the following necessary and sufficient conditions: x is a member of R if and only if x is a set which lacks itself as a member. An initial intuitive perusal of sets in general and the set R in particular would suggest that most (if not all) sets would be in R since most sets (perhaps all), so it seems, lack themselves as members. So far, so good. Yet of course there is a serious problem here. The problem (the paradox) is detected when we ask the seemingly harmless question, Is *R* a member of *R*? Because if *R* is in *R* then *R* isn't in *R*, since *R* is the set of *all* sets (therefore presumably including *R*) lacking themselves as members. But if *R* isn't in *R* then it is in *R*, since *R* includes all sets which lack themselves as members and so, therefore, would include *R*. The set-theoretic, self-referential paradox—a sort of modern version of the ancient paradox of the Cretan who declares, "All Cretans are liars" (that is, they lie all the time)—shook modern logic (and Cantor and Frege in particular) to its foundations, thereby dashing efforts to build mathematics on top of this now shaky edifice. The Aristotelian particular, which had proved to be such an extraordinarily serviceable concept for thousands of years (including, especially, the centuries during which it was used in the development of modern science), had fallen down on the job of defining sets or groupings of particulars.

Other philosophers, Hegel among them, had previously ventured misgivings about the relationship between parts and wholes. But this latest failure, which had occurred within the rigorous precincts of mathematics/logic/science, added new weight to the problem of particulars—and, of course, sets. Russell and Whitehead came up with an ad hoc solution to the paradox, the so-called Theory of Logical Types, which effectively disallows the question "Is *R* a member of *R*?" What this accomplished was to expose still further the arbitrariness of a particular (and set)/identity-based mode of understanding (this particular is the same as that particular).

But the significance of all this was not fully realized until two decades later, when Kurt Gödel (1906–1978) published his "Incompleteness Theorem," a brilliant work which many, including us, regard as one of the most important conceptual breakthroughs of the twentieth century. In it Gödel (1962) established that any effort to create a metamathematical system which reduces (or purports to reduce) an area of mathematics to logic so as to be able to prove it will yield a mathematicized metamathematical system (he showed how to create it by a remarkable procedure since known as Gödel numbering) which itself embodies the paradox of self-referentiality, only this time in mathematical form. In other words, such an effort will yield a mathematically true proposition in proper mathematical form (something like "7 + 5 = 12") which essentially says of itself in mathematical language that it is unprovable. Gödel further demonstrated that any ad hoc type-theoretic effort such as Russell and Whitehead's to resolve such a difficulty logically merely generates yet another paradoxical, mathematicized, *metamathematical* system. There is not, Gödel showed, any systematic way of proving consistently (that is, without contradiction) that anything other than a very simple mathematical system is both complete and sound: that is, all truths of that area of mathematics and only truths of that area of mathematics (and/or the ability to generate them) are reducible to a metamathematical logical system.

Interestingly, Gödel's work did not close down either mathematics or logic. On the contrary, it stimulated new branches of both, including, for example, recursive function theory, which is the mathematical foundation of cybernetics and computer technology. But it did give pause, if only indirectly, to a few of those interested in foundational questions in logic, mathematics, and philosophy—none more so, arguably, than Ludwig Wittgenstein.

THE EARLY WITTGENSTEIN AND THE PHILOSOPHY OF LANGUAGE

Ludwig Wittgenstein (1889–1951), a genius born into a socially prominent Viennese family possessing enormous wealth and culture, became interested in foundational questions by way of his youthful work in the field of aeronautical engineering. Frege urged the young Wittgenstein to study with Russell at Cambridge (and urged Russell to be his mentor). Wittgenstein's early work, the *Tractatus Logico-Philosophicus*, published in 1921, was his only book to appear during his lifetime. The *Tractatus*, written under the inspiration of Russell (who was still under the influence of the *Principia*), can be seen as an effort to do for language what the *Principia* had done, more or less successfully (for better or worse), for mathematics. In it Wittgenstein sought to reduce language to its logical form. (Remember that Gödel's "Incompleteness Theorem" had not yet appeared.)

The philosophical study of language was then still in its infancy. Yet Wittgenstein already had the insight which dominated his entire intellectual life: the "troublesomeness" that is called Philosophy (with a capital *P*) is rooted in the confused way that language is conceived by people in general and by philosophers in particular. In the *Tractatus*, Wittgenstein was implicitly attempting to solve all the outstanding problems of philosophy by showing the logical form of language. That is, his concern was not simply with philosophical language, nor with any particular natural language (or any particular unnatural language, such as mathematics), but with language in general—with language in the abstract or, if you will, language as "the form of thought." As such, the *Tractatus* was, in effect, an effort to create (or at least to establish the foundations for) a new, non-Aristotelian logic. As we have suggested, such a project was entirely consistent with what many logicians and mathematicians of the day were seeking to do.

Ironically, Wittgenstein's writings were subsequently used by his followers (whom Wittgenstein had never wanted to have) to create still another field within philosophy, what has become known as the philosophy of language. The attempts of Russell and Whitehead to reduce mathematics to its ultimate logical form (what Russell called "logical atoms") and, thereby, to eliminate metaphysics from philosophy (to get the Greeks out of it) stimulated (via Wittgenstein) the formation of a new school of philosophy known as *logical positivism*. Referred to as the Vienna Circle because they worked in Vienna until Hitler forced them to leave, the logical positivists (such as Carnap, Hempel, Schlick, Waismann, and Neurath) interpreted Wittgenstein's *Tractatus* as a directive to transform philosophy (now without the metaphysics, but not without the particular, which had become a logical atom!) into a servant of science.

But Wittgenstein himself had already abandoned the *Tractatus* altogether to devote himself to his ultimate philosophical "duty": the destruction (in postmodern terminology, deconstruction) of philosophy and the curing of philosophers of their obsession with language. This he pursues in his later writings, which also stimulated the growth of the philosophy of language, only this time his self-proclaimed followers went in the direction of what is called "ordinary language."

THE SHORT, UNHAPPY LIFE OF LOGICAL POSITIVISM

If the Vienna Circle was done in by Nazism, logical positivism was done in by its own liberalism. For in reality it was nothing more than an effort to salvage or revise philosophy by turning it into an abject glorification of science. In this attempt, not only did logical positivism contribute mightily to its own demise, it actually opened the door wider to the postmodern critique of science. While Gödel (who was not in the Vienna Circle) was effectively establishing rigorous limits of certainty for mathematicized science, the Vienna Circle, blindly following Wittgenstein's *Tractatus* (and, at least at times, seemingly oblivious to problems of self-referentiality), proceeded to construct logical foundations for all of modern science.

Members of the circle were particularly concerned with matters of scientific reductionism. Consequently, they elaborated the Kantian distinction between analyticity and syntheticity. As well, they refined the notion of reductionism by attempting to give a logical (foundational) characterization to sense experience itself. Particularity and identity, now in logical atomistic guise, remained intact. In the service of science, these and other philosophical analyses spun like planets around positivism's sun— the so-called Theory of Verifiability. This central principle asserted that meaningfulness be identified either "by definition"—the analytic—or as the verifiable. According to the theory, a proposition is verifiable if something counts as evidence—ultimately reduced to empirical evidence—for the truth or falsity of the proposition.

Enormous creative energy was devoted to clarifying the key conceptions involved in the verification principle. In an age of self-referential and critical sensibility, it was no surprise that before very long the question was asked regarding the logical status of the verifiability principle itself. Was it true by definition? If so, that might reduce its relevance to actual science. Or was it itself verifiable by an appeal to empirical evidence? This, of course, raised issues of circularity and regress.

The debate raged from the 1930s through the 1950s. The positivists generated ever more subtle notions of confirmation (for example, Popper's Theory of Falsifiability), and their analytical critics found fault. It was the American logician W.V.O. Quine who put the matter (and logical positivism) to rest. In his brilliant essay "Two Dogmas of Empiricism" (he presented an early version of it in 1950), Quine (1963) systematically deconstructed logical positivism by analytically and logically demonstrating that reductionism and the analytic–synthetic distinction—the cornerstones of post-Kantian empiricism and, therefore, of logical positivism (also known as logical empiricism)—are essentially untenable.

Thus were logic and mathematics (by way of Gödel) and empiricism (by way of Quine), which together constituted the absolute bedrock of modern science, thoroughly and rigorously challenged from within. Gödel and Quine went even further than that to challenge philosophy itself. But still they did not seek to abandon it. For Gödel, philosophy was the ongoing evaluation of logical–mathematical analysis. Meanwhile, Quine's notion of philosophy, "empiricism without the dogmas," was a kind of pragmatic philosophical–sociological–cultural mode of analysis continuous (in contemporary logical form) with the work of the early American pragmatists (such as William James, Charles Pierce, John Dewey, George Herbert Mead, and C. I. Lewis). Ultimately, Quine's work would be cleverly identified (by Donald Davidson, who much respected Quine) as "the last gasp of empiricism." It was left to the brilliant Wittgenstein to bury philosophy. He would do it out of duty, creating a profound alternative to philosophy: philosophizing without philosophy, the continuous activity of playing language-games.

THE LATE LUDWIG WITTGENSTEIN

Wittgenstein's untimely death from cancer in 1951 spared him the pain of seeing his later work distorted and deformed into so-called ordinary language philosophy by John Austin and others who claimed to be his followers, much as his early work had been misused (from Wittgenstein's point of view) in the creation of Vienna Circle–style logical positivism. Sadly, however, he also missed the opportunity to see his investigations become (as they now are) a major component of the emerging postmodern critique of science and psychology. For, while Wittgenstein's later writings addressed issues of concern to psychology, they were distinctly antipsychological.

Likewise, his views on philosophy, language, and philosophical scientific methodology were explicitly critical. However, Wittgenstein was not merely writing as a critic. We (and others, including Baker, 1992, and

Peterman, 1992) hear his voice as also that of the therapist: that is, his critique took the form of a nonsystematic, "client-specific" treatment plan for both philosophers and ordinary people. For Wittgenstein, philosophy is the disease, language the carrier, philosophical scientific methodology the hospital which science neither wants nor needs. And psychology is the pseudoscientific, bogus cure. Precisely how pseudoscientific and how bogus is the subject of the following chapters, an inquiry into the sordid life and impending ignominious death of the "bad (commodified) seed" born to philosophy and science.

Together with Lev Vygotsky, Wittgenstein has become a most distinguished grandfather of postmodernism. He is a presiding influence on so-called philosophical psychology, a term used to describe the work of the Wittgensteinian philosophers who began writing on psychological matters in the years immediately following his death and continue to do so. More recent times have witnessed the emergence of "psychological philosophy," a term we use to describe the work of a growing number of contemporary psychologists who, like us, have been profoundly influenced by Wittgenstein's thought (for example, Gergen, 1994; Jost, 1995; Shotter, 1991, 1993a and b; van der Merwe and Voestermans, 1995). These days, philosophical psychologists and psychological philosophers are increasingly joining forces in the effort to create a new, relation-based (as opposed to a judgment- or truth-based), nonsystematic understanding of understanding. Wittgenstein's language-games, and his notion of "form of life," are proving invaluable in this enterprise.

Critical scholars in various parts of the European academic world (Jacques Derrida, Michel Foucault, Jurgen Habermas, and Martin Heidegger, to name a few) have been likewise raising issues about philosophy, science, and psychology in different ways. They or their followers can also lay claim to igniting the postmodern revolt against modern science (and the 350-year-old absolute authority of the scientific paradigm). But America had by then become the home away from home of modern science and psychology. The Wittgensteinian revolution (which, as we approach the twenty-first century, is turning out to be vastly more important than either the Marxian or the Freudian ones) was, from the late 1950s through the 1970s, quietly germinating within the American university system. Its history inside that system and, at least as importantly, outside it, is one of the things that must be understood if we are to understand understanding at all.[3]

It was not until several years after Wittgenstein's death that his work, along with the writings of the first wave of his posthumous followers, became generally available. At the time, the "happening" philosophical topics (at many American universities) were the philosophy of mind (philosophical psychology), the philosophy of language, logic, and the philosophy of science. One of the most important subtopics being hotly debated was explanation. Was there a difference in accounting for human action and explaining nonhuman events? If so, what was it?

An important essay by the distinguished positivist philosopher of science Carl Hempel called "The Function of General Laws in History" (1965; first published in 1942) began appearing in various anthologies. In it Hempel argued that while general laws and empirical observation are typically less evolved in the "science" of history than in science in general, the characteristic unstated explanatory model of history (that is, writing and research) is roughly the same as in physics, biology, or chemistry. This seminal essay on the structure of explanation marked a turning point in the emergence of twentieth-century philosophy of history. (Prior to this point, analytic philosophers did not think highly of the philosophy of history that had been produced.)

Donald Davidson, a former colleague of Hempel's who is now one of the world's most distinguished professional philosophers, continued in Hempel's path. According to Davidson (1980), explanations or accountings of human actions given in terms of reasons are both causally and structurally the same as, or very similar to, explanations of events (especially nonhuman events) in the so-called hard or natural sciences. That is, the model of explanation operative (or at least said to be operative by methodologists and philosophers of science) in the hard sciences—sometimes called a "causal" or a "deductive–nomological" model—suffices, in the form of reasons, for history and the softer social sciences and/or ordinary, conversational accountings of human actions. In other words, while reasons may not be the same as causes, they play the same role in explaining human actions as causes play in explaining physical events.

At this point, you will recall, logical positivism had already been all but destroyed as a philosophical "school." Davidson apparently saw himself as having leaped beyond Humean empiricism to a kind of analyticism which was more than consistent with empirics but which broke completely with the metaphysics of empiricism. We believe that he succeeded in making that analytical leap. Ultimately, however, Davidson (who spoke of Quine's "last gaspism") himself became one of philosophy's most significant "last gasps."

The neopositivist, deductive–nomological thesis of Hempel and Davidson was beginning to come under attack from philosophers of mind/philosophical psychologists, including those who had been strongly influenced by Wittgenstein (particularly his later writings). Something of considerable importance was clearly going on, but it was not at all clear what that something was. What everyone would have to have known then in order to comprehend it was that, under the emerging influence of Wittgenstein, the stage was being set for the overthrow of philosophy. At the same time, the philosophical roots of postmodern social psychological critical and theoretic deconstructionism were beginning to take hold. Three decades later, in the 1990s, they would become the basis for a radical challenge to psychology and, in turn, for a radical challenge to science itself.

A number of new Wittgenstein-influenced books on the subject of "explanation in history" began to appear. One of the most important was *Laws and Explanation in History* (1957) by the Canadian philosopher William Dray. Obviously influenced by so-called ordinary language and ordinary language philosophy (which, as we have noted, is usually said to have derived from Wittgenstein's later work), Dray argued that not all explanations, and especially not all historical explanations, are causal answers to why questions at all. Instead, accounting for something in history often merely involves saying, in some detail, what happened or how it happened or, indeed, simply how it was possible that it happened. None of these, Dray said, required causal–deductive underpinnings; neither did all historical explanations.

Michael Scriven (1959), a philosopher of science at Indiana University, backed Dray up (or vice versa) by insisting that Hempel confused a historical explanation with the grounds which might justify either the explanation itself or the giving of the explanation. And so on, and so on. A number of philosophers began to get into the act by writing about the philosophy of history in general and historical explanation in particular. Among other things, those who argued against Hempel insisted that the context in which an explanation is given is a critical factor in the analysis of the explanation itself. This argument appeared to some to be problematic in that it confused the critical distinction between what an explanation is and what the activity of explaining is. But what, some began to ask, if there is no distinction? What if the philosophical–explicative activity (for example, the explication of explanation) cannot ultimately yield an abstract *explicandum*? That is, what if it cannot yield some kind of philosophical definition? What if it can only yield itself as activity—or, perhaps, more activity? What if, following the later Wittgenstein, the entire philosophical activity cannot yield philosophical truths, only more and more activity?

Dray and Scriven were arguing, at least by implication, that context could somehow be explicated philosophically. But, for some, their context turned out to be just as troublesome as Hempel's explanation. For the analysis of context failed to take into account the context in which context was itself analyzed. Perhaps even activity itself was just another word or concept?

Enter Lev Vygotsky and activity theory.

So far as anyone knows, Vygotsky (1896–1934) never heard of Wittgenstein (who, as far as anyone knows, never heard of the Russian with whom he would turn out to have much in common). Censored under Stalin, Vygotsky's foundational works in psychology and culture were largely unavailable in English and other languages until the late 1970s. Today,

however, Wittgenstein and Vygotsky, in tandem, are, in our opinion, bury-
ing psychology—dead or alive.

As with the death of philosophy, and closely connected to it, the demise
(still-in-process) of psychology demands a new, nonsystematic method to
answer the still relevant questions that it once took care of, questions about
human life in general, and the life of the mind in particular. For as Wittgenstein and many who followed him teach us, their deaths are inseparable
from the overall failure of systemization itself that we can see manifest
everywhere, from the sabotage by Gödel of the effort to systemize mathematically the foundations of mathematics and logic to the Soviet–Stalinist
destruction of international communism. Thus it is that science, the embodiment of systemization in modernist culture, is itself under devastating
assault by Wittgenstein, Vygotsky, and their critical theoretic descendants
(the present authors included). If there is such a thing as the postmodernist
story, in our opinion, that is it.

For the moment, however, we turn to the unheard-of story of psychology,
which is descended, as we have earlier noted, not only from philosophy but
from science as well. Theirs is a remarkable family indeed, one so riddled
by murderous power struggles, incestuous couplings, intrigues, and be-
trayals as to rival those which figured in the classic tragedies of ancient
Greece. And surely that's appropriate enough. For it was in what is now
called Greece, you will recall, that human beings first began (Western)
philosophizing some 2500 years ago—an activity that, with Plato, would
become systemized in the form of philosophy.

As we have pointed out, there may not be any explanation for why the
human capacity for abstract Western-style thought should have made its
first appearance in that place and at that moment. For our purposes, it is
enough simply to note that it did. Nor is it possible, in our opinion, to say
with any certainty why it was that the dualistic, particularistic form of
thought which is philosophy should have come to define reason, driving
all other forms of thought from the field. Again, what is certain is that it did.

We saw as well that modern science was born of philosophy about 350
years ago. Assuming philosophy's dualistic stance, guided by the logic of
the particular and accompanied by the technology that was the material
expression of (or, at least, companion to) its method, science undertook to
observe/describe/control the natural world. Thus did modern man (per-
sonified by the scientist) knowingly conquer nature. The astounding accomplishments of science in the early years of this century precipitated a
major "family" crisis. For science, the child, had by then achieved sufficient
stature and power so as to challenge philosophy's millennia-long ideologi-
cal/methodological domination of the world.

In the early part of the twentieth century these two titans, philosophy
and science, entered into a power struggle that lasted for several decades.
Religion (scholasticized Christianity) in battle with fundamentalism, and

politics (bourgeois democracy) in battle with communism, each in its own way, remained aloof. Traditional religion held itself above the fray, content to be the official (and well-kept) consort of the modern secular state. Politics maintained its neutrality, prepared to be the patron of whatever form of corporatism would best serve its interests (ideological and otherwise).

On the defensive, philosophy attempted to perfect itself by appropriating the means of science and in doing so inadvertently discovered its own profound weaknesses—"genetic" flaws from which science also suffered but which were masked by its extraordinary practical achievements. Science, meanwhile, strode masterfully from one triumph to the next, reaching its practical–theoretical apotheosis in the late 1930s and 1940s with the discovery and harnessing of nuclear energy.

Eventually, science would succeed in unseating philosophy from its throne. Philosophy was gradually relegated to the underfunded periphery of academic life, regarded simultaneously as a monument to be venerated and a joke. But even jokes have cash value in our thoroughly pragmatized and commodified culture. When Richard Rorty, currently America's philosophical spokesperson and superstar, sheds his intellectually sophisticated cover, he reveals the philosophical school of thought known as American pragmatism to be every bit as vulgar (but not as honest) as the ordinary American working-class attitude: "If it don't make no money, it don't mean nothing." In *Consequences of Pragmatism* (1982), Rorty revises the American philosophical pragmatic tradition from James to Quine, a tradition that sincerely (if incorrectly) sought to define key philosophical conceptions such as truth in terms of values or value terms. In its place Rorty substitutes a practical-minded nihilism which is entirely indifferent to the truth question and wholly concerned with the money question. According to Rorty, analytic philosophy "now has only a stylistic and sociological utility" (p. 217); what distinguishes philosophers from others is neither a subject area nor an attitude, but a talent (philosophers are a "corps d'elite united by talent rather than a list of shared problems and prior results—the *Inspections des Finances* of the academy, so to speak," pp. 219–220) whose best hope is "Andy Warhol's promise that we shall *all* be superstars, for approximately fifteen minutes apiece" (p. 216). He calls for the elimination of Philosophy in favor of philosophy and Experts in favor of experts—but only if the cash value remains constant. Philosophy, it turns out, is "just what we philosophy professors do" (1982, p. 320). We wonder whether American pragmatization and philosophy deserve a better end than this.

The wunderkind science, by contrast, became enormously popular: tens of millions of people would view science on exhibit at one or another World's Fair; they would see it romanticized in the movies and, beginning in the 1950s, could watch it at home on television. In contrast to the image of the philosopher as an innocuous, even slightly pathetic, dreamer the scientist appeared in popular culture as a man of action, a hero or an evil genius, who could change the course of destiny.

Yet while science, having overthrown philosophy, would continue to enjoy enormous prestige and to exercise tremendous power throughout this century, it was psychology—the lackluster child of a moribund philosophy and a science that, for all its dazzling accomplishments, had inherited philosophy's fatal flaws—which would take over the world. A seemingly minor character, psychology walked onto the stage of history virtually unnoticed while the battle between philosophy and science was at its height. Struggling mightily with one another, they were unmindful of the nonentity that had entered the scene; to imagine that psychology was a rival to be feared by both would have seemed preposterous and absurd.

For psychology, the child of such extraordinarily gifted and creative parents, was itself nothing very special. It never showed any signs of the brilliance, the integrity, the humaneness which had characterized philosophy and science at their best. This is not to say that psychology is some sort of monster, for it possesses no grandeur of any kind. It is simply mediocre: silly, trivial, superficial. As such psychology is, if you will pardon the philosophical expression, ideally suited for a world in which reason, which has been the prevailing form of thought for the last 2500 years, appears to have reached its limits and biggest-bang-for-a-buck pragmatism is the only game in town. Neither terribly intelligent nor unduly burdened by principle, and rampantly opportunist (a case in point being its relationship with the modern state, as we show in the following chapters), psychology, a socially constructed (commodified) myth disguised as science, came to rule the world in the second half of the twentieth century. If reason has been the form of thought for two millennia and more, with scientific reason prevailing since the eighteenth-century Enlightenment, it is psychologized reason which has dominated the last fifty years. Yet this is despite the fact that unlike science, psychology has produced virtually nothing of value; it has solved, we would argue, no human problems.

The principal instrument of psychology's rule is nothing other than the scientifically discredited identity logic of the particular. Psychology transformed that logic, which it inherited from philosophy and science, into a pseudoscience of the individual, and sold it to the highest bidder. Today there are few places on earth where commodities such as identity, for example, and other products of the logic/myth of the particular have not been successfully marketed.

What follows is an account of the transactions which made psychology the best-selling myth the world has ever known.

NOTES

1. See Marx's *Theses on Feuerbach*. For example, in Thesis III Marx says, "The coincidence of the changing of circumstances and of human activity or self-changing can be conceived and rationally understood only as *revolutionary practice*" (Marx, 1973, p. 121). See also Theses I, V, and VI.

2. The process of mathematicizing logic in preparation (intended or unintended) for defining mathematics in terms of logic is hardly considered improper (that is, circular). Indeed, it is a characteristic practice of modern mathematicized science (and modern scientific or metamathematics, that is, mathematics that is primarily concerned with its own foundations). For example, the proof of Fermat's last theorem much reported-on in recent years is based on work in so-called proof theory (a relatively new and foundational branch of mathematics), which extends the conception of mathematical proof in ways that support (indeed, make possible) the proving of Fermat's and other heretofore unsolved puzzles. This technique of creating the conceptual and technological tools necessary to achieve the desired results in an area where the tools are applied is typical of modern mathematical/technological science. It is, moreover, characteristic of the modernization of mathematics, which came to include logic (mathematical logic) as a branch of mathematics itself.

3. Many of the ideas presented in this brief history of "the Wittgensteinian revolution" within the American university system were first presented in Newman (1996) *Performance of a Lifetime.*

Part II

PSYCHOLOGY'S UNHEARD-OF STORY:
THE STATE AND THE MIND

A favorite off-duty pastime of many sophisticated and enlightened psychologists—especially those who are clinicians or psychotherapists—is to make fun of diagnosis. They do not only do this at cocktail parties and family barbecues, some even begin professional talks with an especially ludicrous quotation from the *DSM-IV*, the fourth revision of the *Diagnostic and Statistical Manual of Mental Disorders* (American Psychiatric Association, 1994). A nearly nine-hundred-page compendium of hundreds of categories and subcategories of mental illness, the *DSM-IV* is the bible of clinical psychology, psychiatry, and psychiatric social work. The following syndromes usually get a good laugh:

  Hypoactive Sexual Desire Disorder . . . a deficiency or absence of sexual fantasies and desire for sexual activity (302.71, p. 496);

  Dissociative Disorder Not Otherwise Specified . . . Number 6. Ganser syndrome: the giving of approximate answers to questions (e.g., "2 plus 2 equals 5") when not associated with Dissociative Amnesia or Dissociative Fugue (300.15, p. 491);

  Disorder of Written Expression . . . a combination of difficulties in the individual's ability to compose written tests evidenced by grammatical or punctuation errors within sentences, poor paragraph organization, multiple spelling errors, and excessively poor handwriting (315.2, pp. 51–52)

But once the laughter dies down comes the rueful acknowledgment that, absurd as they may be, such diagnoses are a necessary stock in trade. It is not that they believe in diagnosis, some psychologists will explain (sometimes self-righteously); besides, what they write down on the form has little or no effect on their work with clients. But if they didn't use the *DSM-IV*, they point out, they'd soon be out of a job. For in order to receive payments from medical insurance companies or the government for clients they see in therapy, clinicians must come up with a diagnosis from the *DSM-IV*: no diagnosis, no reimbursement. Moreover, as Gergen (1994) and others have pointed out, clients themselves typically demand to know "what's wrong" with them; they often ask for a diagnosis. Of course, these same psychologists say, they avoid the absurd in favor of a "reasonable" and hopefully innocuous diagnosis, such as major depressive disorder:

> If Manic, Mixed, or Hypomanic Episodes develop in the course of Major Depressive Disorder, the diagnosis is changed to a Bipolar Disorder. However, if manic or hypomanic symptoms occur as a direct effect of antidepressant treatment, use of other medications, substance use, or toxic exposure, the diagnosis of Major Depressive Disorder remains appropriate and an additional diagnosis of Substance-Induced Mood Disorder, With Manic Features (or With Mixed Features) should be noted. (*DSM-IV*, p. 339)

In our opinion, any ordinary person looking at the *DSM-IV* with even a half-open mind would recognize it as sham science (for one thing, it is insufficiently mathematical to be called science). Laced with inconsistencies, contradictions, and arbitrary distinctions, the *DSM-IV*—despite its claims to rigor and objectivity—is essentially subjective and normative. How, then, did it become the official word in clinical psychology, psychiatry, and social work? How did something so obviously unscientific in so many ways become the scientific guide to mental health practice in the United States?

We are not pointing a finger here at individual practitioners for naiveté, ignorance, or questionable ethics. Rather, we are concerned to tell the mostly unheard-of story of how psychology created its subject matter; successfully sold its expertise in this subject matter to government, educational and social service delivery institutions, the military, and the public; and came to be a model for scientific endeavors in the human–social realm.

We believe that this history is critical for understanding the current efforts to create a postmodern unscientific psychology. What brings together the various and valuable postmodern analyses and critiques of psychology is their challenge to psychology's pretense that it is a science. Moreover, postmodernists point out that psychology is socially constructed on a purely pragmatic basis and that this fact has critical implications for the continued existence of the discipline and institution.

What is significant is not that psychology is socially constructed, but that it is a socially and pragmatically constructed myth which has succeeded in disguising itself and becoming accepted as a social-scientific discipline. This rather remarkable feat (psychology became Psychology) was accom-

plished within a century. During that time psychology broke with traditional ontology and, invoking the logic of the particular and, in particular,
the self, created an entirely new ontology of godlike psychological objects;
it created new investigative practices that could only be validated through
what established scientists would call sleight-of-hand techniques; it made
and continues to make knowledge claims that are more comprehensible
within a framework of self-fulfilling prophecy than within a scientific
framework; and, most importantly, it did this by having cemented a sym-
biotic relationship with the state through federal, state, and local legislative
bodies which is unlike that of any other social institution or human service,
including medicine and education. In the following four chapters we will
touch upon each of these accomplishments, as we trace its evolution—more
a money-making scam than a mere story or harmless myth.

4

The New Ontology and Psychology's Mythology

WHERE WE ARE NOW

A look at the official program for the 103rd Annual Convention of the American Psychological Association (a guide of five hundred plus pages to five days of scholarly presentations) suggested that this convention would be pretty much like its recent predecessors. The weather would be sweltering (held in mid-August, in 1995 the convention took place in New York City), the numbers huge (more than eight thousand speakers would make presentations to fifteen thousand to twenty thousand attendees). The symposia, invited lectures, workshops, and paper presentations sponsored by the various divisions and committees of the American Psychological Association (APA) were listed in the subject index under headings that subdivided psychological research and practice in ways that were recognizable, if only to the initiated (examples: Community—Rural/Urban; Developmental—Stages/Infant; Disabled—Rehabilitation; Education—Learning; Ethnic Studies—Cross-Cultural; Industrial/Organizational—Personnel; Motivation; Neuropsychology; Social—Attribution; Social—Group Processes; Sexual Behavior/Functioning; Teaching of Psychology).

But things were not all business as usual during those five muggy days, despite appearances. For the American Psychological Association had been "infiltrated" by postmodernists. An unprecedented number of presentations by psychologists explicitly challenged psychology's claim to be a science, attributed responsibility for the crisis which the century-old discipline is experiencing to psychology itself, and called its continued existence into question.

In the past there have always been a few such iconoclastic presentations at APA conventions. But until now they had been sponsored by the smaller and more esoteric divisions of the association (theoretical and philosophical psychology, humanistic psychology, psychology and the arts) and sparsely attended. What was significant this year was that major divisions, including general psychology, experimental psychology, personality and social psychology, consulting psychology, psychotherapy, psychologists in independent practice, and psychology of women, were cosponsoring miniconferences and symposia on such topics as "Mental Health Expertise: Does Our Science Justify Continuing What We Do?"; "Is There a Crisis in Psychology?"; "Illusion of Science in Clinical Assessment—Diagnosis and the DSM"; "Consulting for a Paradigm Change—The Overreliance on the Medical Model"; "Struggling with Relativism and Politics—Constructionist, Hermeneutic, and Feminist Approaches"; and "Language in Psychology—Setting the Ontological and Epistemological Bounds." Interestingly, however, there were no listings in the subject index under headings such as "Critique," "Crisis in Psychology," or "Postmodernism." Nor were there any listings for the psychological traditions and approaches from which many of the critiques were made: social constructionism, deconstructionism, feminist psychology, hermeneutics, discourse analysis, and narrative therapy. This absence of information made it difficult to find out where the postmodernist sessions were taking place. Still, many hundreds of people took the trouble to get to them.

Responses to the presentations were mixed. There were those who agreed with the critique but, unabashedly pragmatic, pointed out that without the imprimatur of science psychologists would no longer be experts and they would no longer get paid. The defenders of the status quo (the hard-core modernists) were, by and large, defensive; they argued variously for a return to empiricism, recommended emulating Newtonian physics, or vigorously denied that science is socially constructed (their conclusion being that it is, therefore, "the same" in Brooklyn, Bangkok, and Bangladesh). The majority of participants, however, enthusiastically supported the substance of the critique as well as the fact that such discussions were taking place.

Psychology is, in our view, in serious trouble. It has been for some years now, but 1995 was the year that the American Psychological Association could no longer deny what was happening. One indication—the infiltration of its annual convention by postmodernists—was likely unintentional. But in its publications, the APA officially recognized that all is not well with psychology—especially clinical psychology—and announced what it was going to do to remedy the situation.

Recently a single issue (July 1995) of the association's monthly newspaper, the *APA Monitor*, contained three articles whose subtext was the current crisis in psychology: "APA Campaign Stresses the Value of Psychology,"

"APA Initiative Will Expose Media to the Rigors of Psychological Science," and "APA Grant to Promote Science on the Radio." The articles included the news that the association is allocating nearly $2 million to boost psychology's image—$1.5 million for a public education campaign to "raise the public's awareness of the value and scientific basis of psychology" (p. 14), $170,000 for a special science initiative whose aim is "to improve journalists' understanding of scientific psychology and help them further appreciate the scope of the field" (p. 33), and $100,000 to a public radio show so it can "include more of scientific psychology in its programming" (p. 33). Like other articles in the *Monitor* appearing during that year, these reveal both the crisis in psychology and the inability (or unwillingness) of the psychological establishment to comprehend the nature of it.

The impetus for the various public relations campaigns is the seemingly sudden and economically motivated loss of faith in psychology of the federal and state governments, the corporate sector, the media, and the public as evidenced by recent policy changes. First is the nationwide transference of the mental health care delivery system from private practitioners to managed care companies. Second are legislative proposals to eliminate allocation of federal funds for behavioral science research and to merge the Department of Education with the Department of Labor (which would effectively end research in educational psychology).

With the advent of managed care, the federal government, insurance companies, and health maintenance organizations (HMOs) will no longer provide payments for mental health services directly to psychologists, psychotherapists, psychiatrists, and social workers. Rather, payment will go to managed care companies, which, in turn, will not only pay mental health practitioners on a fee for service basis, but decide how many hours of treatment are called for. For example, if Ms. Brown, a bank supervisor, currently seeks psychological help, she can contact a professional recommended by a friend, look in the phone book, or ask her medical doctor for a referral. As long as the professional she sees for therapy is licensed or certified, her costs will be covered (at least in part) by her carrier. Under the new model, however, Ms. Brown's carrier will have a relationship with one or more managed care companies. Now Ms. Brown will be given a choice of which professional service provider to see from among the managed care companies' list of practitioners. The person she chooses will receive a fixed payment determined by the company's estimate of the time needed for effective treatment.

Clinicians are concerned with what they perceive as a loss of professional autonomy and a decline in the quality of care for consumers. They seem to have been caught off guard by the abruptness with which the transformation of the American health care system is taking place. Perhaps they expected a public outcry. Instead, the move to managed care has served to make clearer the declining faith in the effectiveness of mental health services in general and psychology in particular. The fastest growing treatment modality in the United States for alcohol, drug, and other "compulsive behavior" problems, for example, is self-help, primarily through the non-professional (but legitimized by the mental health profession) Alcoholics Anonymous and its numerous spin-offs (Narcotics Anonymous, Overeaters Anonymous, and so on). And when Americans do turn to professional treatment, more often than not it is drug therapy—not psychotherapy—that they choose, a fact the APA could not help noting. An article in the June 1995 issue of the *APA Monitor* pointed (somewhat self-servingly) to the public's desire for a "quick fix" as the presenting problem with which clinical psychologists and other practitioners have to contend.

The official position of the psychological establishment is that the current crisis in psychology has little to do with psychology and much to do with its image. The public is misinformed about psychology; its understanding is "limited at best." People need to be educated about "psychologists' unique training and skills, the science base of practice and the value of psychological assessments, interventions and services" (*APA Monitor*, July 1995, p. 8). This sentiment is echoed by psychologists themselves: 49 percent of psychologists who attended "conversations" sponsored by the APA said that the public was "confused" about psychology (*APA Monitor*, November 1995).

In the establishment's rush to defend psychology as science, there is no mention of its profound failures. The ongoing, acrimonious debate between psychologists and psychiatrists over which is more effective, talk therapy or psychotropic drugs, never takes into account that they *both* have been tragically ineffective in treating emotional pain and psychopathology. We are no closer to understanding or stopping the violent behavior of individuals or groups, decreasing school failure, or lessening the quantity or quality of all kinds of emotional suffering despite the billions of dollars and hours spent in psychological research and practice by an ever-expanding number of psychologists and other mental health professionals. Neither is there mention of the fact that to thousands of psychologists (most of them, incidentally, APA members)—critical theorists, feminists, neo-Marxists, sociocultural psychologists, activity theorists, social constructionists, and others in or near the postmodern camp—the problem is not that psychology is perceived as not being scientific, but that psychology *is* (pseudo)science. From the postmodernist vantage point, psychology's failures (and the societal response to them) are rooted in its misguided efforts to emulate the natural sciences; this is the origin of its ecological and historical invalidity.

THE NEW ONTOLOGY

Unlike people living at the dawn of the twentieth century, we now live in a world filled with mental objects of a very particular sort—psychological objects. For every obscure psychological entity like the Ganser syndrome, there are hundreds more commonplace ones—personality, neurosis, depression, panic disorder, intelligence, practice effects, rating scales, test scores, ego, id, stages of development, learning disability, midlife crisis, and, of course, addiction—that ordinary people speak about and live with on a day to day basis. Having become insinuated into ordinary language and the popular culture, these inventions of the laboratory and the clinic are taken to be as real as trees and stars. How was this remarkable "act of creation" accomplished?

The trees and the stars give us a clue. As one human science methodologist has noted, "The scientific study of human and social phenomena began after the scientific study of the natural world had been successful" (Polkinghorne, 1983, ix–x). The emergence and phenomenal achievements of modern science and technology during the rise of mercantilism and industrial capitalism were perhaps the most important factors contributing to the application of a natural science model to human behavior and human action. While there were those who argued against this secondhand use of the scientific paradigm and for a unique approach to human phenomena during the eighteenth and nineteenth centuries and into the twentieth, ultimately there was no stopping "the scientific model."[1] The natural science paradigm was imported wholesale into the study of human beings. In our view, this was a tragically wrong turn for our entire species—one that now, in the final years of the twentieth century, has brought us to a dead end. We (the authors) are not alone in this belief. The current spate of postmodern critiques of science bear witness to the fact that matters are terribly, terribly amiss.

In the 1920s and 1930s Vygotsky attempted to create a more human psychological science; he wanted, he said, to "discover how science has to be built" (1978, p. 8). Vygotsky, however, was caught in a struggle between two intellectual traditions: a natural science model rapidly on its way to determining and defining psychology, and an even younger science— Marxism, the science of revolution—already becoming calcified, revised, and paradigmized along the lines of the science which it had officially repudiated as being in the service of its class enemy, the bourgeoisie. Although Vygotsky never completely escaped the traditions to which he was heir, in our opinion he came remarkably close to doing so. In Chapter 9 we will focus our attention on Vygotsky's postmodernist significance (along with that of Wittgenstein) as an important bridge in the evolution of an unscientific psychology. Here we only want to draw attention to a striking observation Vygotsky made that is relevant to the task at hand.

The observation appears in a discussion of science and its relation to revolution and history. This is a subject likely to strike the psychologist of the 1990s as bizarre, quaint, or irrelevant, but it was central to the methodological break with a natural science paradigm that Vygotsky was able to make. "A revolution solves only those tasks which have been raised by history; this proposition holds true equally for revolution in general and for aspects of social and cultural life," Vygotsky said (quoted in Levitan, 1982).

This characterization of revolution as socially and culturally situated is more postmodern than modern. Revolutions—whether they be political, cultural, or scientific—Vygotsky tells us, are neither capricious nor moral. They do not merely produce better systems. Revolutions occur when the institutions of a given society and culture can no longer successfully engage the sociohistorical issues that must be dealt with in order for people to get on with things.

History has frequently thrown up (new) questions for which human beings, or at least powerful elements within a particular society or culture, have needed answers in order to keep going economically, scientifically, philosophically, culturally: "How did the world begin?" "How can we get to the East?" "What is illness?" "How can we cure this disease?" "How can we make sense of our dreams?" "How can we increase profits?" "Can one draw or paint process?" "Is there, or could there be, life on the moon?" "Why do human beings talk?" "What do babies know?" "How can we teach children to read?" and so on. Sometimes, when the existing societal arrangements (the answering machines) fail to provide anything resembling an adequate answer, an extended period of stagnation or decay sets in; people persist in looking in the same places in the same way for the answers.

When there is some kind of breakthrough, a recognition that the existing societal arrangements cannot produce any, then revolution may occur. But this is hardly inevitable; the failure of the existing answering apparatus to deal with the questions raised by history is a necessary but not a sufficient condition for revolution. There must be at least the hint of some alternative in the air—a new paradigm, a new approach, a new way of seeing—something positive, which has sufficient currency to be thought of as a possible answer.

Thomas Kuhn's classic work, *The Structure of Scientific Revolutions* (1962), describing how the history of science progresses through a series of paradigm shifts—the revolutionary process whereby one worldview breaks down and is replaced by another—is invaluable for an appreciation of how, as modern science was being created over the course of the seventeenth, eighteenth, nineteenth, and twentieth centuries, the existing philosophical and scientific apparatus failed to answer some of the critical questions. Numerous other works in the history and philosophy of science are also helpful (for example, Butterfield, 1962; Feyerabend, 1978; Lovejoy, 1960). A number of scholars have written extensively about paradigm shifts in other areas such as medicine, art, and literature.[2]

Postmodern critiques of psychology suggest that the necessary conditions for revolutionary change currently exist. For at the same time as a technologically sophisticated medical model threatens the very existence of clinical psychology as we know it, as abnormal psychology is turning from a social paradigm back to an asocial paradigm (Prilleltensky, 1994), and as the modernist nature–nurture dichotomy thrives (with cognitive science and genetic biology sweeping away the remnants of behaviorism), simultaneously a distinctly critical psychology (an antipsychology or even a no-psychology) movement is rapidly growing. (Judging by the amount of space set aside by bookstores to accommodate the number of books devoted to the critique of psychology, it is becoming a field unto itself.) Many theorists and practitioners simply no longer believe in psychology or its foundational concepts and methods (such as development, the individual, the self, stages, dependent and independent variables, rationality, predictability, objectivity, proof, quantifiability, universality, patterns, empirical evidence).

This lapse of faith in psychology's ability to provide answers to the questions history has raised—about our sociality, our antisocialness, emotional pain, violence, identity, learning and educational failure, prejudice and bigotry, sexuality, creativity, depression, memories (false or true), and a host of others—marks a significant moment in the breakdown of the existing paradigm (including the recognition that it is breaking down). In our view the new critique represents a change in focus from ideology to methodology. The valuable critiques of psychology produced during the 1960s and 1970s exposed primarily its ideological biases (its Eurocentrism, racism, sexism, classism, and homophobia) and pointed out, correctly in our opinion, that as such psychology was simultaneously irrelevant and harmful to most of the world's people.

These days, postmodern deconstructions of psychology are more likely to expose its methodological biases, and to conclude that psychological science is, at best, anachronistic. A positivist, empiricist, and structuralist method permeated with philosophical assumptions, goes the postmodernist argument, cannot begin to answer the kinds of questions being raised about human beings today (if indeed it ever could) because human behavior and activity are far too complex for psychology's thoroughly modernist pseudoparadigm. If human beings are social–cultural–historical entities who construct our world—which includes ourselves and our science—then human beings cannot be studied by means of a natural science paradigm which excludes the human and the social.

Are the conditions sufficient for a revolution in psychology? The necessary breakdown is occurring. At its best, postmodernism is a rigorous critique of the psychologizing of life through the mistaken attempt to apply a scientific model to phenomena that are, in their essence, relational rather than individuated (particularized). Unlike prior scientific/intellectual revolutions during which one paradigm came to be replaced with another, a critique of paradigmism itself is central to postmodernism. The most provocative writings do more than point to the inapplicability and error of the modernist paradigm; they point to the inapplicability and error of the *paradigm* as a conceptual/methodological tool. They thus simultaneously challenge psychology's philosophical underpinnings and its scientific outer garments.[3] It remains to be seen whether a nonparadigmatic positive (but not positivist), practical–critical activity alternative to psychology will develop sufficiently to be the catalyst for the continuous completing of a scientific revolution.

What are the characteristics of modern science that make its adaptation to the study of human–social phenomena ecologically and historically invalid? What characteristics of the mother (philosophy) did the child science take on, and how were they passed on to the younger child psychology? What historical conditions produced the need to understand human–social phenomena, especially "the mind"? How did psychology come to embrace the natural science model, and then distort it nearly beyond recognition? How is it that in a culture which is so exceedingly overpsychologized, establishment psychology is fighting for its (scientific) life? These are some of the questions we will explore as we attempt to set forth a social–cultural–historical analysis of the myth/hoax that is psychology.

We will argue that the mythic nature of psychology derives not from a mistaken but successful application of a natural science paradigm to the human–social realm, but from the impossibility of applying such a paradigm. Drawing upon a variety of sources, we will try to show that modern psychological practice does not meet the standard criteria of modern science for the straightforward reason that it cannot. Throughout the history of psychology, therefore, psychologists abandoned the criteria. But they retained the rhetoric, and attempted to resolve the contradiction by creating new technology (as physics did), inventing data-generating apparatus, and producing knowledge claims about people which violate the laws of both mathematically based and empirically based science.

Interestingly, psychology's relationship to philosophy was the mirror image of its relationship to science; psychology abandoned philosophical rhetoric but held on to philosophy's a priori unscientific criteria. Proclaiming itself the scientific (and therefore the only true) way to approach the study of human actions and behavior, psychology officially severed its ties with philosophy while steadfastly engaging in philosophical abstraction and systematically incorporating such centuries-old philosophical presuppositions as mind–body dualism, systemization, proof, causality, first causes, and explanation into its practice.

The construction of the new mythology was intimately related to the ongoing work of creating a professional/intellectual niche for psychologists. Psychology successfully persuaded political, industry, and social policy leaders; the academy; and the public to believe that "what was good for psychology was good for America." More than the practitioners of any other profession or discipline, it was psychologists who had the "expertise" to promote the general welfare through the promotion of psychology (the APA's official statement of purpose). Even during its current crisis, as its failures become more obvious and its bogus nature more exposed, the institution of psychology remains the most powerful producer and disseminator of ideology in the postindustrialized world.

THE HEGEMONY OF KNOWING

Knowledge—what it is, how it is acquired, its relationship to what there is to be known, why it is important—is central to understanding both the development of modern Euro-American psychology and its critiques. From ancient times to the present (as we examined earlier), what has counted as knowledge in Western science and philosophy has changed considerably, as has the family of concepts associated with knowing.

What has changed hardly at all over the last 2500 years, however, is the hegemony of knowing in Western culture: the insistence that knowledge is necessary to understanding and making sense of the world (and thereby, presumably, to living). The acquisition of knowledge—through recalling past experiences, perceiving, explaining, categorizing, interpreting, describing, and so on—is considered to comprise one or more such mental acts. The dominant understanding of understanding is cognitive; it occurs, supposedly, in the mind of the individual and comes about through or is identical with knowing. Even those who would agree that understanding is jointly produced through social interaction and relationships still often hold to the belief that there is something in people's heads called knowledge/understanding. This cognitive bias, in our opinion, is among the most antidevelopmental (antihuman) characteristics of modernism which permeate psychology. Accordingly, we find that what is especially provocative and significant about the postmodern critique of psychology is the extent to which it challenges the cognitive paradigm of understanding.

In their introduction to *Therapy as Social Construction*, McNamee and Gergen (1993) discuss how modern psychology's cognitive bias (over)determines the therapeutic process and (mis)shapes the relationship between the client and the scientist–therapist.

> For it is the scientist who observes most acutely and systematically, who applies the most rigorous and rational procedures in evaluating and synthesizing information . . . who builds safeguards against emotions, values, and errant motives, and stands independent from the objects of observation lest his or her conclusions are contaminated. It is this image of the expert, independent, and individual knower that therapeutic practitioners have largely adopted in the present century. It is the therapist who carefully observes and deliberates, and who offers his or her conclusions about the adequacies and inadequacies of independently situated others. And it is the

common individual who suffers from inadequacies, who may regain a fulfill-
ing life by giving way to expert knowledge. (pp. 1–2)

The image of the therapist as an expert required, of course, something to
be knowledgeable *about*, something to be expert *in*. Psychology had to
create a new ontology in order to carve out a niche within both the scientific
and public domains. In order to produce knowledge (a necessary condition
for respect and legitimacy), it had to create its own subject matter and
investigative practices.

In his invaluable history of psychological research from the nineteenth
century through the middle of the twentieth, Danziger (1994) describes in
great detail the evolution of psychology's knowledge-producing apparatus
and the social–cultural–economic forces accompanying its development.
Here he draws attention to a contradiction with which scientific psychology,
unlike botany and physics, for example, had to contend (notice the role
played by mathematicization in the legitimizing enterprise):

> In the judgment of the lay public everyone had to rely on psychological
> knowledge in making his or her way through the world. How could anything
> offered by experts compete with a lifetime of experience in human affairs?
> This ever-present background challenge had effects on the investigative
> practices of psychologists that should not be underestimated . . . these
> practices . . . served to demonstrate a crucial distance from those mundane
> situations in which everyday psychological knowledge was acquired. This
> was achieved largely by drawing on the mystique of the laboratory and the
> mystique of numbers, both of which had been well established prior to the
> appearance of modern psychology. The very artificiality of laboratory situ-
> ations became a plus in establishing the credentials of knowledge claims
> emanating from this source, and the imposition of a numerical form on
> otherwise trivial knowledge gave it an apparent significance with which lay
> knowledge could not compete. (pp. 184–95)

However, the distance and artificiality cannot be so great that the knowledge produced by these means is judged too remote from ordinary life to
be of any value. Danziger continues: "The discipline's ability to make fairly
reliable predictions about human beings outside the psychological laboratory depended to a large extent on the closeness of the context of investigation to the context of application. It was often the case that psychological
knowledge had some technical utility only insofar as its investigative
practices were continuous with relevant social practices outside the investigative situation" (p. 189).

Thus, the new ontology of psychology was inextricably tied to its creation of new investigative practices, which, in turn, had some connection to
previously existing social practices. Mental testing (one of psychology's
most lucrative investigative practices and the context for the construction
of numerous psychological objects) provides a clear illustration. Its evolu-

tion into a knowledge-producing apparatus in the early-twentieth century depended in part on the prior existence of the social practice of the academic examination as a means of sorting and selection, and the social practice of the medical examination as a means of assessment (Danziger, 1994; see also Burman, 1994; Morss, 1990; Rose, 1990).

Furthermore, as Gergen (1994) notes, the discursive elements of existing social practices were taken over by psychology. With the appearance of so-called scientific terms such as *clinical depression*, the more vivid and nuanced language used by ordinary people—"having the blues" or "feeling down"—becomes devalued.

> A concept such as rationality is removed from its everyday context, replaced by technical terms such as "cognition" or "information processing," thrust into artificial intelligence formalizations, measured by dichotomous listening devices, and submitted to experimental investigation. As the language is technologized, so it is appropriated by the profession. The language of cognition or information processing, for example, becomes the property of the profession, and the professional now lays claim to knowledge that was once in the common realm. The professional becomes the arbiter of what is rational or irrational, intelligent or ignorant, natural or unnatural. (p. 152)

In tracing the history of how psychology accomplished this appropriation and projected itself as the possessor and producer of expert knowledge about the human–social realm, we will draw upon a variety of sources. We have found three recent works to be especially valuable for this purpose: Danziger's (1994) historiography, to which we have already referred, provides precise details of the social–cultural–historical production of scientific psychology in its first fifty years; Gergen's (1994) social constructionist analysis, as we have seen, emphasizes the discursive dimensions of paradigm shifts in psychology; and Burman's (1994) deconstruction of developmental psychology is an ideological critique that addresses the culture and gender biases of research in child development and parenting. From different perspectives, each makes a strong argument against establishment psychology's claim to be a science.

MAD ABOUT METHOD

As it became an autonomous field of inquiry in the first quarter of the twentieth century, psychology was constrained by existing scientific and intellectual practices that it took over from already existing fields, most notably philosophy and physiology. It extended these practices in its own name and produced new practices appropriate to its peculiar location. Danziger (1994) notes, for example, that psychology gained legitimacy for its knowledge claims not through the production and distribution of sophisticated theory but almost entirely through establishment of the objectivity of its method: "Claims in psychology have depended almost completely on the rational virtues of its methodology. It was only because of the logical–technical features of its investigative practices that psychology could give some plausibility to its claims for scientific status" (p. 5). Danziger contrasts this "methodolatry" of psychology with the situation in the natural sciences, where theoretical discourse has been at least as common and sophisticated as discourse on method.

In analyzing psychology's obsession with method as a means of producing itself (including its scientific legitimacy), Danziger traces the historical production of the psychological laboratory and the development of the unique social arrangement known as *psychological experimentation*. Originally a collaborative effort among scientists who took on various tasks (such as interchangeably assuming the roles of what we now call "subject" and "experimenter") out of purely practical considerations, the psychological experiment rapidly became institutionalized. The structure so familiar to us today—the rigidified roles of the naive experimental subject who serves as the "source of data" and the experimenter who manipulates the experimental conditions, their interaction strictly governed by rules—was not there when psychology was born in 1879 in Wilhelm Wundt's Leipzig laboratory (Danziger, 1994).

Wundt—in the psychological folklore "the father of psychology"—did indeed play a significant role in solidifying the natural science paradigm within psychology. However, it was neither Wundt's questions nor his method that would become the backbone of psychological research. Quite the contrary; as Danziger puts it, "Virtually everything that happened in modern psychology was a repudiation of Wundt, explicitly or implicitly" (1994, p. 34). Rather quickly, the inquiry that played a significant role in psychology's beginnings was transformed into another task entirely, one more akin to human engineering than scientific investigation.

Wundt's enterprise stemmed from a desire to study and understand the human subjective experience. In this pursuit he sought to devise a method for studying private individual consciousness, to create conditions under which internal perceptions could be transformed into something like scientific observation. Wundt's interest was the actual perceptual experience itself, not the self-reflective reporting of experience. To construct a science of mental life, he set up the psychological experiment as a means of manipulating the conditions of internal perception so that they approximated the conditions of external perception.

Intellectual curiosity about this sort of human subjectivity arose from developments within philosophy (with which Wundt was familiar). Two centuries earlier, Locke had distinguished between two sources of knowledge: sensation (which gives us knowledge of the external world) and reflection (which gives us knowledge of how our own minds operate). A philosophy of mind, based on evidence from reflection, was thought to correspond to the philosophy of nature, based on evidence from our senses. But until Kant, no hard and fast distinction between the two had been made.

In Kant's attempt to synthesize empiricism and rationalism, he created a distinction between philosophy and psychology and between psychology and (natural) science (Danziger, 1994). Acknowledging that there were a world of private experiences and an "inner sense" through which this world was made manifest, Kant asked whether experiences conveyed by the inner sense could function as the basis for a mental science analogous to the way experiences of the outer senses functioned as the basis for the physical sciences. His conclusion was that they could not, because science required a systematic ordering of information capable of being expressed in mathematical terms, something he deemed impossible with mental life. The empirical basis of mental life, Kant said, was not *sufficient* for it to be scientific; it was, however, necessary to be able to account for the origins, source, or cause of our experiences being what they are.

Wundt took up the challenge, attempting to discover the psychological determinants of experience. Modeling his inquiry on the physical sciences, he sought, by using the existing techniques of the physiological laboratory, to uncover the laws of psychic causality that physiology, physics, and the other natural sciences had neglected. Never relinquishing his ties to philosophy, Wundt wanted to achieve "a rejuvenation of philosophical inquiry by new means" (Danziger, 1994, p. 39) rather than to create a new discipline. While his vision was experimental, it was not necessarily quantitative. Nor did he desire to omit completely the social and cultural factors involved in subjective experience.

Ultimately, Wundt did not succeed. The social conditions in Germany necessary for the enterprise to be successful no longer held; the acceptance of psychologically oriented scholars into university philosophy departments was short-lived, and "experimental psychology in Germany found itself rejected by the forces that were to have provided it with an institutional home base. It was increasingly forced to make its own way as an independent discipline" (Danziger, 1994, p. 40).

Thus Danziger argues that the social–cultural–intellectual environment—especially the structure and organization of academia—had much to do with the direction in which psychology would eventually go. Nearly all the early American psychologists received their training in Leipzig with Wundt, and the system to which they returned influenced not only what it was they took away with them but how they interpreted it.

Philosophy was not strongly entrenched in American universities as it was in German institutions. What had replaced religion in the United States was not philosophical inquiry but (the glorification of) science much as pragmatism replaced what Santayana (1911) called America's "genteel tradition."[4] Moreover, the American universities were beholden to businessmen and politicians; they or their representatives made decisions about appointments, departments, and projects. Accordingly, it was necessary to market scientific psychology as a new discipline capable of yielding something which the members of this "business class" would recognize as being of value to them (Buss, 1979; Danziger, 1979, 1994; Napoli, 1981; Sarason, 1981).

Evidently, the American psychologists understood what their marketing strategy had to be. The great achievements of the natural sciences in the nineteenth century had helped to foster "scientism"—the glorification of science in the belief that the natural science methods were the only ones by which useful and reliable knowledge about anything could be produced. Simultaneously had come the devaluation of the humanities and social disciplines such as philosophy, history, linguistics, and anthropology. In other words, the social conditions required that psychology be practically useful (to those with power) if it were to exist. But to be practically useful was to be scientific, for within both philosophy and the sciences the equation of truth (what science seeks) and usefulness—pragmatism—was already gaining wide acceptance. The impact on psychology was profound. Not only were many psychologists concerned with practical applications from the very beginning, but even those who clung to the notion of intellectual inquiry for its own sake looked to the natural sciences for guidance and direction.

The growth of psychology as an academic subject was swift. In 1882, Johns Hopkins University began the first American doctoral program in psychology, granting its first Ph.D. in 1886. Less than twenty years later, more than one hundred Ph.D.'s were awarded in psychology (surpassed only by chemistry, zoology, and physics among the sciences) and forty-seven new psychological laboratories had sprung up (Napoli, 1981, p. 14). The American Psychological Association was formed in 1892; by the turn of the century psychologists were regularly publishing scholarly journals. As the new discipline gained academic recognition, it simultaneously generated interest among nonacademics in its potential practical utility.

Whether or not psychologists were always conscious of the pressures upon them, within a short time psychology's knowledge goal was transformed. From investigating the human experience through the careful study of individuals who were themselves interested in this question, psychologists quickly turned to positing universal human characteristics and attributes through techniques for mass testing and aggregating data. The transformation from studying individuals as *subjects of experience* to studying them as *objects of intervention*, says Danziger, was necessary to provide "knowledge that could be quickly utilized by agents of social control so as to make their work more efficient and more rationally defensible. Knowledge that led to behavioral prediction suited this purpose, but knowledge obtained in situations where the participants collaboratively explored the structure of their experience did not" (1994, p. 66).

Who were these "agents of social control"? What kind of knowledge claims did they require to justify their work? And what data-generating mechanisms did psychologists construct in their entrepreneurial zeal to be accommodating? The exploration of these questions requires that we examine how some of psychology's most widespread and destructive myths were constructed. As well, it brings into greater clarity the nature of psychology itself. As we shall attempt to show, the relationship between the myths of psychology and the myth that is psychology is not one of identity; nor is it simply additive. Our analysis is derived from interweaving some of the major critiques of psychology (which tend to emphasize the myths it has produced) and historical documents and analyses (which reveal it to be comprehensible only as a pragmatically driven scam or hoax). In the next three chapters we will explore, in turn, the relationship of the myth/hoax of psychology to three of its most influential mythical conceptions: the myth of the individual, the myth of mental illness, and the myth of development.

NOTES

1. Arguments against the adoption of a natural science paradigm to study the human–social realm began almost as soon as modern science gained hegemony. The eighteenth-century scholar Vico is typically cited as the most significant forerunner to the early antipositivist, antiempiricist movement. In *The New Science*, written in 1725, Vico put forth a historical–cultural view of human phenomena emphasizing the primacy of our meaning-making capacity. Vico's ideas have become increasingly popular among postmodernists (for example, Shotter, 1993a). Other antipositivists whose work prefigures the twentieth century's mostly philosophical opposition to positivist psychology include Brentano and Dilthey.

2. Among the many works discussing paradigm shifts in the move toward modernism we recommend the following: In medicine, Brown, *Rockefeller Medicine Men* (1979); Cassell, *The Nature of Suffering and the Goals of Medicine* (1991); Golub,*The Limits of Medicine* (1994); and Foucault, *Madness and Civilization* (1965) and *The Birth of the Clinic* (1975); in painting, Berger, *The Success and Failure of Picasso* (1966); Cooper, *The Cubist Epoch* (1970); Golding, *Cubism: A History and an Analysis* (1968); Schwartz, *The Cubists* (1971); in theater, Brecht, *Brecht on Theatre* (1994) and Suvin, "The Mirror and the Dynamo" (1972); and in literature, Benjamin, *Illuminations* (1969).

3. Kuhn, while not considered a postmodernist, served as a bridge between the philosophical and scientific communities. Influenced strongly by Quine, who, in turn, was influenced (albeit in many cases, negatively) by the Vienna Circle, Kuhn's classical work was published by the University of Chicago's *Encyclopedia of Science*, edited by key members of the circle.

4. "America is not simply, as I said a moment ago, a young country with an old mentality: it is a country with two mentalities, one a survival of beliefs and standards of the fathers, the other an expression of the instincts, practice, and discoveries of the younger generations. In all the higher things of the mind—in religion, in literature, in the moral emotions—it is the hereditary spirit that still

prevails, so much so that Mr. Bernard Shaw finds that America is a hundred years behind the times. The truth is that that one-half of the American mind, that not occupied intensely in practical affairs, has remained, I will not say high-and-dry, but slightly becalmed; it has floated gently in the back-water, while, alongside, in invention and industry and social organization the other half of the mind was leaping down a sort of Niagara Rapids. This division may be found symbolized in American architecture: a neat reproduction of the colonial mansion—with some modern comforts introduced surreptitiously—stands beside the sky-scraper. The American Will inhabits the sky-scraper; the American Intellect inhabits the colonial mansion. The one is the sphere of the American man; the other, at least predominantly, of the American woman. The one is all aggressive enterprise; the other is all genteel tradition" (Santayana, 1911, pp. 39–40).

5

Psychology and the Individual

The notion that psychology's object of investigation is the individual has been both the basis for its legitimacy as a field of inquiry and a locus of much of the criticism leveled against it. Psychology is typically described (for example, in introductory texts, dictionaries, and encyclopedias) as being concerned with individuals or groups of individuals—how they behave, how they develop, and, in particular, how they differ from each other. Responding to psychology's seeming obsession with the ahistorical, asocial, isolated individual, many postmodern critics (as well as some of their modernist precursors) have questioned whether there even is such a particular/thing.

Psychology has been taken to task for allowing the assumption of the individual knower to permeate theory and practice in virtually every area of its domain. In relation to psychotherapy, and clinical and abnormal psychology, we have already glimpsed the social constructionist critique (for example, Gergen, 1994; McNamee and Gergen, 1993). In addition, workers in the areas of family and systems therapy (for example, Poster, 1978), critical psychology and psychiatry (for example, Ingleby, 1980a; Parker, 1989; Parker and Shotter, 1990), and "prevention" and community psychology (for example, Albee, 1981; Sarason, 1981) not only critique the traditional practice of treating the individual but argue that social units of various configurations, such as the family or the community, are as well the proper unit of study and of cure. Within developmental and educational psychology, there are writings on development and learning as socially constructed activities or processes, especially by Vygotskians and cultural–

historical psychologists (for example, Lave and Wenger, 1991; Moll, 1990; D. Newman, Griffin and Cole, 1989; Newman and Holzman, 1993; Rogoff, 1990; Tharp and Gallimore, 1988; Wertsch, 1991). Feminist and neo-Marxist psychologists (for example, Burman, 1990, 1994; M. Gergen, 1988, 1995; Ussher and Nicholson, 1992; Venn, 1984; Walkerdine, 1984) and feminist epistemologists (for example, Harding, 1986, 1987; Harding and Hintikka, 1983; Keller, 1985) often explicitly critique psychology's conception of the individual knower/learner. More generally, work in the sociology of psychological knowledge frequently incorporates similar critiques (for example, several chapters in Buss, 1979; Gergen, 1982).

We are among the more vocal critics of psychology's obsession with and glorification of the individual (Holzman and Newman, 1979; Newman, 1991a; Newman and Holzman, 1993). We agree that psychology developed alongside and played a central role in the development of the ideology of "rugged individualism" that accompanied the expansionary years of American and international capitalism. Nevertheless, we believe that to locate the problem entirely in the myth of the individuated subject is mistaken. For to do so, in our opinion, is to miss the magnitude of psychology's distortions and to understate profoundly the destruction which psychology has wreaked on our culture.

Psychology's obsession with and glorification of the individual—a construct derived directly from the logic of the particular—is a hoax. The contradiction is this: while it has been successful in infusing us with a sense of "identity" and the experience of ourselves as individuated things separate from "the other," psychology itself has never been particularly concerned with individuals as individuals. Its concern has been methodological—the individual is a useful construct in making knowledge claims about groups or formulating general laws of behavior. Psychology's intense and extensive study of the individual has not been done in the name of, nor has it empirically supported, human diversity and uniqueness. Its object of investigation has not been the individual, nor has it really discovered anything about the actual and potential ways in which people differ from one another. Far from contributing to a culture that supports individual differences and fosters individual expression, psychology has been instrumental in contributing to a culture of conformity.

THE ISOLATED INDIVIDUAL

To substantiate this claim, we need to look closely at the concept of the psychological subject. Recall that Danziger described a shift very early in the history of psychology from an interest in the individual as the subject of experience to a concern with the individual as the object of intervention. The information required by the "agents of social control" (primarily in industry, the military, and education, as we will see shortly) was not about individuals but about types of people; it was not about their *experiences* but their *attributes*. Who will make the best military officers? What are the characteristics of good insurance salesmen? What method can be used to sort children for teaching purposes under laws of compulsory education? With seemingly little hesitation, psychology self-interestedly accepted the challenge to deliver the goods. What it would take was a significant alteration in psychology's relationship to the individual subject.

Danziger (1994) tells us that two already existing social practices—quantitative social research and the questionnaire method—proved invaluable in this effort. As early as the mid–nineteenth century, statistical data on public health and social problems such as crime, suicide, and poverty were being gathered by the socially concerned in North America and Europe. Instead of relying solely on official statistics, they began to use questionnaires as a means of gathering their own data.

According to Danziger, the scientific appeal of statistical tables depended upon the numerical regularities that emerged when the actions of large numbers of individuals were aggregated—regularities that were interpreted as reflecting the essential lawfulness of human conduct. Soon it was being claimed that the accumulation of large numbers was necessary in order to reveal the scientific laws which were supposed to underlie human conduct.

In Danziger's view, the move from social to psychological statistics was not simply administrative but required new conceptions. Once statistics (for example, on crime) were gathered, the problem of how to account for differential but stable rates remained. Quetelet, the pioneer of statistical social science, came up with a new conception that was at least a partial solution—"propensities" toward certain actions that could be attributed to an "average individual." Differential rates of crime could then be said to depend on variations in the average "propensity to crime," which itself might be influenced by such factors as age or gender. This invention was to have enormous methodological significance for psychology. Danziger writes: "What Quetelet had done was to substitute a continuous magnitude for the distinct acts of separate individuals. Suicide, crime, homicide, and other social acts were not to be understood in terms of the local circumstances of their individual agents but in terms of a statistical magnitude obtained by counting the number of heads and the number of relevant acts in a particular population and dividing the one by the other" (1994, p. 76).

The making of inferences about individuals from statistical regularities that are observed to occur in groups required a point of view about how totalities (sets) and particulars (members of sets) are related: namely, that particulars form totalities and that group characteristics are the sum of individual attributes. The adoption of this point of view enabled psychology to develop a "scientific" method that was not experimental in Wundt's sense.

A new method for justifying psychological knowledge claims had become feasible. To make interesting and useful statements about individuals it was not necessary to subject them to intensive experimental or clinical exploration. It was only necessary to compare their performance with that of others, to assign them a place in some aggregate of individual performances. Individuals were now characterized . . . by their deviation from the statistical norm established for the population with which they had been aggregated. (Danziger, 1994, p. 77)

As Danziger points out, however, this methodological approach was too crude to be widely accepted by the scientific community; it did not meet the criteria of the natural sciences. Yet it clearly possessed social relevance and practical applicability. This emergence of two competing investigative practices, the experimental and the statistical, and the competing pressures on psychology from an expert scientific community and a lay public (the historical contradiction of a scientific psychology born of its decision to emulate the natural sciences) converged. The invention of the *experimental group* resolved these conflicts, if only temporarily.

It is one thing to study groups which "occur" naturally (that is, societally), such as children of different ages or males and females, and to make claims about them from aggregating data. Such collective subjects of psychological research are preexisting societal categories which have a certain utility and meaning in the culture. It is quite another thing to *create* categories, to invent groupings of people that do not have a prior existence or meaning in the culture at large but become cultural products solely by virtue of the psychologist's intervention. Here again we see set theory at work (underground). For example,

> a group mean is obviously not the attribute of any actual persons who contributed to its constitution but the attribute of a collectivity. But what kind of collectivity is this? It is the group of individuals who happened to participate as sources of data in a particular psychological investigation. Their common activity in the experimental situation defines them as a group . . . the collectivity of which the group mean is the aggregate is one that is defined by laboratory practice rather than by social practice outside the psychological laboratory. (Danziger, 1994, p. 85)

We are persuaded by Danziger's argument that such a practice involved a conceptual shift of great magnitude and had tremendous significance for the direction psychology would take.

> It points the way to a science that supplies its own categories for classifying people and is not dependent on the unreflected categories of everyday life . . . [T]here is now the possibility that psychologically constituted collectivities will compete with and even replace some of the more traditional categories of social groupings. Categorizing children or recruits by intelligence quotient

was an early example of such a process. In terms of the internal development of the discipline, the artificial constitution of collectivities by the research process itself provided the basis for a science of psychological abstractions that need never be considered in the context of any actual individual personality or social group. (p. 85)

In the decades since, psychology has constituted thousands of categories for classifying people (those contained in *DSM-IV* are a relatively small sample) which have supplanted everyday ones. The creation of various types of artificial groups (experimental, treatment, control, psychometric) has allowed for the generation of knowledge claims built on the sand of psychological artifacts and philosophical abstractions. Such investigative practices create knowledge claims that are completely determined by the practices which produce them. For example, findings of research involving experimental and control groups are interpreted in terms of the differences created by the researchers between the groups; findings of research involving psychometric groups (comprising individuals selected by the researchers on the basis of performance on a psychological task) are interpreted in terms of the stable characteristics of the group created by the researchers. Data that do not "fit" can always be treated as error or artifact (one way of resolving what the ethnomethodologist Garfinkel, 1967, referred to as "the et cetera problem" of operational definitions). This attempt to solve the problem (or paradox) of operational definition is, like Russell's "type theory" in mathematics and logic, an example of an ad hoc solution.

Armed with the tools required for generating data relative to abstract attributes of equally abstract populations of people, psychology packaged these data as findings and sold them as knowledge claims about individuals. That is the hoax. Psychology, from its earliest days, has not been concerned with individuals—that is, with the person. American psychology aspired to be a socially relevant—but not a social—science (Danziger, 1994, p. 88). Accordingly, psychologists used the individual (it is living, breathing, socially situated people, after all, who were recruited for psychological experiments and still are) as the medium through which—they claimed—abstract laws of human conduct were made manifest. It is these "laws," and not individual human beings, which became and to a large extent continue to be the subject matter of psychology.

THE CRITIQUE: THE SOCIALLY SITUATED INDIVIDUAL

For the moment, let us look at psychology from this point of view (which many psychologists share): instead of investigating human experience or individual differences, psychology *should* seek to discover the underlying and abstract laws of human action and behavior. Even granting that this is a reasonable intellectual activity and one that is, perhaps, societally useful as well, is psychology on the right track?

It seems to us that serious problems remain. The study of human–social phenomena is a qualitatively different activity from the study of physical phenomena. (If it were not, there would be no rationale for a separate science of psychology.) We (the authors) are among many who have pointed out that it is human beings who study human beings—and that makes us, uniquely, the subject *and* the object of investigation, the studiers *and* the studied. Even if there were underlying and abstract laws to be discovered (we happen to think there are not), not only would they have to be of a qualitatively different nature from the laws governing physical objects, but the procedures for discovering them would need to be sensitive to the unique position we are in (scientifically speaking and otherwise) relative to ourselves since the time long ago when, as Jaynes speculates, the twin capacities for self-consciousness and abstraction transformed human experience.

While any and every scientific endeavor is a social practice, in the case of psychological investigation there is a self-reflexivity (which is not present in botany, astronomy, or physics, for example) that places the sociality of the investigation in relief. It is precisely this sociality that psychology has gone to great lengths to deny in creating its ecologically invalid method, and it is this denial that is a major focus of postmodern critiques.

Some critics have approached the issue of sociality from a macrolevel, pointing out that both psychology and psychologists themselves are socially situated. For example, Sarason (1981), in speaking of the ways that psychology is ahistorical and asocial, reminds us that the position of psychologists in the social order (coming from and relating to a narrow and relatively privileged segment of society) has a significant impact on what they do. In a series of essays, *Psychology Misdirected* (simultaneously a critique of and an apology for psychology), he argues that psychologists' failure to be aware of how their conceptions and theories are shaped by their experiences and social location has led psychology astray. Other writers, more hard hitting, accuse psychologists of becoming involved in questionable enterprises and of holding to dubious theoretical positions out of sheer self-interest.[1]

That psychology serves to preserve the status quo seems obvious. That psychologists (as a professional group and, in many cases, as individuals) act in their own self-interest is equally apparent. That many acts of psychological and physical violence have been done to ordinary people (sterilization of "the feebleminded," lobotomies and electroconvulsive shock treatment, stigmatization and deprivation of educational opportunity, and racist immigration policies are the most notorious) in the name of promoting human welfare as defined by scientific psychology's expert knowers is clear as well. What we think is more difficult to see (and what we are attempting to show) is the relationship between psychology as social practice in this global, recognizably ideological and political sense and in the more local sense of the social practices it invented. The evolution of the myth/hoax of psychology (not merely its substantive myths) is located in the history of this relationship.

The sociality of psychology is, of course, always present. Even the sterile laboratory is socially situated. Several recent inquiries into the psychological experiment are especially helpful in investigating psychology's subject matter.

In *Deconstructing Developmental Psychology*, for example, Burman (1994) takes apart one of the classics of infancy research to illustrate two themes: the influence of the view that the infant is a biological organism, and the research experiment as a social practice. The research in question, known as the "visual cliff" experiments, first published in 1960 by Gibson and Walk, spawned a series of studies by these authors and others, and has been standard fare in psychology texts for many years.

The Gibson and Walk research was designed to investigate how human beings perceive depth: is our ability to process and interpret visual cues about depth innate or learned; is it species-specific? They created an apparatus that appeared (to adults) to be a cliff by placing a checkerboard some distance underneath a clear glass floor. Infants were placed at the "shallow" or "deep" end and their mothers, placed at the opposite end, were instructed to call their infants to them. In the first experiment, only three of twenty-seven infants crawled out over the cliff; the rest cried or moved away from the cliff. Gibson and Walk claimed to have demonstrated that most infants can discriminate depth through visual cues by the time they can crawl, although they did not argue that this ability was innate.

According to Burman, modifications and replications of the initial experiment as well as critical discussions of Gibson and Walk's claims were carried out for fifteen years, all within a framework that suppressed "the analysis of the task as a social situation" (1994, p. 31). She describes a more recent study that incorporated the variable of face recognition into the visual cliff research; the investigators found that there was a direct relationship between whether or not infants crossed the cliff and the expression on their mothers' faces (for example, smiling, fearful, angry).

The implication, writes Burman,

is that presenting the task as an epistemological enquiry ignores motivating factors, and reduces what is clearly a complex communicative encounter, dependent on particular aspects of a relationship, to a question about individual perceptual competence. . . . Moreover, this experiment illustrates how misleading it is to regard the infant alone as the appropriate unit of analysis. Rather we must look at the whole material and communicative system within which the infant acts. (1994, p. 31)

Yes, and no. What we find most interesting about Burman's analysis is that it unwittingly recapitulates the laboratory paradigm (which views things from the level of the biological organism) at a social or communicative level. But integral to the experiment as a social practice is the ontology it has created. Burman has abandoned neither the psychological subject nor the psychological object. For the former, she prefers "the whole material and communicative system within which the infant acts" to Gibson and Walk's infant. For the psychological object, she prefers "the task as a social situation" to their task of discriminating depth. Burman appears to have overlooked an important feature of the myth/hoax of psychology, one that seems to us at least as important as the biologizing of childhood: a critical component of the social practice known as experimentation is the creation of a *psychological task*.

In our view, establishing a psychological task (regardless of how social it may be) makes it impossible to study human beings as human beings. For to be human is not only to be socially situated; it is to be historical. What we mean by human historicality is the revolutionary activity of changing the totality of circumstances that determine the changers (Newman and Holzman, 1993). The investigative paradigm of psychology, which has as its central premise the changing of particulars, makes it impossible to study human activity.

It is from this revolutionary activity-theoretic point of view that we take issue with Burman's otherwise insightful deconstruction. In a similar vein, we have previously criticized the social–cultural–historical methodology of the "ecological validity" project conducted in the 1970s at the Laboratory of Comparative Human Cognition (Cole, Hood and McDermott, 1978; Hood, McDermott and Cole, 1980). These researchers (who included one of us—Holzman, formerly known as Hood) argue persuasively for the unit of psychological study being "the person–environment interface" or "the scene" (similar to Burman's "material and communicative system") and for the use of ethnographic methods as opposed to interpretive and biased experimentation. In pointing out its limitations, we acknowledge that capturing the socialness of human beings through creating more social units of analysis and using ethnographic descriptions are likely to eliminate some of the biases of establishment science. But neither practice eliminates the scientific bias "embedded in objective description, for description itself is an interpretation" (Newman and Holzman, 1993, p. 188). To the experimenters, the (social) situation is still an experiment. There remains a real discrepancy between the analytic and instrumentalist nature of the scientific enterprise and the behavior, activity, and experience of the participants.

A somewhat different, but not opposing, view is that of the German psychologist Klaus Holzkamp. His enterprise, called "critical psychology," was carried out in the mid-1960s but has only recently become available to an English-speaking readership, primarily through the writings of Brandt (1979) and Tolman and Maiers (1991). Holzkamp was concerned with the political implications of applied psychology. He also examined the "external relevance" of experimental psychology—is psychology relevant to people outside the laboratory? (This is similar to the ecological validity question.) Both of these concerns were united by Holzkamp's belief that theories should be evaluated on the basis of their representativeness.

In this context, Holzkamp described the psychological experiment in contractual terms. Essentially an agreement between the experimenter and the experimental subject whereby the subject agrees to "expose himself [*sic*] to the life situation which E has produced for S as 'experimental procedure,'" the experiment creates the subject as "an imagined individual who is exposed to environmental conditions which *it has not created itself . . .* [and whose] *responses are fully determined* by the . . . experimental conditions" (quoted in Brandt, 1979, p. 82, emphasis in original).

What happens, according to Holzkamp, is the following: on the basis of this agreement, the subject "no longer acts in typically human ways but merely as an organism." Furthermore, the experimenter disregards the fact that the restricted actions of the subject come from the agreement they made (Brandt, 1979, p. 82). On this basis, the boundaries between animal and human psychology can be erased, and psychologists obtain similar results for animals and humans. To Holzkamp the similarity in findings is explained by a critical difference—*"human beings behave in the experiment according to agreement only like organisms, while rats 'are' organisms"* (quoted in Brandt, 1979, p. 82, emphasis in original).

Research showing that human beings do not behave in the experiment "like organisms" does not, in our opinion, discredit Holzkamp's argument. Looked at from within the experimental paradigm, people do behave in this way. Viewed from outside, they do not. To say that people do *x* or *y in* the laboratory is to make the mistake of taking the laboratory for a physical space. But the laboratory is a methodology that can be applied equally to events which go on in a physical laboratory and in everyday life settings. It is an ecologically invalid research practice (Cole, Hood and McDermott, 1978). From our relational, Wittgensteinian perspective (which we will present in Chapter 9), the laboratory experiment is a *form of life* or, more accurately, a *form of alienation.* People "behaving like organisms" is a form of life/form of alienation, albeit usually a nondevelopmental one. From this perspective, the emptiness of psychology's knowledge claims is apparent; they violate psychology's own rules of investigation.

THE SELLING OF INDIVIDUAL DIFFERENCES

The history of psychology is not part of our general cultural knowledge. Nor is it regularly studied with any seriousness in undergraduate or graduate psychology courses. (This lack of historical perspective is, of course, not unique to psychology but is pervasive in American educational culture.) There is, however, a rich and fascinating literature exploring developments within the field itself, the relationship of psychology to economic and political events, and the complex interplay between psychology and the overall culture.

Over the last fifty years, there have appeared dozens of histories of psychology and related fields, written from establishment as well as critical perspectives by psychologists themselves, historians, and journalists (see, for example, Baritz, 1960; Cushman, 1995; Danziger, 1979, 1994; Dawes, 1994; Freedheim, 1992; Herman, 1995; Hilgard, 1978; Hunt, 1993; Kamin, 1974; Koch, 1959; Koch and Leary, 1992; Morawski, 1988; Napoli, 1981; Prilleltensky, 1994; Sarason, 1981). Much of this literature draws heavily on archival materials from scholarly journals, popular magazines, and newspapers; the APA, the National Research Council, and other organizations closely tied to psychology's emerging legitimacy; and personal records of psychologists and others. Evidently, the pioneers of the discipline and profession were meticulous in documenting their progress; available materials include official lectures and addresses; APA committee meetings; correspondence and memoranda between psychologists, government and military personnel, industry tycoons, attorneys, philanthropists, and journalists.

By nearly all accounts, what put psychology on the map was the study of so-called individual differences—and World War I. From as early as 1890, American psychologists with applied interests had begun consulting (on a relatively small scale) in intelligence testing and vocational selection with business management, advertising executives, public school administrators, and directors of training schools and institutions for "the feeble-minded." Immediately after Congress declared war in 1917, the APA president, Robert Yerkes (who was not doing applied work himself), called the APA executive council together and charged the members with developing a plan for involving psychologists in the military effort.

They foresaw that their expertise would be useful in selecting recruits and assigning officers and personnel for special combat. The existing Binet intelligence test, which was designed to be administered individually, was too slow and cumbersome for this massive endeavor. The committee set to work devising a standardized test that could be administered to groups and produced the Army Alpha Test. The army approved a test trial and commissioned Yerkes a major; in this capacity, he supervised the army's testing program.

Despite competition with psychiatrists, who claimed intelligence testing as their domain, doubts expressed in military circles about the value of such testing and confusion as to why it was a personnel and not a medical (that is, psychiatric) issue, the army intelligence testing program was retained. Over 350 professional psychologists and graduate students were employed in the project, which by war's end had tested nearly 2 million men. Immediately after the war, many of these psychologists completed their tour of duty by treating patients individually in the forty-three army hospitals; they administered tests, helped those with learning problems, and tried to raise morale (Napoli, 1981, pp. 26–27).

Whether the project was actually of any use to the army is questionable. While nearly eight thousand men were declared unfit for duty on the basis of their low scores, how the army used the data on the rest is unclear. In his well-documented analysis "Ideology and Intelligence Testing," Samelson (1979) notes that there is no way of knowing with any certainty how personnel officers made use of the intelligence ratings in assigning recruits. According to army documents, reporting of test results was erratic and often erroneous (at one camp, there was a 20 percent error rate in scoring), instructions to army personnel were vague, and it was widely believed that there was more to making a good soldier than intelligence. (It was the opinion of some officers that "men of slow mentality who have little education often make better soldiers in the end than those with more flashy minds who would probably be rated higher," Samelson, 1979, pp. 143–145.)

As to the validity of the tests, this too is questionable. Comparisons of test results with officers' judgments and with performance evaluations of recruits during training camp were inconclusive. Attempts to conduct validation studies from troops returning after the armistice were aborted and, consequently, there are no data on the predictive value of the tests relative to soldiers' performance in combat. Add to all this the unsurprising fact that there was a very high correlation between test scores and amount of schooling. Samelson concludes that merely recording educational level of the recruits would have been as useful, as well as far less labor-intensive and costly.

The army intelligence testing project was of tremendous value to psychology, however. As one historian bluntly put it: "If psychology had not in fact contributed significantly to the war, the war had contributed significantly to psychology" (Camfield, 1970, quoted in Samelson, 1979, p. 154). The enterprise gained for psychology prestige, popularity, and a greatly expanded network of powerful contacts in the military, government, and industry. It also gave a boost to the eugenics movement, of which several leading psychologists of the time were enthusiastic proponents—Yerkes, for example, was a member of the Eugenics Research Association and had been appointed to the Committee on Eugenics of the National Commission on Prisons prior to the declaration of war (Kamin, 1974). There is no doubt that the psychology–military connection during World War I both built upon and helped to expand the market for psychology's new product—the mental test as a definitive measure of "individual differences."

Two eager buyers were industry and education managers. The tremendous growth of industry and the establishment of compulsory education at the turn of the century presented challenges of an enormous and unprecedented scope to those charged, respectively, with the related tasks of making a profit out of labor and turning poor immigrant children into literate (or at least compliant) adults. Reluctant at first to turn for help to those outside their own spheres, industrial and educational administrators were far more receptive to applied psychologists after World War I.

According to several social–cultural analyses of applied psychology, other factors that contributed to the acceptance of testing included the overall climate of progressivism, the growth of government, the closing of the American frontier, the glorification of science (and its association with progress), and the need to make "order out of chaos." Many writers are of the opinion that psychology was overtly concerned with establishing close ties to capitalism during these years (see, for example, Baritz, 1960, *The Servants of Power*, and Napoli, 1981, *Architects of Adjustment*). For these historians, and more recent cultural analysts who confront psychology as ideology (for example, Billig, 1982; Bulhan, 1985; Cushman, 1995; Sampson, 1993), psychology is comprehensible only in relation to the complex social–cultural–economic–political processes of which it was and is a part. We agree. Indeed, much of our own writing has been devoted to such analysis (Holzman and Newman, 1979; Holzman and Polk, 1988; Newman, 1978; Newman, 1991a; Newman and Holzman, 1993). Here we want to focus on some specific conjunctures of events, through which psychology evolved into a servant of political–social liberalism during the period of economic development and growth. We think this will be helpful in understanding how psychology, as the ultimate commodity, serves those who preside in this current moment of economic, social, and political crisis.

Industry leaders in the first two decades of the twentieth century had two main concerns: increasing production and stopping trade unionism. They realized that they had to "begin managing men and women as well as machine and process" (Baritz, 1960, p. 15). To deal with the tremendous turnover among auto workers in Detroit as a result of the industry's expansion, for example, in 1914 Henry Ford increased his employees' wages from $2.30 to $5 a day. The wage, however, was contingent on clean living; Ford sent investigators to workers' homes to check up on their sex lives, drinking habits, and so on. His hopes that these actions would increase productivity and loyalty to the company were realized, although increases in the cost of living forced him to authorize the $6 day in 1919.

Such a policy could not succeed indefinitely; while some companies followed Ford's lead, ultimately it proved too costly. What Ford did accomplish, according to Baritz, was to bring personnel issues to the forefront. It occurred to some manufacturers that instead of putting so much effort into controlling and training workers, they could concentrate on making good hiring decisions: "to select workers half as good as their machines" was good business (1960, p. 35).

The two psychologists traditionally credited with giving birth to industrial psychology are Hugo Munsterberg and Walter Dill Scott. Both had trained with Wundt in Leipzig and settled at American universities, Munsterberg at Harvard and Scott at Northwestern. As important as what they said in lectures and wrote in publications was how their connection to the "captains of industry" helped to create the demand for their psychological products.

Munsterberg first surveyed hundreds of executives about the psychological traits they thought necessary in employees. He was less impressed by their answers than by their great interest in the topic, which indicated to him that he should go further (Baritz, 1960). Munsterberg subsequently published his ideas for a psychology of industry as *Psychology and Industrial Efficiency* and simultaneously began working for industrialists. Drawing on the techniques of intelligence testing, he developed selection tests for various businesses, including the American Tobacco Company (traveling salesmen) and the Boston Elevated Company (train conductors).

Scott entered the door of industry through advertising. After being approached by a Chicago advertiser to deliver a lecture on how psychology could be useful to advertising, he was invited by a large advertising firm to write a series of magazine articles on the subject. Already a professor of psychology at Northwestern, in 1909 he received the additional appointment of professor of advertising. Over the next few years, Scott devised selection procedures and personnel rating scales for leading companies, including Western Electric, National Lead Company, and the George Battern advertising agency (Baritz, 1960; Napoli, 1981). The university–industry connection continued to be built as others across the country saw an opportunity for mutually aided growth.

The wartime testing project had given welcome publicity not only to testing and selection procedures but to psychologists (Scott was awarded the Distinguished Service Medal for his war work). It also provided an opportunity for establishing connections with government and quasi-government organizations, including the National Research Council. Formed in 1916 under the auspices of the National Academy of Sciences and the Engineering Foundation to "inventory and mobilize the scientific resources of the nation" (Baritz, 1960, p. 45), the National Research Council for several decades continued to play a leading role in linking psychology with industry and the military.

Over a period of seventy years, industrial/organizational psychology made itself tremendously useful to corporate America. As we shall see in Chapter 6, America's business leaders also found Freudian psychology invaluable in their successful efforts to construct the consumer through advertising. The alliance of psychology and industry likewise advanced the legitimacy of psychological knowledge. The early psychologists constructed answering machines that proved capable of solving some specific tasks raised by history for certain people in positions of power. One element of the answering apparatus was the notion that there existed expert knowledge about what we now call cognitive, personality, and social skills and that the services of those who possessed such knowledge could be bought (monetarily or otherwise) and organized in the interests of solving social and economic problems. Mass education was one of these problems.

That psychology and education would form an alliance seems obvious to us today. Learning is understood as being at least partially—if not completely—a psychological phenomenon. Teaching methods, learning styles, curriculum development, assessment, and evaluation are integral to the process and institution of education; they are understood as practices at the intersection of psychological science and educational theory.

In the early twentieth century, psychology and education did form an alliance, but it had little to do with any of these issues. On the ideological–political level, the mental hygiene movement that had begun with efforts to reform asylums had branched out to education and child care. This social movement for a better future interpreted social and interpersonal problems as the consequences of personal maladjustment in childhood, which could be remedied through the intervention of appropriate agencies of social control. Private foundations began to grant large amounts of money to mental hygiene programs, particularly educational ones (Danziger, 1994; Rivlin and Wolfe, 1985).

The goals of the mental hygiene movement (like those of industry) led psychologists to extend intelligence testing into the realm of human "traits" or "character." Tests, inventories, and rating scales were constructed as means of assessing and measuring personality for the purpose of personnel selection and for the assessment of maladjustment. The new techniques enabled psychologists to make a particular sort of knowledge claim.

In asserting that they could measure the specific amount of some personality trait, says Danziger, psychologists "supplied a reified category that translated the general social requirement [for certain people to behave in a particular way] into psychological terms. Numerous instances of the socially desired outcome were aggregated to contribute to an abstract quality of [for example] 'ascendance,' or its opposite, that was now thought to reside not in interpersonal situations but within strictly autonomous individuals" (1994, p. 163).

During the first two decades of the twentieth century, schools were being transformed into bureaucratically administered institutions modeled on the factory. By 1918, all forty-eight states had enacted compulsory education laws. Growing urban industrialization and immigration created a need for rapid assimilation of the young (especially the foreign-born and poor) into American culture (especially the culture of the factory) (Greer, 1972; Rothstein, 1994). The literature of the time compares school superintendents to factory managers, teachers to industrial workers, and children to the "raw materials" which were to be "shaped and fashioned into products to meet the various demands of life" (Rothstein, 1994, p. 49). School administrators strove to achieve overall "work efficiency" (Danziger, 1994; Napoli, 1981). To accomplish this, they needed ways to diminish "wasted time," streamline the use of physical space, sort pupils, compare different educational programs and the groups exposed to them, and justify their interventions (Danziger, 1994; Rivlin and Wolfe, 1985).

The stage had been set for psychologists to respond. In addition to the legitimacy which psychology had gained from the army mental testing project (despite its lackluster results) and the promise of personality testing, psychology had already been involved with schools on a small scale. From as early as the 1890s psychologists had collaborated with teachers on large, census-type child studies. While these endeavors produced no scientifically recognized findings, they did popularize the presence and idea of a psychology–education connection (Danziger, 1994).

Psychologists needed to develop new investigative practices if they were to satisfy the management needs of school administrators. Neither the laboratory experiment nor intelligence and personality tests could meet their challenging demands. The idea of creating groups of children, placing them under differing conditions of instruction, and measuring their performance both before and after the intervention is attributed to the British school inspector W. Winch (Danziger, 1994). The school environment was conducive to this grouping and measuring practice (large numbers of children were already grouped together in controlled situations), and psychologists found they could carry out systematic manipulation there. More important for the evolution of psychology, the environment shared certain characteristics with laboratory experimentation; it was not long before group work was brought into the laboratory. This is the origin of the *treatment group* and the fancy statistical footwork that are the mainstays of psychological research today.

In both cases, the school and the laboratory, human action was reduced to performance (output), which was converted into the measurement of a specific human capacity. Rather quickly, that capacity was generalized into an abstract "learning" or "forgetting." The merger of the experimental method (born in the laboratory) and the aggregating of data (born in the intelligence test) was in its origins thoroughly instrumental and practical. Designed to meet the administrative needs of an industrial-style educational system, it succeeded. However, working within schools meant working within the constraints of a school system with its own agenda, rules, and authorities. Clearly, this had its limitations. Within the psychological laboratory, however, the situation was very different:

> In the safety of university laboratories a kind of experimentation that had originated in relatively mundane practical concerns developed into a vehicle for maintaining fantasies of an omnipotent science of human control. . . . To [the more ambitious American psychologists] the performance of children on school tasks under different conditions was simply one instance of the opera-

tion of generalized "laws of learning" that manifested themselves in the entire gamut of human behavior. This faith enabled them to continue to use a style of experimentation that had already proved its practical usefulness and to reinterpret the results of such experimentation so they now provided evidence bearing on the nature of the fundamental laws of behavior. (Danziger, 1994, p. 115)

Among the most successful entrepreneurs of educational efficiency/scientific psychology was Edward Lee Thorndike. Like many of his contemporaries, Thorndike had established his credibility through the army testing project. (He chaired the Committee on Classification of Personnel.) He also lent his services to industry, having developed personnel tests for the insurance company now known as Met Life in 1915 (Baritz, 1960). As a professor at Columbia University's Teachers College in the 1920s and 1930s, Thorndike was similarly well connected to school administrators and used the popular press as well as academic journals to propagandize for what Danziger calls his "metaphysics of quantification." Thorndike believed that measurement was an essential property of things: "Whatever exists at all exists in some amount" (quoted in Danziger, 1994, pp. 146–147). Thorndike's work contributed significantly to the establishment of a new discipline within psychology, the quantitative psychology of learning.

Solidifying the Psychological Paradigm

According to several historians of psychology, the increased production, sophistication, and elaboration of mental testing produced important conceptual and methodological changes that helped to solidify the psychological paradigm (and the myth/hoax of psychology). First, the concept of individual differences was reconceptualized in such a way that the individual literally was defined away (Burman, 1994; Danziger, 1994; Soldz, 1988). Individuals were no longer characterized on the basis of their unique qualities (either on a specific performance or in a more general sense). Now individual performance was defined relative to a group mean. This meant that the characterization of any individual was as much a function of how others performed as it was of anything the individual did, and that the qualities an individual shared with others were the basis for determining the characteristics of the individual. To make a scientific/meaningful statement about an individual was to compare that individual with others.

The popularity of mental testing in the first two decades of the twentieth century also played a significant role in solidifying the concept of intelligence as an objective, operationally measurable dimension of human beings. While neither this nor the necessary accompanying identification of reality with measurability was a new idea, both gained scientific mileage from the project. Even as behaviorism became dominant within academic psychological science, the influence of this notion of intelligence as fixed and as measurable never waned, either with the applied "experts" or in the public mind. The recent flurry of controversy over Herrnstein and Murray's 1994 *The Bell Curve* is just one manifestation of its potency.

Indeed, intelligence and the practice of intelligence testing have been socially constructed as a major arena in which the ongoing nature–nurture fight is carried out. Proponents of testing and behaviorists are typically presented as opponents in everything from their political and moral agendas to their conceptual views on what constitutes human nature to their investigative practices. Surely, there are major differences, but the similarities and continuity from one practice to the other are important in considering psychology's construction of its subject matter in general and its "construction of the subject" (as opposed to the study of human beings) in particular.

Intelligence testing brought a new method to the study of individual differences and a new conception of how to assess them, both of which were extended into personality testing and carried over to the "more scientific" practice of behaviorism (and, as we shall see later on, to the study of psychopathology). Behavior, functionalism, the assessment of personal qualities based on performance in a restricted milieu—all were new. Both mental testers and behaviorists carried out investigative practices which presumed that overt responses to standard stimuli presented under controlled conditions could yield understanding of human beings.

Underlying the earlier practices of measuring the size of people's brains, categorizing people according to body type, and interpreting their handwriting or facial expressions was the notion that mind and body are linked and, furthermore, that a neurological or bodily structure revealed itself in overall personality or capability. Administering intelligence quotient (IQ) tests and conducting operant conditioning experiments, on the other hand, presume no such mind–body connection (let alone unity). Furthermore, they assume that human capacities (general laws) are revealed in how people function in a particular situation. The impact of this conceptual change is difficult to overstate in our current world of performance evaluation.

How did this type of performance assessment come to prevail? In identifying another way that intelligence testing contributed to the formation of the modern psychological paradigm, Samelson (1979) provides a clue (although he does not draw the connection that we do). He describes a 1920s debate between the two psychologists Boring and Brigham. Boring took the opportunity of reviewing Brigham's research to call for clarification in the way psychologists define intelligence. He believed that Brigham confused two meanings, one related solely to test performance, the other a broader definition of intelligence as native and existing prior to and independent of any test. Boring urged Brigham to abandon the narrower definition lest psychologists be vulnerable to criticism of drawing inferences from test results because of what is generally known about "the nature of intelligence." But only a year later, according to Samelson, Boring reversed his position (after public criticism of Brigham's eugenics-laced reports) and asserted that intelligence is what intelligence tests measure (1979, p. 157).

Boring's change of mind may have been a matter of simple opportunism. According to Samelson, however, it also marked the early use of what would become one of psychology's most effective techniques. "[It] would allow psychologists to make pronouncements about important phenomena of the real world (intelligence, aggression, learning, and many others); but when they were pressed hard about the relevance of their empirical data, operational definitions would allow them to retreat to the argument that they claimed for their concepts only what they had created in the laboratory" (p. 158).

This ad hoc form of reasoning, operational definition, was heavily critiqued in the 1950s by philosophers of science, who chastised psychologists for holding to a philosophical conception that had long been discredited by philosophers and physicists (Polkinghorne, 1983).

In presenting this early chapter in psychology's story and deconstructing some of the investigative practices and knowledge claims of the time, our aim has been to bring together and add to the existing postmodern critiques of psychology's (constructed and commodified) object of analysis—the individual. As we see it, modern psychology has simultaneously been attentive to and turned away from individuals. To the extent that it has ignored and attempted to eliminate from its investigations the essential sociality and historicality of human beings (including psychologists' own), it has focused on the isolated individual it has constructed. At the same time, the abstracted individual psychology has constructed—fundamentally operational, normative, and comparative—is far removed from even the highly isolated, overly individuated, "normally" alienated member of postmodern culture that psychology also helped to produce. Psychology's individuals—as mythic as the gods of ancient Greece, or the particulars of modern science—are also a sham, a thoroughly nondevelopmental story.

Earlier we said that psychology proclaimed itself free of its mother, philosophy, and allied itself with its sibling, science. But the evolution of psychology's conception of the individual and the paradigm of individual differences reveals the opposite to be the case. To the extent that the natural sciences which psychology sought to emulate were imbued with philosophical presuppositions, psychology adopted them. Moreover, the reified objects and sleight-of-hand techniques invented by the early psychologists (and still in use today, sometimes in more sophisticated versions and sometimes not) have little to do with the methods of the chemist, the physicist, or the biologist. In fact these objects and techniques are not applications of a natural science model to human–social phenomena; they are disguised philosophy, a priori metaphysics in psychological form.

As we turn in Chapters 6 and 7 to how psychology has constructed mental illness and human development, we will repeatedly encounter these metaphysical constructs: the experimental subject; individual differences; treatment groups; statistical significance; operational definitions—and the philosophical assumptions on which they rest.

NOTE

1. See, for example, the chapters in Ingleby's *Critical Psychiatry* (1980a); Prilleltensky's 1994 examination of the ethics and politics of seven fields of applied psychology; much of Albee's work in primary prevention and social change (1986) and Albee, Joffe and Dusenbury (1988); and the ideological critiques of many feminist, African American, Third World, and Marxist psychologists (for example, Burman, 1990; Cushman, 1990; Fulani, 1988; M. Gergen, 1988, 1995; Henriques, Holloway, Urwin, Venn and Walkerdine, 1984; Parker, 1989, 1992; Parker and Shotter, 1990; Rose, 1990; Sampson, 1991; Sinha, 1986; Ussher and Nicholson, 1992; and Wilkinson and Kitzinger, 1993). The work of Frantz Fanon (1963, 1967) and Bulhan's (1985) discussion of Fanon are particularly valuable.

6

Psychology's Best-Seller: Mental Illness and Mental Health

Perhaps more than any other area of human–social functioning in which psychologists have involved themselves, it is the investigation and treatment of mental illness (emotional disorders, psychopathology) and the regulation of mental health which have contributed to the construction of individualism, the normalization of alienation, the giving of new life to ancient philosophical abstractions and dualities, and the dominance of modern philosophical rationality (the identification of knowledge with systemization and explanation).

Wittgenstein, who had a special interest in the language and philosophy of psychology, observed that "a whole mythology is deposited in our language" (1971, GB 35).[1] While he was speaking of language in general, he might well have been speaking directly of clinical psychology, clinical social work, psychiatry, and the other components of the contemporary mental health profession (which only came into its own after his death). Dualistic discourse—normality–abnormality, cause–condition, mind–brain, rational–irrational, inner–outer, self–other, repression–expression, reality–fantasy—has become inseparable from the ordinary, everyday experiencing of "I" and "other." For all the fragmentation of the self that has occurred in recent decades, for all the diversity of social roles we play in an increasingly deconstructed culture, our experience as individuated entities (our identity) is still very much tied up with the status of "our minds" relative to other minds. And we still rely on the mind experts to tell us how to think about ourselves.

Just how powerful is the discourse of the mental health profession is apparent in the rapidity with which changes in professional jargon become part of the popular culture. Entire frameworks, not merely specific terms, are transformed; most recently, the illness metaphor is being replaced by deficit disorder terminology. With the exception of schizophrenia and depression (which neuropsychiatry and genetic biology currently control), these days emotional/mental states are as likely to be described in ordinary discourse in terms of deficiency (for example, "attention deficit disorder") or damage (for example, "hyperactivity" or "codependency") as they are in terms of suffering and illness.

But we are getting ahead of our story. The multibillion-dollar industry which supplies us with mental states of this particular sort—whether as illness, health, disorder, or deficit—and is one of the largest employers of professionals in the United States—had very humble beginnings.

The mental hygiene movement and Freud, in different ways, challenged the rigid sane–insane dichotomy that had been in place until they came along, raising critical questions about the nature of emotionality, personality development, and behavior. Both the movement and the physician also contributed to attempts to create alternatives to the inhuman ways in which the "insane" were treated until about one hundred years ago in Europe and North America. Many of us are familiar with the horrors of lunatic asylums, where the insane were isolated from the population at large, confined, and often kept in chains. This is not to say that no one was thinking about or working toward amelioration of severe emotional suffering—only that there was nothing approaching a movement until the late nineteenth century.

As the number of people classified as insane increased, and the size of the institutions established to colonize (and later treat) them also grew, there was a deepening concern with how mad people were treated (Magaro, Gripp and McDowell, 1978). In the United States, for example, the insane population, estimated at around 24,000 in 1860, had swelled to nearly 100,000 only twenty years later. (As in Europe, it was becoming commonplace to institutionalize the poor with the insane.) Despite a proposition put out in the 1850s by the Association of Medical Superintendents (the managers of asylums) that no asylum be allowed to contain more than 250 people, in New York State the Willard Asylum opened in 1865 with 1500 beds. Within twenty years, it would be dwarfed by state hospitals across the country built to house as many as 10,000 patients (Magaro, Gripp and McDowell, 1978, pp. 26–41).

While asylums were, in principle, calm and tranquil spaces set aside for patients to recover their moral/mental faculties, in practice they were places of confinement, deprivation, and punishment. On the theoretical level, two alternative views of madness coexisted: according to one, a deteriorated brain could not be mended; according to the other, psychological processes temporarily disordered by pressures in the environment could be reversed if the person were removed from that environment and placed in one where it was possible to manipulate conditions in such a way as to restore sanity. But, as the following excerpt from a description of the second view shows, it evidently took more than tranquillity to "destroy improper associations and restore proper ones: A system of humane vigilance is adopted . . . [we must] convince the lunatics that the power of the physician and keeper is absolute; . . . punish disobedience peremptorily, in the presence of the other maniacs; . . . allow limited liberty [to convalescents]; introduce . . . employment in agricultural pursuits" (quoted from Deutsch, 1949, in Magaro, Gripp and McDowell, 1978, p. 27).

As the story is told, the advent of mental hygiene gained support from the 1908 publication of *A Mind That Found Itself* by Clifford Beers, a Yale University graduate student who had spent three years in asylums for manic–depressive symptoms. According to Kovel (1980) and others, Beers's exposé of maltreatment (published with the help of Adolph Meyer, a psychiatrist at Manhattan State Hospital) was the catalyst for the mental hygiene movement and the beginnings of psychiatry's connection with state power through the U.S. Public Health Service. At the same time, the medical approach also gained a boost from the discovery that paresis was caused by syphilis and could be cured with penicillin; for the first time, medicine had identified without question both cause and cure of a severe mental disturbance. For the next forty years, people suffering from mental illness continued to be jointly cared for by asylum administrators and physicians; patients simultaneously were under "custodial care" and served as guinea pigs for increasingly invasive experimental treatments (including ice baths, insulin, electroconvulsive therapy, and lobotomy).

The young profession of psychology had little to do with (this) madness. For one thing, psychiatry had cornered the market on it. For another, in its early years psychology had nothing to offer. It still had to establish its scientific legitimacy and to prove its utility to those in charge of America's economic and social expansion before it could compete for the job of ameliorating what was then considered a social nuisance (although it was to become a massive and highly lucrative industry). As we have tried to show, psychology managed to accomplish this in the areas of education and industry while continuing to advance its position within academia.

For most of the first half of the century, however, clinical psychology was more an "ugly duckling" than anything else. Of the three applied areas of psychology— industrial, educational, and clinical—the last was the smallest and had the lowest status (Baritz, 1960; Furumoto, 1987; Napoli, 1981). Clinical work generated neither the prestige for the profession nor the immediate benefit for bureaucrats that industrial and educational psychology did. Clinicians tended to work in state hospitals, houses of detention, and delinquency centers, where they were subservient to psychiatrists and mostly administered mental tests. Their work was considered menial labor by their fellow psychologists.

Furumoto's (1987) analysis of women and the professionalization of psychology from 1890 to 1940 implicates a strong gender bias in the occupation of psychologists during this period. According to Furumoto's data, during this period psychology was more open to women than other sciences; there were more women Ph.D's in psychology than in physics or chemistry, and the percentage of women in the American Psychological Association was significant (13 percent in 1917, and nearly 22 percent by 1938). Although academically trained, women were unable to obtain academic positions except at women's colleges, and so they tended to do applied psychology—"not the work for a man" (p. 106)—where they were in the majority in all areas. More men, however, worked in industry (and kept their university appointments) than in the educational or clinical arenas. Virtually no women were involved in the World War I testing project, out of which male psychologists made important and lasting connections with government, military, and industry leaders.

From the outset, the relationship between academic psychologists and clinicians was somewhat tense. One measure of the tension is the position of clinical psychologists within psychology's major professional organization, the APA. Right after World War I, a clinical division was formed which was open only to Ph.D.'s with an interest in testing. In the 1930s, clinical psychologists left the APA and formed their own association; they stayed away until 1954, when they rejoined. The related fields of abnormal psychology and psychotherapy did not form a division within the association until 1946. It dissolved soon after, merging with the returning clinical psychology division.

Given the dominance of psychiatry, the hopelessness that pervaded mental institutions, and the lack of a specifically psychological approach to psychosis, it is not all that surprising that psychology had little to do with mental illness framed as such. Not only did psychology require scientific recognition and the acknowledgment of its utilitarian value; psychologists also needed a new concept of abnormality. Otherwise there was little basis on which they could compete with those already claiming to be experts on psychosis. The invention/discovery of *neurosis* and its incorporation into the mental illness–mental health framework gave psychology a "mental condition" about which it could develop expertise. Freud's revolutionary ideas about human personality and the radical treatment he developed, psychoanalysis, produced a new market (ordinary neurotics) for the mind experts.

The impact of Freud and psychoanalytic theory on American culture, the American "psyche," and the varied fields of psychology, psychiatry, social work, education, and literary studies has been written about extensively. For some cultural analysts, it would be difficult to overstate Freud's influence. For example, in *Constructing the Self, Constructing America: A Cultural History of Psychotherapy*, Cushman (1995) argues:

> Freud had unknowingly started something that will transform psychotherapy, influence the shape of popular culture, revolutionize advertising theory and personnel management, and eventually even contribute to saving capitalism from a second devastating depression. . . . American capitalism used Freud's concept of the unconscious to shift the nature of the American economy and its cultural–political landscape. (p. 142)

Freud delivered invited lectures at Clark University in 1909. Almost immediately psychoanalysis and the concepts of infantile sexuality and the unconscious began to be popularized through newspaper and magazine articles and, eventually, in theater and film (Cushman, 1995; Torrey, 1992). The mental hygiene movement linked its social reform efforts to Freud's views (Cushman, 1995; Kovel, 1980; Napoli, 1981; Torrey, 1992). Among the general public, it was members of the urban intelligentsia and the literary–cultural community who most enthusiastically embraced Freudianism. Some psychiatrists left asylums to become trained as psychoanalysts so they could cater to this educated clientele. Others adapted Freudian concepts to traditional psychiatry; according to some critics, they Americanized, medicalized, and sanitized psychoanalysis (Cushman, 1995; Ingleby, 1980a; Kovel, 1980; Turkle, 1980).

And what of psychologists? The consensus is that through the 1940s Freud had very little direct impact on either academic or applied psychology (Magaro, Gripp and McDowell, 1978; Napoli, 1981; Rose, 1990; Venn, 1984), although from time to time it was unsystematically and opportunistically applied (Venn, 1984). By the time clinical psychologists entered the mental health field in any significant numbers, Freudianism had transformed American social theory and popular culture, a disease model for understanding emotional suffering and problems was entrenched (both as part of the American Freudian view and in non-Freudian psychiatric views), and psychology was firmly established as a legitimate and useful social science. Psychologists were now in a position to expand their sphere of influence exponentially; they had a disease to call their own, to cure, and to make knowledge claims about. The disguised philosophy known as psychology would flourish along with the growth of psychology; the new subject matter it had inherited, abnormal behavior, suffered from all the defects of a disease ontology.

THE NORMALIZING OF ABNORMALITY

The modern ontology of mental illness–mental health is a peculiar synthesis of Freudian theory and a scientific–technical model. A look at how this synthesis was constructed will help us to see the dialectical interplay between the presuppositions which psychology took directly from philosophy and the presuppositions underlying the science which psychology tried to emulate. For the process by which abnormality became normalized is a major chapter in the story of the construction of the modern individuated (psychologized) subject and the commodification of human subjectivity.

Freud's immediate popularity notwithstanding, the Freudian paradigm did not become woven into the fabric of American life all at once. Throughout the early decades of this century, different aspects of Freud's theory gained prominence in certain disciplines, and different concepts were popularized at different times. Interestingly, very little changed for those locked up in mental institutions or for university students of human behavior during the 1920s, 1930s, and 1940s. The serious consideration of Freudian theory and practice by scientists of human behavior did not occur until after World War II; initially, his profound influence was primarily a social and cultural mass phenomenon (Magaro, Gripp and McDowell, 1978). We turn now to an exploration of how this change occurred, and how it laid the foundation for the mental health industry.

The early burst of popularity enjoyed by psychoanalysis in the 1920s was closely associated with and contributed to the sexual revolution of that decade (Torrey, 1992). When the revolution peaked, so did popular articles on psychoanalysis—the annual rate of such articles in the 1930s and 1940s was only one-third the rate from 1915–1922 (Torrey, 1992, p. 36). Freud remained popular mostly among urban intellectuals. In Torrey's view, the transformation of Freud's theory "from an exotic New York plant to an American cultural kudzu" (p. 104) was made possible by the association of Freud with the nature–nurture controversy.

Two highly politicized social issues of pre–World War II America served to link Freud with this controversy. One was eugenics, and the other was criminal behavior. We temporarily leave the subject of mental illness (and psychosis, neurosis, asylums, and psychoanalysis) to tell this part of the story.

The Eugenics Movement

As Torrey sees it, the nature–nurture debate became "Freudianized" and politicized primarily through the rise and fall of the eugenics movement (1992, p. 58). Far from being confined to academic discussions, competing theories about the causes of human behavior were linked to the issues of race and immigration in the period between the turn-of-the-century influx of Southern and Eastern Europeans and World War II. (Prior to this period, the scapegoats of American racism were mostly Blacks and the Irish.)

Many proponents of the belief that intelligence, personality, and moral behavior are genetically determined were eugenicists who not only believed in the superiority of the "Nordic" race, but advocated "cleansing" the United States of "inferior" races. The eugenics movement counted prominent figures within government, business, industry, and academia among its leaders and supporters.

The Eugenics Research Association and the Galton Society were two early "scientific" organizations formed immediately after World War I with the dual purpose of discussing the latest scientific research and providing it to relevant government agencies (including the House Immigration Committee). In this alliance of scientists and politicians, we again encounter psychologists such as Yerkes, Brigham, and Thorndike as well as quasi-scientific organizations such as the National Research Council of the National Academy of Sciences. All were leading advocates for the view that limiting inferior stock was good for America (Kamin, 1974).

Torrey (1992) provides a vivid account of the blatant racism (particularly the anti-Semitism) of America's leaders and their propagandizing for sterilization and restrictive immigration laws. Organizers of the First and Second International Congresses on Eugenics (in 1912 and 1921 respectively) included the presidents of Harvard, Columbia, Stanford, and other leading universities, and prominent public figures such as Alexander Graham Bell and Herbert Hoover. In 1921 Vice President Calvin Coolidge, writing in the popular magazine *Good Housekeeping*, warned that "our country must cease to be regarded as a dumping ground. . . . The Nordics propagate themselves successfully. With other races, the outcome shows deterioration on both sides" (p. 51).

Henry Ford (selected, along with Theodore Roosevelt and Thomas Edison, in a poll of the time as one of the five "Great Americans") used his newspaper the *Dearborn Independent* to foment anti-Semitism, calling Jews a "race of people that has no civilization . . . no universal speech . . . no great achievement in any realm except the realm of 'get'." The House Committee on Immigration followed suit and declared that Jewish immigrants were "abnormally twisted, filthy, un-American, and often dangerous." The secretary of labor, who played a key role in getting Congress to enact the first Immigration Act (in 1921) limiting immigration by country of origin, characterized new immigrants as "rat–men." The more restrictive Johnson–Reed Act was passed three years later, and within one year Italian and Jewish immigration to the United States decreased by 89 percent and 83 percent, respectively (p. 55).

The legitimacy of the claim that intelligence was genetically determined and associated with race derived from the data generated by psychologists prior to and during World War I. The eugenicists used these data in their arguments for a "pure America." As is clear from the preceding examples, however, their propaganda linked alleged low intelligence with so-called immoral behavior, laziness, squalor, and criminal behavior, marking millions of people as unfit for the rights and responsibilities of American citizenship. Their arguments were persuasive. In 1928 (five years before sterilization was legalized in Nazi Germany), twenty-one states had passed compulsory sterilization laws; among those who were prohibited from having children were the feeble-minded, crippled, blind, homeless, rapists, drunkards, epileptics, and moral and sexual perverts. By that year an estimated 8500 people had been sterilized (Torrey, 1992, pp. 47–48).

Freud's theory that early childhood trauma determines adult personality and behavior dovetailed with and reinforced the arguments of those who opposed these barbarous policies and practices. For example, the work of the pioneering anthropologists Franz Boas, Ruth Benedict, and Margaret Mead (who was originally trained as a psychologist) was partially devoted to refuting the eugenicists' claims about heritability. The issue of how to account for human behavior was "red-hot" in the context of an increasingly polarized international political situation. The social scientists who adopted an environmental position also tended to support liberal views, and to be social activists for individual freedom; many were socialists, communists, or anarchists. And many became enamored of what was understandably seen as Freud's humanism. The eugenicists tended to be openly conservative in their views on politics *and* sexuality.

Within a decade, the popularity and official support for eugenics began to decline. The threat of "inferior blood" all but disappeared as fewer and fewer immigrants arrived on America's shores. (During the Great Depression the rate of emigration *from* the U.S. was greater than the rate of immigration *into* the country.) Mass poverty and unemployment were, by far, the more pressing issues of the day. Moreover, some of the movement's most ardent and openly racist proponents, such as psychologist Brigham and Henry Ford, reversed their positions in a highly publicized (and in Ford's case, at least, in an obviously opportunistic) manner. By the end of World War II, the Nazi atrocities were regarded by many to be the "logical" conclusion to eugenics—the horrific, genocidal extension of one extreme of the nature–nurture controversy. In the decades to come, nurture would prove to be not only politically correct but also politically advantageous for those concerned with America's economic progress and its ascension to great power status on the international stage (Cushman, 1995; Torrey, 1992).

Popularizing Neurosis—Cause, Rehabilitation, and Prevention

The humanism of Freud's ideas—for example, his notion that every individual (except those with the most severe psychosis) could be helped through the reexperiencing of early childhood traumas—was linked with visions of progress on the individual, societal, and global levels. Along with the intellectuals who underwent psychoanalysis in the pursuit of their own personal growth, there emerged a movement to create an emancipatory theory of human civilization through a synthesis of Marxian and Freudian thought.

Among the most prominent of the nearly two hundred psychoanalysts who made their home in the United States after fleeing Nazi Germany were Marxists who had already begun the effort to effect such a synthesis. They quickly became influential within American political and psychoanalytic circles. The establishment in 1934 of the *Partisan Review*, a magazine devoted to radical politics and culture, marked the formal recognition by leading intellectuals that the emancipation from human suffering which is central to the vision of both Marx and Freud was realizable. (The marriage lasted until 1952, when the magazine officially repudiated Stalinist repression, totalitarianism, and Soviet-style Marxism; from that point on, it began extolling American democracy and promoting Freud exclusively.)

The Freudian vision of personal liberation, the Freudian belief in unconscious motives and drives, and the Freudian "discovery" that repressed sexuality is omnipresent were disseminated to the public through cultural products created by intellectuals who had been profoundly influenced by these ideas. As poets, playwrights, and novelists learned about Freud and/or underwent psychoanalysis themselves, they incorporated themes of early childhood trauma, the Oedipus complex, psychoanalytic treatment, and other elements of the Freudian repertoire into their work. Torrey (1992) takes us on a tour through fifty years of Freudianized literature, theatre, film, and television; we learn that the first play to use Freudian conceptions, *The Fatted Calf*, opened on Broadway in 1912; in 1916 *Suppressed Desires* became the first production about psychoanalysis; Theodore Dreiser's *The Hands of the Potter*, published in 1919, was about a sexual psychopath whose behavior was attributed to a "great force" that Dr. Freud was studying (pp. 30–31); and the list goes on. Moss Hart, Lillian Hellman, Tennessee Williams, and Eugene O'Neill were among the many playwrights whose work, permeated with Freudian themes, would help to popularize Freud in this country.

The linking of madness and criminality that had lunatics and thieves housed together in asylums and that took an even more barbaric form with the eugenicists did not dissolve. Freud gave the connection new life and a new, more humane shape. Prior to the post–World War II period, psychoanalysis was put into practice mostly in juvenile centers and prisons. Freud lent legitimacy and precision to the view that criminal behavior was not hereditary but was due to social forces, especially family relations and early childhood experiences. Some psychiatrists came to regard criminal behavior as being rooted in psychic trauma which had been caused by repressed sexual desires and could be cured through psychoanalysis. In 1917 a pioneer of "Freudian rehabilitation" for criminal behavior, the British psychiatrist William Healy, was made director of the Judge Baker Guidance Center. Affiliated with Harvard University, the center was a model for other clinics around the country set up to prevent juvenile delinquency. A significant development attributed to Healy is the incorporation of social workers as members of treatment teams. Opening up the "mental realm" to practitioners of social work in this way dramatically changed the direction of that profession (Torrey, 1994, p. 149).

Other prominent psychiatrists with psychoanalytic training, notably Bernard Glueck and William A. White, applied this treatment model to adults in prisons. Both of them, along with Healy, testified at the sensational 1924 murder trial of Nathan Leopold and Richard Loeb. The impact of their appearance for the defense on the mass psychology of Americans, writes Torrey (1992), was considerable: by questioning the assumption that individuals are responsible for their own actions it brought this issue to the attention of the entire nation; and it greatly helped to legitimize Freudianism (pp. 153–57).

The trial was a bona fide media event for its time; the two Chicago newspapers even invited Freud to come to America to psychoanalyze Leopold and Loeb for the edification of their readers and said he could name his own price. Freud declined (Torrey, 1992, p. 154). The lawyer for Leopold and Loeb was the famed Clarence Darrow, who mounted a defense of the two young men based primarily on psychiatric evidence. During the trial and after, Darrow emphasized the importance of bringing science and psychiatry to bear on criminal cases. (A year after the trial he was a guest speaker at the American Psychiatric Association's annual convention.)

Darrow and his psychiatric witnesses argued that Leopold and Loeb were not responsible for their actions as a consequence of their emotional immaturity, which was caused by early childhood events; they were mentally ill; they might have had a homosexual relationship; the murder was "the inevitable outcome of this curious coming together of two pathologically disordered personalities" (quoted in Torrey, 1992, p. 155). In ruling for the defense and sentencing Leopold and Loeb to life imprisonment (instead of the death penalty), the judge cited the relevance and value of the analysis of their life histories. He thereby set a precedent for the eventual marriage of psychiatry and the law, establishing the validity of the psychiatric defense. Psychiatric evaluation of convicted felons was subsequently mandated in several states, and many prisons set up psychiatric treatment facilities. No longer were insanity and criminality on an equal footing as two distinct "genetic impurities" of the species. The institutions of psychiatry and the law had jointly constructed a new entity—the pathologically disordered personality—which lay somewhere between the psychotic and the law-abiding neurotic.

As significant as these changes were within criminology, the trial served to further the development and propagation of the Freudian paradigm. Torrey (1992) quotes a historian who observed that the Leopold and Loeb case provided "a sort of crash course in psychoanalysis for the ordinary American" (p. 157).

Twenty years later American consumers were treated to another Freudian blitz in the mass media, this time centered on an issue much closer to home—the well-being of themselves and their children. Psychoanalysis again became a leading topic in popular magazines and newspapers; it started, according to Torrey (1992), with *Time* and *Life* magazines, owned by Henry and Clare Boothe Luce. Articles by psychoanalysts, celebrities, and ordinary people, some explaining Freudian concepts in detail and others describing successful treatment, appeared regularly. Torrey quotes from the comedian Sid Caesar's "What Psychoanalysis Did for Me," which appeared in *Look* magazine: "Once I made clear to myself that those childhood incidents were in the past, I found I could start a new life. . . . My work began to improve" (p. 119).

Even more of a mass phenomenon was the burgeoning interest in child rearing and the possibility of *preventing* neurosis. Prior to the postwar period, the idea of applying Freudian conceptions to child rearing had some support among analysts but never achieved much popularity (Torrey, 1992). To the extent that parenting and child rearing practices were promulgated, it was by the behaviorists.

With the publication in 1946 of *Baby and Child Care* by the pediatrician Benjamin Spock, a Freud adherent, the thinking and practice of millions of parents underwent a major transformation. Spock's advice took the form of proclamations about what babies and very young children feel and think in this or that situation so that parents could anticipate their child's needs and thereby prevent trauma. The doctor said, for example, that every little boy worries that something will happen to *his* "wee wee" unless he's given a good reason for why his sister doesn't have one. (The reader is not told what a good reason might be.)

In this way, Spock put forth a Freudian view of development. Packaged under the rubric of parenting skills, the notion of a universally fragile, psychically driven human organism in perpetual conflict with "the social world" was disseminated to millions, eventually all over the world. (An international best-seller, *Baby and Child Care* is often cited as being second only to the Bible in sales.) The idea that the emotional trauma of early childhood, so detrimental to healthy adult functioning, could be minimized is another way in which Freud became connected to the idea of progress. Neurosis was natural. It could be cured, in adulthood, through psychoanalysis. Now came the good news that, up to a point, it was preventable.

Constructing the Consumer

At the same time that intellectuals, producers of culture, and those working in what are now called the helping professions were finding

Freud's theory useful, America's business leaders were discovering its utility as well. The intelligentsia and the professionals took the unconscious to be a liberating conception, and the notion that a universal, biologically determined sex drive explained human behavior to be of therapeutic value. Industry, with typical American pragmatism and greed, latched onto the unconscious and drive theory for its own economic purposes. From as early as the 1920s, Freudian concepts were used to sell products; human liberation became identified with consumerism. From the marriage between Freud and advertising came the dual imperative of contemporary culture: the repression of the sex drive and the expression of the drive to acquire. Thus was constructed the modern individual, a being naturally driven to accumulate, possess, and consume objects.

It all began with tobacco. The man known as the father of public relations, who remains its most widely respected authority (Fry, 1991), was Freud's nephew Edward Bernays. In 1929 Bernays was contracted by the American Tobacco Company to develop an advertising campaign that would promote smoking by women (Ewen, 1976; Torrey, 1992; Cushman, 1995). In consultation with a prominent Freudian, A. A. Brill, Bernays looked to the Freudian unconscious as an instrument with which to dispel the taboo which forbade women to smoke. Cigarettes, they "discovered," are phallic symbols, smoking a sublimation of oral eroticism. Bernays shrewdly connected smoking as a symbol of masculinity with the emancipation of women, which at the time was a major public issue. He launched the campaign with a contingent of cigarette-smoking women marching down New York City's Fifth Avenue in the Easter Parade. Afterward, he pronounced it a success: "Our parade of ten young women lighting 'torches of freedom' on Fifth Avenue on Easter Sunday as a protest against women's inequality caused a national stir" (quoted in Ewen, 1976, p. 161).

Cushman (1995) notes the significance of the psychoanalytic elements of Bernays's advertising campaign in creating the modern *consumer self*. If it was unhealthy to deny oneself sensual gratification, as Freud had taught, then neurosis could be prevented by substituting a socially acceptable gratification (such as smoking a cigarette) for a socially unacceptable desire (such as suckling). In this way, Cushman argues, smoking was constructed as a "solution to the pressures of modern civilization . . . only one of a number of supposedly 'natural' desires that advertising first created and then justified so as to encourage the consumption of leisure commodities" (p. 156).

In the wake of his triumph, Bernays called for the implementation of a mass psychology to control public opinion and stimulate consumption. He saw the potential for using the science of psychology "to control and regiment the masses according to our will without their knowing it" (quoted in Ewen, 1976, p. 83). The captains of industry were clear about the kind of control they wanted to achieve—the imposition of consumerism as an alternative to more radical modes of social change, the inculcation of the ideology of mass consumption as a commercially viable substitute for "class thinking."

In *Captains of Consciousness*, a valuable history of advertising and the consumer culture, Ewen lets us listen in on some of the conversations Bernays was having with business leaders and economists in the 1930s, discussions in which they described advertising as "the answer to Bolshevism," "a fundamental process of Americanization," and lauded consumption as "a democratizing process." Edward Filene, the department store founder, even went so far as to argue that consumption was far more democratic than representative government because through consumption people were not only electing "their industrial government" but were also "constantly participating in it." Ewen writes, "Participation in an industrially defined marketplace had become a modern expression of popular political activity, yet it was an activity that maintained American industrial barons as the social directors of the nation, for 'participation' in no way implied control or determination" (1976, p. 92).

These early uses of psychology (especially elements of Freudianism) by corporate capitalism help to reveal how the social construction of the (psychically driven and cognitized) individuated subject was an essential part of making social control invisible. Integral to the mass psychology of manipulation was the legitimizing of expert knowledge about human behavior. That human beings behave as individuals, as isolated particulars, responding to feelings, thoughts, beliefs, and opinions which originate within each of us, is among the most deeply held assumptions in our culture; it is accepted, by and large unthinkingly, as objective truth.

THE SUBJECT MATTER OF PSYCHOLOGY REVISITED

With this somewhat simplified and necessarily selective summary of the transformation of American culture in the first half of the twentieth century—its Freudianization—we return to the subject matter of psychology. Mass culture had accomplished the normalizing (and humanizing) of abnormality, which contributed substantially to the socially constructed myth of the isolated individual. Elements of this elaborate myth—a family of reified mental objects, abstract mental structures, dualistically divided and causally determined relationships—became embedded in the culture. Freud's worldview—his notion that human beings are individuated biological organisms compelled to exist in a social world, that the actions of individuals can be explained by the universal and inevitable intrapsychic conflict generated by the human condition—seeped into America's social institutions. The "prime cause" was taken out of heaven and brought down to earth, where it was relocated within the individual human being. Thus was philosophy thoroughly commodified and born again.

The stage was now set for the introduction of psychology's long-running best-seller. Both the public and the state were ready. The public recognition of something called mental health had been achieved, and with it came the possibility of creating a public need for mental health services. The rejection of 1 million men as mentally unfit for military duty in World War II provoked the government's concern with mental illness. Additionally, congressional hearings on the horrific conditions within state mental hospitals required some kind of action.

In 1946, Congress passed the country's first mental health legislation. The National Mental Health Act, which included the establishment of the National Institute of Mental Health (NIMH), was designed to promote mental health through science. Funds were to be allotted for "researches, investigations, experiments and demonstrations relating to the cause, diagnosis, and treatment of psychiatric disorders" (quoted in Magaro, Gripp and McDowell, 1978, p. 63). Four years later, the National Science Foundation (NSF) was established. Although formally they are nonmilitary organizations, both the NIMH and NSF have, since they were founded, been institutionally bound in varying ways to the Department of Defense.

A principal beneficiary of the government's new-found concern with the mental health of the population, psychology thereby became linked ever more closely with the state. NIMH instituted grants to leading universities across the country to set up training centers, not only for psychiatrists in medical school but for psychologists as well. Throughout the 1950s–1970s, when the federal government was becoming increasingly involved in funding research, higher education, and professional training, the field of psychology grew enormously. It may well have benefited more than any other discipline, in part because of its multidisciplinary status (Gilgen, 1982). This status made it eligible for federal (and private) funds not only as a science, but also as a helping profession and as one of the humanities.

Statistics on the growth of the mental health–mental illness industry, and within it the growth of psychology, since the National Mental Health Act was passed are instructive. In 1945 there were only 9000 psychologists, psychiatrists, and psychiatric social workers combined. By 1992, their number had increased to 200,000 (Torrey, 1992, p. 204). The number of recognized mental illnesses also rose considerably in the same period. The first *Diagnostic and Statistical Manual of Mental Disorders*, published in 1952, listed 50 to 60 classifications. By 1987, the number had tripled; the 1994 *DSM-IV* contains over two hundred. Along with the expansion in the ranks of professionals and the proliferation of mental disorders, the number of Americans in some kind of treatment for mental illness also increased. In 1957 the percentage of the population utilizing professional mental health services was 14 percent; by 1977 it was over 25 percent (Gergen, 1994, p. 159). Hunt (1993) reports on the current estimate of how many Americans have been in some kind of treatment: one out of three. These figures *do not include* addiction and drug treatment programs.

What was the position of psychoanalytic theory during this expansionary period? Despite the central role it played in transforming thinking about what makes us human, and despite the fact that virtually every psychological theory and treatment approach since Freud has reflected his impact (even if only as "a reaction formation"), Freudian analysis has never enjoyed anything resembling mass popularity as a treatment modality. Even at its height in the 1950s, among the 14 percent of the population utilizing professional mental health services it is estimated that no more than ten thousand people were in traditional psychoanalytic treatment (Hunt, 1993).

The postwar growth of the dominant professional associations is similarly impressive. In the mid-1940s, the American Psychological Association had 4200 members. By the mid-1970s, membership had increased by 850 percent to 40,000 members (Gilgen, 1982, p. 31). In 1994, it had reached 132,000. There are indications that membership growth may have peaked, in part because of declining numbers of doctorates awarded in psychology (Albino, 1995). The American Psychiatric Association also experienced tremendous growth, doubling or tripling its membership each decade since the 1940s.

How psychologists earn their living has also changed from the early days, when most of them worked in academic settings. It is worth noting that psychology's close association with the military, which began during World War I, has not waned. According to APA reports, currently the largest employer of psychologists in the world is the Department of Veterans Affairs (Fowler, 1995). Among APA members, 30 percent are employed in academic settings (one-third of them describe their work as scientific research); 25 percent are employed in health care settings; and one-third are independent practitioners (Albino, 1995, pp. 622–623). Federal requirements for Medicaid and Medicare payments, state regulations for the licensing of psychologists, and federal funding for scientific research have resulted in a very intimate connection between psychology and institutions of government. The vast majority of psychologists either work directly for federal or state agencies or have their work largely determined by those agencies.

The number of women already trained in or studying psychology is steadily increasing. Yet, similar to the period 1890–1940 described by Furumoto (1987), women psychologists remain underrepresented in high-ranking positions. The APA's expressed concern over the increasing numbers of female psychologists is worth examining. The fact that women currently comprise 42 percent of the APA membership is, according to the "Five Year Report," "a membership development that has led to both pleasure and alarm" (Albino, 1995, p. 622). The task force set up to study the issue of gender and the profession reports that, on the one hand, this indicates the strides made by psychology in eliminating gender biases; on the other hand, there is concern with "the effects of larger societal attitudes toward a profession dominated by women." In an effort to dissociate itself from these larger societal attitudes ("we're not sexist"), the report summarizes the "findings" of the task force: It is not the case, as many evidently believe, that increasing numbers of women in a profession brings down salaries. Rather, the situation is quite the opposite: opportunities for women seem to increase when the salaries and prestige of a profession have already started to diminish. Warning psychology and psychologists "not to fall into unproven stereotypes regarding the relationship between gender and prestige of a profession," the report offers instead a "proven stereotype" in its efforts to comprehend and slow its demise. (The very low proportion of what the APA refers to as "ethnic minority" membership—5 percent—is also a source of expressed concern.)

Several pages later in the same report, the APA describes how the current "corporate" association has changed in the course of one hundred years: "[It is] a very different creature from the simple scientific and professional association founded by G. Stanley Hall and his colleagues a century ago. We have become a real estate developer, a major book publishing house, and a powerful legislative advocacy voice for science, practice, and social policy in Congress and the courts" (Albino, 1995, p. 631). In our view, the APA's current corporate identity is firmly rooted in the history presented here; it was hardly a "simple scientific and professional association" even at the moment of its birth.

Classificatory, Interpretive, and Explanatory Myth Making

If psychology's connection to industry and education best illustrates its readiness to accommodate itself in the most vulgarly pragmatic, commodified way to the marketplace and the state, it is the evolution of *clinical* psychology and psychotherapy that shows off psychology's willingness to create a thoroughly fictitious taxonomy (a system of classification) in the name of being scientific. The effort to create an "objective science of the subjective" produced new modes of understanding and variations of old modes which in turn required a new ontology. (If it didn't, why have a separate "science" called psychology?)

Yet even those qualities (for example, consciousness, intentionality, and emotionality) that prima facie distinguish human subjectivity from nonhuman, inanimate phenomena and human subjectivity from medicalized, biologized phenomena—diseases are in lungs, livers, brains, and so on, while subjective states are, most would say, not *in* anything but *of* the person—often generated not so much an "objective science of the subjective" as a "subjective pseudo-science of the unreal." This being so, psychology (in particular, clinical psychology and psychotherapy) is essentially religious. While it functions as a modernist, secular religion, structurally and ideologically it has come more and more to resemble premodern, prescientific (indeed, prescholastic) religion. The fictional ontological elements (the labels) of clinical psychology look like and operate as Homeric gods—everyday Olympian characters which do not so much explain in modernist scientific fashion why something happens as substitute themselves for more ordinary descriptive language so as to create the pre–Judeo–Christian religious illusion that something has been accounted for.

The marriage of Freudianism with science and technology is the centerpiece of psychological fictionalization. While Freud's worldview was (like that of many other religions) pessimistic and not particularly developmental, his theoretical pronouncements and clinical practice were unquestionably humane relative to how people suffering from emotional pain were treated during his lifetime. We agree with those who argue that mental illness, psychopathology, neurosis, schizophrenia, and the rest are not scientific, but essentially moral, categories (for example, Goffman, 1961; Ingleby, 1980b; Szasz, 1961). They are, however, more humane moral categories than insanity and lunacy. To give credit where credit is due, Freud brought the "madman" into civil society (Deleuze and Guattari, 1977) and broke down, to some extent, the barrier that had been erected to separate those designated mad from other human beings.

That said, Freud thought of himself as a scientist and his work as scientific. Although he tended in his later years to present psychoanalysis more as a general theory of humanity and civilization than as a cure for neurosis, this shift was a move away from medicine but not from science (Timpanaro, 1976). Freud's new ontology of intrapsychic structures (id, ego, and superego) simply extended the cognitive epistemological bias of philosophy, its powerful offspring modern science, and the embryonic social science of psychology into the area of subjectivity and emotionality. As such, it was entirely compatible with the rationalistic, deductive set of Kantian categories which were already widely accepted. The Freudian concern with the conscious (the spoken word, for example) and the unconscious (the force or drive behind it) was fully consistent with structuralist science, which located the understanding of phenomena (and the language used to describe them) in the supposedly systematized relationship they had with the underlying forces said to produce them.

It was Freud's new method of analysis, *interpretation*, a method he thought to be uniquely necessary for understanding subjectivity, that violated the basic tenets of science. With the interpretive method, he effectively created an alternative to the empiricistic–positivistic conception of explanation, and un-self-consciously contradicted his own scientific worldview. American psychiatry and psychology, with typical American entrepreneurial ingenuity, managed to incorporate aspects of the interpretive method and Freudian theory into the positivistic paradigm. What resulted were the objectification (actually, the fictionalization) and medicalization of subjectivity and emotionality. Freud's methodological contradiction was "resolved" by the clinical merger of Freudianism, first with a positivistic medicalized psychiatry and later with a positivistic behaviorist psychology.

But not all psychologists and psychiatrists were willing to resolve the contradiction by denying the uniquely subjective characteristics of human life—for example, by denying consciousness. In particular, many clinicians (psychotherapists and social workers as well as psychologists) chose not to reduce psychology to some other existing system such as medicine, neurology, behavioral science, or physiology. Instead, they created more and more obviously fictionalized entities; in effect, they became humanistic priests of varying sects within the new religion. It is in the practical work of clinicians that we see most clearly the structure of late modernist myth making.

In our view, the "myth of mental illness" pales by comparison with what is, from a postmodern perspective, the myth/hoax of psychology itself—an interpretive, classificatory, and explanatory pseudoscience. Ironically, it is in studying "pure" clinical psychological work (psychology uncontaminated by any other system or discipline) that we will find it to be permeated with metaphysics (in the plainly pejorative positivistic sense). In our view, the postmodernization of psychology (the deconstruction of the myth/hoax that is psychology and the construction of a nonphilosophical, unsystematic, unscientific practice of method) requires curing mental illness of its philosophy (as Wittgenstein aimed to cure philosophy of its mental illness), abandoning scientific psychology, and creating a noninterpretive, nonclassificatory, nonexplanatory approach.

Classification

But even those who took the easy way out by fully or partially reducing psychology to medicine were not without metaphysical trouble. For what did it mean to "medicalize" Freud? This question entails another: What is medicine? While a social constructionist, activity-theoretic analysis of modern medicine is beyond the scope of this book, it will be helpful to take a brief look at Michel Foucault's social–cultural history of medicine and illness. In our view (to anticipate Part III), curing mental illness of its philosophy requires (as a necessary, though not a sufficient, condition) that we deconstruct and reconstruct its discourse. It is in this activity that Foucault's *The Birth of the Clinic: An Archaeology of Medical Perception* (1975) is so valuable.

In this early work (originally published in French in 1963) Foucault unravels the story of the birth of modern scientific medicine during the cultural, political, and economic upheavals that accompanied the emergence of the bourgeoisie in the France of the late-eighteenth and early-nineteenth centuries. The focus of this fascinating history is how medicine "took on a philosophical density that had formerly belonged only to mathematical thought" (p. 198) and how a new discourse of illness was socially constructed as the perception and treatment of disease were transformed.

Modern medicine locates disease within the individual, but this was not always the case. Foucault has discovered seventeenth- and eighteenth-century metaphorical descriptions that speak of immutable laws and essences and relate to disease as a naturally occurring phenomenon which follows an inevitable life course (like a plant) and which may merely "happen" to inhabit individual human bodies. The shift to the modern (anatomoclinical) method came about through the objectification of disease. According to Foucault, that transformation, in turn, represented a monumental epistemological change in the relationship between perception and discourse, between seeing and saying—what he calls *the gaze*. The origins of modern clinical medicine are to be found in the transformation of the gaze from passive to active, from seeing only what was visible to seeing what is invisible (what is seeable but not seen).

Foucault describes the perceptual changes that took place in the new construction of medical knowledge. For example, the elements of a pathological phenomenon were restructured from a botany of symptoms to a grammar of signs; tissues were isolated and examined; disease was situated in parts of the body and its causes and effects sought in a three-dimensional space (p. xviii). Scientifically structured discourse about disease and illness accompanied this new way of seeing. Objectifying disease through the gaze—revealing what had previously been neither seeable nor speakable—opened up language to a new domain, "that of a perceptual and objectively based correlation of the visible and the expressible. An absolutely new use of scientific discourse was then defined: a use involving fidelity and unconditional subservience to the coloured content of experience—showing by saying what one sees" (p. 196).

The discourse of objectified illness was only one of the transformations that took place in the construction of modern medicine. Foucault describes how the clinic and hospital were restructured during and immediately after the French Revolution, changes that would eventually give rise to the institutions and institutionalized meanings of health, illness, disease, and cure that are still with us today. Here is where the social contract originated which is the basis for how clinics, hospitals, and other institutions treat illness; here is where the political as well as the philosophical objectification of illness began.

It was during this time that a distinction emerged between "officers of health" and "doctors." Officers of health were practitioners. That is, they treated people. They had no need of theory; a "controlled empiricism"— knowing what to do by example—was sufficient. Doctors, on the other hand, supplemented theoretical training with experience gained in the clinic. By virtue of their clinical experience, they (and the clinic) possessed "a gaze that was at the same time knowledge, a gaze that exists, that was master of its truth, and free from all example, even if at times it had made use of them" (pp. 81–82).

Accompanying the new distinction between officers of health and doctors was a restructuring of medical treatment and training. Hospitals were where people were treated, clinics the places where doctors were trained. This institutional restructuring was coherent with the embryonic bourgeoisie, its liberal ideology, and its instrument, the social contract. What emerged was a set of contractual relationships: between rich and poor, the individual and the state, the healer and the sick, and the healer and the state.

The government was relieved of its obligation to provide funds for hospitals, which were entrusted to municipal administrators: "The system of obligation and compensation between rich and poor no longer passed through the law of the state, but, by means of a sort of contract . . . it belonged more to the order of free consent" (p. 83). Foucault tells us that at the same time, a more covert social contract grew up between the hospital and the clinic, because the idea of a clinic for the poor created a moral dilemma. Here is how Foucault describes the dilemma as it presented itself toward the end of the eighteenth century:

> A certain balance must be kept, of course, between the interests of knowledge and those of the patient; there must be no infringement of the natural rights of the sick, or of the rights that society owes to the poor. The domain of the hospital . . . bristled with obligations and moral limitations deriving from the unspoken—but present—contract binding men in general to poverty in its universal form. If, in the hospital, the doctor does not carry out theoretical experiments, free of all obligation to their human object, it is because, as soon as he sets foot in the hospital, he undergoes a decisive moral experience that circumscribes his otherwise unlimited practice by a closed system of duty. (p. 84)

And what of the clinic? Do the "interests of knowledge" take precedence over the "interests of the patient" in these training centers? "[T]o look in order to know, to show in order to teach," Foucault asks, "is not this a tacit form of violence, all the more abusive for its silence, upon a sick body that demands to be comforted, not displayed? Can pain be a spectacle?" (p. 84). Not only can it be, Foucault concludes; it must, for according to the emerging liberal social contract: "no one is alone, the poor man less so than others, since he can obtain assistance only through the mediation of the rich. Since disease can be cured only if others intervene with their knowledge, their resources, their pity, since a patient can be cured only in society, it is just that the illnesses of some should be transformed into the experiences of others" (p. 84).

The rich, then, gain something from helping the poor. By paying for the poor to be treated, they increase the likelihood that new knowledge will be created about illnesses with which they themselves might become afflicted.

In this way, "benevolence toward the poor is transformed into knowledge that is applicable to the rich" (p. 84).

Foucault sums up the terms of the contract by which rich and poor participated in the organization of clinical experience:

> In a regime of economic freedom, the hospital has found a way of interesting the rich; the clinic constitutes the progressive reversal of the other contractual part; it is the interest paid by the poor on the capital the rich have consented to invest in the hospital; an interest that must be understood in its heavy surcharge, since it is a compensation that is of the order of objective interest for science and of vital interest for the rich. The hospital became viable for private initiative from the moment that sickness, which had come to seek a cure, was turned into a spectacle. Helping ended up by paying, thanks to the virtues of the clinical gaze. (p. 85)

The clinic and clinical experience (the clinical gaze) made scientifically structured discourse about the individual possible, Foucault argues. For now the object of discourse could also be the subject of discourse without any loss of objectivity. This new discourse created both a new ontology and a new epistemology. The realm of the knowable expanded to include what had previously been unknowable (the individual, the invisible). The means of producing knowledge expanded; one could come to know through the gaze, a way of knowing (a source of truth) at once active and alienated. For locating illness *within* the individual body also separated illness *from* the body, that is, from the continuing life process. The physician's initial question changed from "What is the matter with you?" to "Where does it hurt?" (p. xviii). In this change, says Foucault, are captured the workings of the clinic and the principles of its entire discourse.

Thus it was that physical illness became politically and philosophically objectified in modernist thought. The paradigm of objectivity, which would be codified by Kant, was in the process of being constructed. The saying of what is seen is simultaneously a showing of it. Along with other restructurings and redefinings, the discourse of objective illness was critical to the construction of clinical experience as a form of knowledge.

What has become, over the past two centuries, of clinical experience—the "gaze that was at the same time knowledge"? In *Asylums*, his sociological analysis of the mid–twentieth century "total" institution, including hospitals and mental institutions, Goffman (1961) calls it a "magical quality" that physicians (psychiatrists) can call upon to lend added legitimacy to their diagnosis (p. 370). The body having been established as a serviceable possession, so too is the mind. The psychiatric patient "becomes the kind of object upon which a psychiatric service can be performed. To be made a patient is to be remade into a serviceable object, the irony being that so little service is available once this is done" (p. 379).

The clinical gaze has been extended from the body to the mind, from which it is divided. Scientifically structured discourse about mental states constructs—and constitutes—psychiatric knowledge. The psychiatrist shows (the truth about the mind) by saying what she or he sees. In so doing, the contemporary psychiatrist—much like the priest—has considerable interpretive leeway. Psychiatric knowledge cannot be proved or disproved; after-the-fact qualifications can always be made to paint a picture of the patient consistent with the psychiatrist's construction. Within the total institution, the gaze "provides a means of systematically building up a picture of the patient's past that demonstrates that a disease process has been slowly infiltrating his conduct until this conduct, as a system, was entirely pathological. . . . An over-all title is given to the pathology, such as schizophrenia, psychopathic personality, etc., and this provides a new view of the patient's 'essential' character" (Goffman, 1961, p. 375).

As pointed out by Ingleby (1980b) and others, this pragmatic, political, and subjective mode of observation is falsely presented as "purely" scientific and objective.

In applying the medically born clinical experience and clinical gaze to the realm of the mental, the philosophy of mind was merged with medical science. Goffman's analysis is helpful for seeing the philosophical presuppositions of objectification (and their attendant contradictions) when applied to mental states and mental processes—presuppositions which are present but more difficult to discern in medicine. Modern medicine and medicalized psychiatry have taught us to relate to the words *heart, liver, cancer, multiple sclerosis, psychosis, paranoia, schizophrenia*, and *narcissism* as what Gergen (1994) calls mirrors of the real rather than as elements of scientifically structured discourse. The conception of mental object is even more powerful than that embedded in physical objects, however. Few of us are inclined to take "heart condition" or even "multiple sclerosis" to be the essence of a human being, for example, but that is just what most people in our culture do when it comes to mental descriptions.

The interpretive clinical approach (experience and gaze) that reveals supposed truths utilizes positivistic medicine's tools of classification and diagnosis. The notion of disease as an interchangeable, fixed, namable, individuated *thing* that is explainable in terms of what caused it and treatable in itself has come to dominate the contemporary institution of medicine so thoroughly that to most of us (patients as well as doctors) it seems only natural to think about it in this thingified way (Feinstein, 1967). Nevertheless, scientific medicine, in contrast to pseudoscientific psychology, has been of enormous value to human beings—simply pointing to the difference between the relative value to our species of science and myth.

As you will recall from our discussion in Chapter 2, classificatory analysis has been with us since the pre-Socratics; it identifies the things that make up the world. Our species has come a long way since Empedocles' Earth,

Water, Air, and Fire. Nowadays, to paraphrase Shakespeare, we believe there are more things in heaven and earth than are dreamt of in Greek philosophy; in fact, humankind has evolved highly complex systems for classifying all sorts of them in the physical and human–social realm. But our conviction that other things make up the world and, moreover, that they can be systematically classified is not independent of the social activity of classifying them.

Herein lies what is and always has been most philosophically/methodologically troublesome about classification: socially constructed systematizing (which has often been, indisputably, of tremendous utility to human civilization) has invariably come to be understood as corresponding to and revealing some truth about something called *reality*. Nature, including human nature, is presumed to be systematic, to exist and to function as it is (somehow or another) characterized in its classification. But what is the nature of this so-called correspondence with reality? What is the relationship between the map and that which it maps? The fundamental paradox of classification is located in the riddle of the relationship between picture and pictured, word and object, classification and classified, language and reality.

Wittgenstein's explorations of these matters are especially valuable. He begins his *Philosophical Investigations* by examining a quote from Augustine's *Confessions* about the naming relationship between words and objects.

> When they (my elders) named some object, and accordingly moved towards something, I saw this and I grasped that the thing was called by the sound they uttered when they meant to point it out. Their intention was shewn by their bodily movements, as it were the natural language of all peoples: the expression of the face, the play of the eyes, the movement of other parts of the body, and the tone of voice which expresses our state of mind in seeking, having, rejecting, or avoiding something. Thus, as I heard words repeatedly used in their proper places in various sentences, I gradually learnt to understand what objects they signified; and after I had trained my mouth to form these signs, I used them to express my own desires. (1953, *PI*, §1, p. 2)

In his discussion of these remarks, Wittgenstein suggests that he views it as a metatheoretic commitment to a picture theory of meaning, that is, meaning as naming, meaning as corresponding to reality. He says, for example, "These words, it seems to me, give us a particular picture of the essence of human language. It is this: the individual words in language name objects. . . . If you describe the learning of language in this way you are, I believe, thinking primarily of nouns like 'table', 'chair', 'bread', and of people's names of certain actions and properties; and of the remaining kinds of words as something that will take care of itself" (1953, *PI*, §1, p. 2). This theory of meaning has dominated Western thinking (and thinking about language) since the emergence of philosophy (self-consciousness and ab-straction). In more modern times the picture theory of meaning and classi-fication has, to some extent, given way to the pragmatic theory of meaning and classification. The subject of much discussion in the philosophy of science and language, linguistics and psychology, the pragmatic view was succinctly articulated in Quine's "Two Dogmas of Empiricism":

> As an empiricist I continue to think of the conceptual scheme of science as a tool, ultimately, for predicting future experience in the light of past experi-ence. Physical objects are conceptually imported into the situation as conven-ient intermediaries—not by definition in terms of experience, but simply as irreducible posits comparable, epistemologically, to the gods of Homer. For my part I do, qua lay physicist, believe in physical objects and not in Homer's gods; and I consider it a scientific error to believe otherwise. But in point of epistemological footing the physical objects and the gods differ only in degree and not in kind. Both sorts of entities enter our conception only as cultural posits. The myth of physical objects is epistemologically superior to most in that it has proved more efficacious than other myths as a device for working a manageable structure into the flux of experience. (1963, p. 44)

Yet "cultural posits" and "efficaciousness" are themselves cultural posits with complex histories. The history of scientific classification for the past several hundred years has included an interweaving of pictorial and prag-matic justification. So while scientific classificatory "myths" are, according to Quine, *epistemologically speaking,* no better or worse than the Greek gods, they are more rigorously defined, more empirically verified, and more functionally or pragmatically valuable. Modern philosophy (epistemology) never succeeds in explicating nontrivially the true nature of the relationship between "truth" and "reality," but in its proven ability to intervene upon and transform nature, modern science (and perhaps even more importantly, modern technology) makes the philosophical riddle moot or, at least, reconstructs it. For while it is often the case that technology is viewed as an offshoot of science, it is just as plausible to view science as the child of technology in certain critical respects. For example, the practical method of contemporary research scientists is often projected as a thoroughly rational process moving from self-conscious principles of science to discovery and invention. Yet many working scientists, engineers, and researchers will say that such is not the case. Emergence, trial and error, and chaos (as in chaos theory) have as much to do with discovery and invention as anything else. Furthermore, our popular cultural picture of the great scientist often por-trays him as going about the business of inventing and discovering me-thodically, rationally, knowing how to do what he is doing. But according to accounts of their own endeavors by contemporary scientists and descrip-tions by philosophers and historians of science of scientific practice, that is not how science actually works. In his classic *The Metaphysical Foundations of Modern Science* (1954), Burtt speaks of Newton in this way:

> Would that in the pages of such a man we might find a clear statement of the method used by his powerful mind in the accomplishment of his dazzling performance, with perhaps specific and illuminating directions for those less gifted; or an exact and consistent logical analysis of the ultimate gearings of the unprecedented intellectual revolution which he carried to such a decisive issue! But what a disappointment as we turn the leaves of his works! Only a handful of general and often vague statements about his method, which have to be laboriously interpreted and supplemented by a painstaking study of his scientific biography—though, to be sure, he hardly suffers in this respect by comparison with even the best of his forerunners such as Descartes and Barrow—one of the most curious and exasperating features of this whole magnificent movement is that none of its great representatives appears to have known with satisfying clarity just what he was doing or how he was doing it. (p. 208)

In practice, science and technology have always been more pragmatic and functionalistic than epistemologically coherent, even if the picturing of the two has been otherwise. It is only in this century, as modernism turns into postmodernism, that this fact of scientific life has been more fully exposed. The scientific or analytical examination of science (the activity) itself (and its deepest theories and principles) has revealed the substantial gap between the word *science* and scientific activity. From Wittgenstein to Gödel to Quine to Kuhn to Gergen, the scrutiny of science points more and more to its mythic dimension.

Yet if hard science and medical classification are mythic, in Quine's and Foucault's sense—if the precise *relationship* between hard scientific classification and its object *in reality* is inherently obscure—it is at least reasonable to recognize that there is a reality, an object, to which the classification does not, in any precise way, correspond. Tarski's explication of truth as correspondence—"It is snowing" is true if and only if it is snowing—only goes to show how little can be said about truth and correspondence. It is only in this Tarskian sense, it seems to us, that "physical objects" and "Homer's gods" are, for Quine, on the same epistemological footing. For in any more serious sense Quine's claim seems to us to have no particular social meaning. But science and technology as practiced (the historical activity) are not at all *about* traditional epistemology. And traditional epistemology, it seems to us, is not *about* anything at all. Nonetheless, stars and microbes and, perhaps even more importantly, the regularities of their motion, are something—not something only if perceived! The scientific and technological activity of engaging them is (practically and relationally) real enough, even if our method(s) of classification is ultimately nothing more than a functionalistic part of that process and not a precise mapping of reality. In other words, there are stars and regularity of stars in motion and there is a useful classificatory component of astronomy even if we cannot sensibly claim that astronomical classification is an accurate mapping of the heavens. After all, our eyes help us to see even if (and even when) we have little or no understanding of the relationship between our eyes and what is seen.

The complex classificatory systems constructed by the natural sciences and medicine are, epistemologically speaking, no less mythic for the advances in science and technology to which they have contributed. But the classificatory system of psychiatry, clinical psychology, and the mental health professions is far more troubling for both scientific and moral–political reasons. As critics of the classificatory myth of mental illness have pointed out, there is absolutely no objective (pictorial or pragmatic) basis for the classification of human subjectivity (Ingleby, 1980b; Newman, 1991b; Szasz, 1961); psychiatric and psychological classification even fails the tests of the positivistic sciences it seeks to emulate. Psychiatric and psychological classification is the systemization of invented, not discovered, diseases (Szasz, 1961); it provides technical solutions to political problems (Ingleby, 1980b); and it is "as valuable to its owners as oil is to OPEC" (Schacht, 1985, p. 515).

If Quine's claim of equality of "epistemological footing" for "physical objects" and "Homer's gods" is utterly trivial, the contention that "mental objects" and "Homer's gods" are "the same" is not so. We have seen that, after Wundt, psychology moved almost immediately away from the real world to self-consciously made-up categories which it substituted for real, human subjective, conscious life activity. It abandoned its subject matter (and its subject) in favor of a purely fictional creation of an easily manipulated, prescientific set of commodified gods, that is, labels. It has had little or no technological success—pragmatically speaking—except in the most vulgar cash value sense; amazingly, it has sold itself for a very high price with hardly any accomplishments to its credit at all: supply and demand in its most gross form. In all of this, and in virtually every other way, it resembles ancient religion far more than modern physics.

Psychology is prescholastic. Unlike physics, it rapidly realized it had no subject matter independent of itself and moved efficiently to create one in the dress of modern science, in the commodified form of modern capitalism, but in the still familiar ideology of ancient anthropomorphized religion. It is, ironically, a kind of return to fallible humanoid gods and Aristotelian teleology mixed with a hard-core Kantian causality (in the face of modern/postmodern science moving in the opposite direction) to account for human relational activity. Psychology's method is, thereby, anthropomorphized even as its fully fictionalized subject matter treats human life as essentially nonemergent. As a new secular religion, psychology (in particular, clinical psychology and psychotherapy) accounts for nothing. It has the explanatory value of the "dormative powers" that were attributed to wine by certain medieval thinkers to account for why drinking it made people sleepy. Psychology too is circularly, self-servingly, and trivially consistent and, more importantly, commodifiable and useful to the state—especially a liberal bourgeois state committed (at least in theory) to the separation of church and state.

Psychology has no subject matter; not in the sense that there is no such thing as human subjective (conscious) relational experience or uniquely human interaction, but in the sense that such activity, such life, is essentially inseparable from its study by those (human beings) who participate in it. A star is, presumably, "starring" whether it is seen or not. But a human seer (a perceiver) cannot be consciously seeing unless one is seen—if only by "oneself." The study of subjectivity cannot possibly achieve the distance required to be a science. Therefore, psychology, in its vulgar commitment to its own existence and cash value, creates that distance. But in doing so it "loses" its subject matter! Scientific psychology is, in our story, an ancient religion in modern (scientific) dress.

Interpretation

But a new system of classification is insufficient for something to be recognized as a new science. A science must use the system of classification to account for something. It must explain and/or predict something. How did the practitioners—the clinicians and psychotherapists determined to preserve an ironically "pure" psychology—deal with this requirement? Practicing some variation of Freud's method of interpretation was a means of focusing on the uniqueness of human life. Generating general laws of human behavior that could be used in "explanations" which fit into the official deductive–nomological hard scientific form was a way to preserve the aura of science. In fact, much of contemporary clinical psychology and psychotherapy is a hodgepodge of these two approaches, mixed (as we have noted) with morality.

Freud's invention of psychoanalysis created the interpretive method, that is, gaze and/or myth. Critics and proponents alike argue that his approach makes his work more of an art (or literary pursuit) than a science. Certainly, giving meaning (whatever it means) central stage is not in the best tradition of positivistic science. Freud sought to make intelligible (that is, reasonable or rational) the seemingly unintelligible actions of human beings. He thereby set up a duality between a situation as it appears from the outside ("in reality" including "mental reality," that is, consciousness) and the situation as constructed—unconsciously—by the person. The patient's thoughts, feelings, and actions could be accounted for, Freud said, by gazing (that is "showing by saying what one sees"), by interpreting the meaning that things, people, and events have for the person of which she or he is unaware.

A major element of psychoanalysis is clinical transference, whereby the patient's actions and feelings toward the analyst are interpreted, or made sense of as feelings for a significant figure from the patient's past transferred to the analyst. The psychoanalytic method also utilizes specific techniques, including the analysis of dreams and "slips of the tongue," to glean systematic meaning from them. Every dream and every speech error stems from unconscious motives and desires which can be revealed in treatment by a skilled analyst.

The methodological critiques of Freud are legion. From the left, the Italian Marxist philologist–philosopher Timpanaro (1976) makes a strong case for the view that Freud's method of interpretation and the theories which he derived from it are useless because they are immune to falsifiability. A dream about someone's dying is wish fulfillment, the veiled expression of a repressed infantile desire for that person to be dead; a dream about one's own death is a wish for punishment because of a guilt complex. Facetiously, Timpanaro asks what characteristics a dream would have to have to be something other than wish fulfillment (p. 218). Freud's theory of dreams—constructed in such a way that every possible refutation can be shown (through some manipulation) to be only seemingly a refutation—is, to Timpanaro, "non-scientific from the moment of its conception" (p. 219).

Using techniques of textual criticism, Timpanaro provides alternative interpretations for many of the slips of the tongue Freud analyzed in *The Psychopathology of Everyday Life*. He is critical of Freud for deciphering "the language of the unconscious" without ever specifying how it meets the criteria for being a language. Furthermore, in interpreting single slips of the tongue and not "an entire symptomology," Freud is guilty of "a procedure which any doctor would regard as ridiculous, since one can practically never construct a diagnosis from an isolated symptom" (p. 222).

Timpanaro emphasizes the nonscientific nature of Freudian theory in general and Freud's method of interpretation in particular. Psychoanalysis, he charges, has "regressed from a science to a myth"; it has "greatly enriched contemporary man's knowledge of himself" but more in the manner of "Kafka and Joyce . . . than Darwin or Einstein"; it is "a self-confession by the bourgeoisie of its own misery and perfidy, which blends the bitter insight and ideological blindness of a class in decline" (p. 224). Although we are sympathetic to Timpanaro's method and conclusions, we are uncomfortable with what seems to be his acceptance of Freud's pronouncements about human nature and civilization. Mainly, we differ with Timpanaro in what we take to be mythic. Timpanaro, an old-fashioned scientific Marxist, thinks that what makes the interpretive method mythical is its nonscientific nature. We locate the myth in its philosophical, religious presuppositions: classification as a thing-in-itself; inner–outer duality; rationality (making sense); a correspondence theory of truth (the deeper meaning of surface things); and the presumed necessity of accounting for human action at all. It is these philosophical (in our view, metaphysical) abstractions that Freudianism brought to its merger with positivistic medicalized psychiatry.

Interpretation and transference are the stuff of religion, including the still religious economic worldview (capitalist ideology) necessary for comprehending commodities in a fully alienated culture. They are, ultimately, a subjective way of "seeing" the products of a society fully alienated, that is separated from the process of their production. But human life *is* essentially relational process. Hence the Freudian interpretive method is such a good way to falsify reality because reality under capitalism is similarly falsified— with transference as "the normal state of mind" (Newman, 1983). But it cannot account for life as lived.

Explanation

Scientific psychology, as we have seen, was concerned with accountings that took the form of scientific explanations. Psychologists made the pretentious claim that in contrast to medical gaze-based know-how, for example, psychology could and would discover the general laws which supposedly govern human functioning. These laws came to light in the investigative practices, such as the mental test and the psychological experiment, that psychology invented. Correlations, patterns, and aggregates of data points were said to have explanatory status; that is, an individual's problem-solving behavior, personality, or intellectual ability could be explained by comparing data from her or his performance on specific tasks to the performance of others. Behavior was lawful and the laws were to be found in numbers. This "statistical metaphysics" (Kvale, 1992) is one version of the explanatory myth (essentially appealing to "dormative powers") of psychology. Explanatory myths of this kind purport to account for some phenomenon when in fact they do not. The laws are empty, often tautological, and ultimately reduce to nothing. To say that "wine has dormative powers," as we have said, is to say nothing other than that wine puts some people to sleep. The "explanation" yields no greater understanding of wine, only a religious aura of pseudoscientific credibility which the term *dormative* lends to the statement (Newman, 1991b). It is sometimes far more difficult to see the myth of explanation in our overpsychologized culture, where every *DSM-IV* description is taken as explanatory. Furthermore, psychology has succeeded in blurring the distinction between classificatory taxonomic constructions (for example, diabetes) and explanatory taxonomic constructions (see Newman, 1991b, pp. 128–129). How many people recognize "addiction" as an explanatory myth, for example—or see "IQ" (whether 82, 102, or 182) and "*x* is significant at the .005 level" as explanatory myths?

Psychology has taken over what had been a task of classical philosophy—explaining the law-generated relationship between human action and mental states or activities. This enterprise rests on some deep-rooted philosophical presuppositions. To begin with, the search for a law-governed relationship between action and mentality presumes that there is one! Second, the type of relationship is presumed to be patterned, lawful, rule-governed in some fashion. Third, the most common type of presumed pattern is causal; that is, a person's actions can supposedly be explained by discovering what caused them.

Recall the so-called general laws of history (they could as well be of psychology) postulated by Hempel in "The Function of General Laws in History." Their triviality (for example, the historical "fact" "Cortez conquered Mexico in 1519," is put into a deductive–nomological form, including the pseudolaw "When Cortez-like people travel, they . . . ") reveals the extent to which positivists would go to defend the deductive–nomological paradigm of explanation as manifest (surely with its own problems) in the hard sciences, for example, physics. "Cortez-like people" indeed! Such a formulation almost makes "dormative powers" look rich. The artificial generation of "general laws" or descriptions which subtextually imply "general laws," as in *DSM-IV*, is the meat and potatoes of psychology's claim to scientific status. But these pseudolaws are not patterns in life that psychologists have discovered (as physical laws are, in some cases, discernible patterns in nature discovered by physicists) so much as they are trivial noninductive generalizations from singular "facts." Hempel's insistence on deductive explanation and Davidson's related insistence on causality as defining conditions of understanding have attempted to reinforce psychology's claim to being scientific. But as Wittgenstein argues, one can easily believe without believing scientifically. And, we would add, one can understand without understanding scientifically—or causally or deductively–nomologically (Newman, 1965). Science might well be a mode of understanding. But is it a proper mode for understanding understanding or, more importantly, for understanding the life activity of understanders?

The use of maps in our culture is based on a recognized gap between the map and that which is mapped. Thus, the uninitiated child will ask why it takes so long to get from Albany to New York City when they are "so close" on the map. It is actually the *lack of correspondence* between map and mapped, that is, the nonpictorial quality of the map, which gives it value as a representational guide. As the map comes more and more to resemble what it is mapping (imagine a 120-mile-long, 50-mile-wide map of southeastern New York state), its usefulness decreases proportionally. The distance (the gap) between the map and the mapped makes classificatory language in the hard sciences more valuable, if not epistemologically sound. But the fundamental relationality of human life prohibits the discerning of patterns or laws. There are no describable patterns in human life, for there *is no gap* between human life activity and its study unless fictions are created to simulate one—fictions that are not merely myths, in Quine's sense, nor stories in our sense, but "white" or not so white lies in Walt Disney's sense. Psychology ("pure" and the closely related "pop") is a Santa Claus science.

The study of individual differences, mental testing, and the operational definition are all examples of psychology's explanatory myth-making apparatus. The "knowledge" they produce takes an explanatory form in that it is meant to provide an accounting in terms of reason or cause. Freudianism, as we have seen, provided, in some sense, the ultimate causal accounting: intrapsychic conflict and infantile trauma are the causes of adult personality disorders and what only seem to be irrational human actions. Through the interpretive (mythic) method one can always find evidence for this overarching explanatory myth.

The behavioristic perspective that dominated much of psychology from the 1920s through the 1960s would appear to have little in common with Freudian theory or practice. A simplistic (albeit sometimes clever) technology more than a bona fide theory, behaviorism was radically antiinterpretive. The earliest successful proponent and popularizer of behaviorism, John Watson, laid out its tenets as early as 1913: behavior, not consciousness, should be the subject matter of psychology; psychology's method should be objective, not introspective; and psychology's goal should be the prediction and control of behavior (Hunt, 1993). Only controlled observation of behavior was necessary for the task.

As behaviorism evolved and expanded the domain of behaviors it investigated, its investigative practices altered somewhat. But its underlying principle was kept intact: all behavior (and behavior was all, making it virtually meaningless), from the simplest reflex to the most complex human interaction or achievement, could be accounted for in terms of conditioning, the association of stimulus and response.

Watson himself showed some interest in so-called abnormal behavior and believed that an "emotional tendency" could be learned as easily as a simple motor habit (Magaro, Gripp and McDowell, 1978). Of Watson's dubious accomplishments, perhaps the most well known is his (apparently successful) attempt to produce a conditioned fear response in a one-year-old boy. A white rat (toward which the child showed no fear) was placed near him. Then Watson, using a hammer, banged a steel bar behind the boy's head. The child responded fearfully. Next, the rat was placed in front of him and as he reached for it the steel bar was hammered again. Over the course of a few months, the boy was responding with fear not only to rats but to other furry things (rabbits, a seal coat, a Santa Claus mask). No efforts were made to "decondition" the youngster. Here, along with psychiatry's classification and Freud's psychoanalysis, was yet another means of objectifying emotionality.

This incident is a continuing source of embarrassment to psychology today, when rigid rules for the ethical treatment of "human subjects" obtain.

Perhaps in tacit acknowledgment of professional discomfort, in *The Story of Psychology* Hunt (1993) tells us a little more about Watson's character. The infamous experiment eventually cost Watson his academic career—not because a young child was treated with a gross disregard of ethics, but because Watson had violated the sexual mores of the day by conducting an affair with the student who was his collaborator. The ensuing scandal, precipitated by Watson's wife, got him fired. He subsequently joined the Walter J. Thompson advertising agency, where he worked on campaigns for deodorants, cold creams, cigarettes, and coffee, helping "to make the 'coffee break' an American custom in offices, factories, and homes" (Hunt, 1993, p. 280).

During the 1920s and 1930s, other psychologists attempted to use conditioning techniques to change the behavior of mental patients, but any significant use of behaviorism in the treatment of mental illness would await the 1950s and B. F. Skinner, who had been working since the 1930s to advance behaviorism with his claim (and the invention of techniques to prove) that nearly all human and animal behavior can be predicted and controlled if the contingencies of reinforcement are known. The notion that abnormal behavior caused by infantile emotional trauma could be changed through conditioning was an important factor in the early popularity of behavior modification and token economies. Moreover, it provided a means by which Freudian theory could be reconciled with positivistic behaviorist psychology.

Here was an explanatory myth whose grandiosity matched Freud's. The simple law of stimulus–response contingencies (actually a causal relationship, although this was denied) was put forth to explain human behavior. What behaviorism added to scientific psychology's already weighty myth/hoax was the notion that with control and predictability come understanding.

Buoyed by successful achievements in experimental animal behavior and applications of behaviorist techniques in complex human behavior, Skinner made highly speculative claims for behaviorism in *Verbal Behavior* (1957). For many in psychology and psychological philosophy, Chomsky's review of the book two years later sounded the death knell of Skinnerian behaviorism as a systematic scientific theory. Chomsky (1959) systematically showed that Skinner's concepts, if taken literally, do not pertain to verbal behavior and, if taken metaphorically, add nothing to existing formulations. Surely behaviorism continues as a popular and even a "scientific psychology" metaphor. But as the end of the twentieth century nears, many critics of psychology have come to believe that neither Freudian interpretationalism nor Skinner's speculative behavioral generalizations make psychology a science. More and more have come to question whether there has to be or could be a scientific psychology at all.

NOTE

1. The convention in philosophical literature is to cite Wittgenstein's writings by title (abbreviated) and paragraph or page. We have chosen to add to that the year of publication of the particular edition we use. Full titles of abbreviated texts can be found in the Bibliography.

7

Psychology and Human Development: The Ideal(ist) Marriage

The story of scientific psychology and development is a different kind of story from the ones we have already told. For one thing, the main character is more elusive than individual differences and mental illness. The prevailing cultural understanding of human development and child development has been constructed out of philosophical and religious thinking as well as psychological practice. Furthermore, the status of what is called developmental psychology is unclear. Officially, it is a branch of psychology on a level with clinical, experimental, industrial, educational, and so on, although it came into existence later than the others. However, since its earliest days (even before it was named developmental psychology) there have been those who argued that development is not an area of psychology at all but an approach to the investigation of human–social phenomena.

What is also different is that the expert knowledge about development invented by psychologists did not have the same kind of utilitarian value as psychological knowledge about individual differences and mental illness. Economic, political, cultural, and scientific changes created new needs among those in positions of power; sorting people, making predictions about their performance in school or on the job, controlling their behavior, and treating the newly conceptualized mentally ill, as we have seen, all came about as a result of such changing requirements. Psychometrics, industrial psychology, educational psychology, and clinical psychology were shaped by the market's demand for their products. Whether mythic or not, these "areas" of psychology are from a utilitarian point of view *about* something and, as such, could be used *for* something.

It is not clear to us that developmental psychology is about anything in the same way. Its ostensible subject matter is what goes on all the time, and has always gone on: children are born; they are cared for in varying ways and to varying degrees; they grow and mature; they become adults; they die. To study this is at the same time to study everything and nothing. Meanwhile, the market for the knowledge which is thereby produced is everyone—and no one. In other words, development has been going on since long before there was industrial capitalism, not to mention psychology; there was no obvious new practical need for knowledge claims about it. By contrast, the construction of the consumer in the late-nineteenth and early-twentieth centuries required psychology. So did the sorting, testing, and educating of children and the hiring and training of workers for maximum productivity. And so did the creation of a less barbaric treatment of those suffering mental anguish and / or deemed to be mentally abnormal.

Because of this peculiar circumstance, neither blatant opportunism nor wheeling and dealing with government officials and corporate executives was a major factor in the emergence of expert psychological knowledge about development. (The Western cultural attitude of progress may have had more to do with the systematic attention and effort given to fundamental questions about humanness over the last hundred years.) This is not to say that the psychological study of development is less ideological or political than the psychological study of anything else. On the contrary, the argument can be made that it is more ideological, and its impact of greater magnitude, for just this reason. This chapter of psychology's story includes an account of how psychology has constructed the myth of development and the myth of childhood, and how these myths were used in constructing the overall myth/hoax of psychology.

The modern study of human development is unquestionably philosophy's stillborn child. More than any other area of the social sciences, developmental psychology became the testing ground for epistemological questions that philosophers had been asking for centuries. How do we know (see, think, feel) what we know (see, think, feel)? Developmental psychology's own epistemology—"What adults know can be discovered by discovering what babies know" (to put it simply, but not inaccurately)—is in fact a restatement of philosophy's fundamental presuppositions about the mind.

The psychological study of human development is at once a story of deception and of exposure. It is the story of how philosophical thinking about thinking became even more deeply insinuated into Western culture at the same time as it showed itself (to those who were willing to see) unable to hold up under the scrutiny of systematic investigation. It is perhaps ironic that it took twentieth-century scientific research into the development of the human mind to show how the consolidation of ancient and modern philosophical thought (in modern science) impedes historically meaningful discovery.

THE EVOLUTIONARY IMPERATIVE

We begin our story in the present day. Psychology, we are told, is onto something new—a revolutionary new paradigm, a unifying theoretical approach capable of integrating fragmented theories and taking psychological science out of its current state of disarray and confusion forward into the twenty-first century. This new paradigm, presented in scholarly journals (for example, *Psychological Inquiry*, 1995) and the popular press (for example, *Time*, 1995), is called *evolutionary psychology*. According to David Buss, one of its major proponents, evolutionary psychology "provides the key to unlocking the mystery of where we came from, how we arrived at our current state, and the mechanisms of mind that define who we are" (1995, p. 27).

Briefly, Buss's argument goes like this: The fact that people behave implies the existence of inner psychological mechanisms. So do all psychological theories. Because psychological theories imply underlying mechanisms, they also imply a human nature (pp. 1–2). Buss asks what the origins of these mechanisms governing human nature might be. Of the various answers that have evolved over the centuries, Buss concludes that only three are viable: creationism, seeding theory (extraterrestrials visited earth and planted the seeds of life here), and evolution by natural selection. Buss eliminates creationism because it is not a scientific theory. He rules out seeding theory because it does not constitute an explanation but merely pushes the problem back a level (what are the origins of the seed and the extraterrestrials?). That leaves evolution. To the extent that most psychologists would agree that evolution in the broadest sense accounts for "how we got here," the interesting questions have to do with "the nature of the psychological mechanisms that evolution by natural selection has fashioned" (p. 5).

Buss contends that the *evolved psychological mechanism*, a postulate of evolutionary psychology, does away with the false dichotomies of psychology (nature–nurture is his catch-all category for them). Rather than there being two kinds of causes, biological and environmental, there is in fact only one, the evolved psychological mechanism. Such mechanisms reside inside the organism, having been formed to solve "a specific problem of individual survival or reproduction recurrently over human evolutionary history" (pp. 5–6). He identifies ten such hypothesized mechanisms on which research is being carried out. They include "superior female spatial-location memory," which functions to "increase success at foraging/gathering"; "male sexual jealousy," which functions to "increase paternity certainty"; "male mate preference for youth, attractiveness, and waist-to-hip ratio," which functions to "select mates of high fertility"; and "natural language," which functions for "communication/manipulation" (p. 6). That contemporary women and men behave in certain ways does not indicate that they are currently driven, consciously or unconsciously, to maximize adaptation through gene selection (as the sociobiologists contend). Rather it indicates that human beings "are living fossils—collections of mechanisms produced by prior selection pressures operating on a long and unbroken line of ancestors. Today we activate and execute these specific mechanisms" (p. 10).

We are tempted to point out how ludicrous the paradigm and its illustrations seem to be; to note the many violations of modern scientific standards of evidence and argumentation; to uncover the philosophical naiveté of Buss's analysis. (To ask questions about mechanisms, for example, is not the same as asking questions about origins.) But there is a more interesting activity to pursue. Let us examine Buss's "new paradigm" in light of the following observation about developmental psychology by Morss (1990) in *The Biologising of Childhood: Developmental Psychology and the Darwinian Myth*:

> Developmental psychology is built on foundations which are rotten. Not only in its more classic formulations, but also most of its present-day versions, adhere to outdated notions of a biological–philosophical nature. . . . It may be that the discipline is constituted by the appeal to evolutionist logic and the related doctrines, and could have no independent existence. If so, developmental psychology might be seen as a mere hangover from the late 19th century: A blind alley in the upward progress of the social and life sciences. (p. 227)

This is the conclusion to Morss's cogent argument that, far from being Darwinian, developmental psychology throughout its history has adhered to biological assumptions of a pre-Darwinian (in particular, a Lamarckian) nature. Morss reminds his readers, for example, that recapitulation—the notion that the development of the individual repeats the evolutionary history of the species—was not Darwin's idea. Neither was the idea that evolutionary process must be a fixed, orderly, hierarchical sequence; nor the belief in acquired characteristics. Darwin subscribed inconsistently to these elements of evolutionary theory put forth by others. Darwin, Morss tells us, was distinguished from his predecessors by his notion of natural selection, and its implications for a nonteleological mechanism to account for change. What was revolutionary about Darwin's theory was not the concept of heritability but the concept of change (Burman, 1994).

Morss summarizes the views of prominent figures in the history of developmental theory (Hall, Baldwin, Freud, Piaget, Vygotsky, and Werner) in relation to the biological influences on their thinking. He shows, for example, how the evolutionary assumptions of continuity, hierarchy, progress, and recapitulation inform Piaget's view that the mechanisms of intelligence recapitulate biological mechanisms, and the position (widely accepted by psychologists) that the "primitive" awareness of sensation is the earliest form of human thinking.

Although Morss is highly critical of developmental psychology and its pre-Darwinian evolutionary presuppositions, he is not suggesting that it become Darwinian. (He is hardly likely to be an adherent of Buss's evolutionary psychology.) Neither is he rejecting biology outright as having no role to play in the study of human development. But biology, Morss reminds us, has moved far beyond Darwin. What Morss is advocating is that developmental psychology become *post-Darwinian*. This move out of the nineteenth century (and into the twenty-first) might mean "the assimilation of modern biology and the excising of 19th century baggage" or "the excising of biology altogether" (p. 232).

In the light of Morss's historical analysis, what are we to make of evolutionary psychology? If developmental psychology is evolutionary psychology, what, then, is the new paradigm? Furthermore, if contemporary developmental psychology is based on nineteenth-century biological theory, what is it about the current explanatory myths of psychology that makes it seem necessary to resurrect Darwin in the cause of revitalizing the field? What is the hole that evolution by natural selection is supposed to fill? To explore these questions, we turn now to an examination of how the essentially evolutionary view of human development was constructed, deepening the union of biology and epistemology that is developmental psychology.

DEVELOPMENTAL PSYCHOLOGY AND THE CONSTRUCTION OF THE CHILD

What Are Children and What Are They For?

Developmental psychology begins with the child, not only because this was its subject matter until very recently but because, so the story goes, it emerged as a discipline out of "child study." It was, we are told, none other than Charles Darwin himself who started it all with the publication in 1877 of *A Biographical Sketch of an Infant*, excerpts from notebooks of observations of his son, which he had begun recording forty years earlier. Evidently, there had been child studies prior to Darwin's, notably by women, but they are not to be found in the received history of psychology (Bradley, 1989; Burman, 1994).

Darwin was interested in the continuity from animal to human; he was particularly intent on finding evidence that our mental and moral faculties had evolved from our animal ancestry (Morss, 1990). Early development was important; it came to be seen as "the hereditary endowment, a baseline from which variation might emerge in the *adult* state" (Morss, 1990, p. 15). Darwin's interest in children, then, was only incidental. As for most of the developmentalists who followed him (the best known being Piaget), children were of interest only insofar as they were the means through which the laws of nature were expressed.

We are jumping slightly ahead of our story, however. In order for children to be worthy of study (if only instrumentally), they had to exist! That is, there had to be a conception of the child, and of a phase of life identified as childhood which was distinct from adulthood. The French historian Philippe Ariès (1962) links the modern Western conception of childhood to the modern Western conception of the family. Ariès argues that these two notions were socially constructed during the sixteenth and seventeenth centuries "at a time when the family had freed itself from both biology and law to become a value, a theme of expression, an occasion of emotion" (p. 10).

Combing diaries and examining paintings produced over a period of four centuries, Ariès shows the changes that took place in how the European aristocracy related to and talked about children and how artists of the time represented them, as evidence for how children were thought about. It was not until the fourteenth century, for example, that children began to be seen in paintings. Before that, in pictures where it might be expected that children would be represented (such as scenes of certain Christian religious events), they were portrayed as little men. Until the seventeenth century, no ordinary children were depicted in art; the medieval child, a holy child or symbol of the soul, was painted nude. Ariès also quotes extensively from diaries of the time—for example, from the diary of the physician to the French king, Henri IV. These excerpts reveal that no special treatment was accorded to children, and no special reserve was shown in their presence; children were present in all of life, including sex, drinking, violence, and death.

Ariès connects the "discovery of childhood" to various cultural and economic changes taking place in seventeenth-century Europe which diminished the sociality (the public nature) of living and gave rise to the idea of the (more private) family.

The conception of childhood from the mid-1800s through the early 1900s was romantic—the child was "closer" to nature, an immature biological organism, untouched by civilization, en route to knowledge and reason but lacking both (Burman, 1994). Through the early 1900s, many studies of children compared them to apes, "primitive man" ("savages"), and the insane. In their observations, scientists looked for evidence of the recapitulation of certain assumed evolutionary adaptations, such as the tendency for physical and mental development to proceed from simple to complex, from homogeneous to heterogeneous, from holistic to differentiated.

The father of developmental psychology is typically identified as the American psychologist G. Stanley Hall, although development to Hall was not a branch of psychology but an approach, the "one true method" that should replace a psychology erroneously based on static views of knowledge and the soul (Morss, 1990, p. 34). Largely forgotten today, except in historical summaries of psychology (and at Clark University in Massachusetts, where he served as president), Hall was highly influential during the first two decades of this century. (It was under Hall that Clark University sponsored Freud's trip to the United States in 1909.) Hall's significance for our story lies in the fact that he put childhood and development on the psychological map.

A strict believer in recapitulation, Hall supported the idea that human learning naturally followed the evolutionary course of civilization and that "education is simply the expediting and shortening of the course" (quoted in Morss, 1990, p. 33). Education should therefore be "developmental"—it should take children through stages of civilization (cultural epochs) because such a curriculum would match their (recapitulatory) needs (Morss, 1990). Hall imported this model, which originated in Europe, to the United States. He also popularized the psychological census as a means of gathering data on large numbers of schoolchildren in order to gain knowledge about how mental characteristics are distributed.

Child study was soon affected by the advent of more sophisticated statistical methods, which we discussed earlier in the context of psychology's obsession with individual differences, and by the mental testing "craze." By making "mental age" analogous to chronological age, it was now possible to "see" (Foucault's "gaze that was at once knowledge") all kinds of abilities as distributed in quantifiable and measurable intervals (the familiar "milestones," such as the age at which babies hold their heads up, begin to crawl, say one word at a time, and acquire a fifty-word vocabulary). Burman (1994) describes how this period was critical in naturalizing and normalizing childhood as it produced the modernist conception of the child. The evolutionary theoretical foundation of child study, coupled with psychology's new investigative practices of sorting, measuring, and quantifying by means of statistically aggregated data, produced knowledge claims about the supposedly natural unfolding of the human growth process. It also provided a simple baseline—age—which allowed deviations from the norm to be identified. Burman adds a Foucault-like twist to a critical analysis that echoes Danziger: "The normal child, the ideal type, distilled from the comparative scores of age-graded populations, is therefore a fiction or a myth. No individual or real child lies at its basis. It is an abstraction, a fantasy, a fiction, a production of the testing apparatus that incorporates, that constructs the child, by virtue of its gaze" (1994, pp. 16–17).

To our way of thinking, the idealism and metaphysics go beyond the production of the child and childhood. The conceptions of natural and normal are now inextricably linked with evolution (as opposed, for example, to revolution). Natural and normal are defined as continuous, steady, and linear. Things may be in a constant state of motion (a view the world has come to accept since Galileo first dared to argue it several hundred years ago), but motion and change occur at fixed intervals. Furthermore, development (still undefined except as "growth") has been reconstituted in time; to speak of development, it now is necessary to refer to chronological age. Thus, another layer of abstraction has been laid down.

If what is natural and normal is *evolution*, then *revolution* thereby becomes abnormal. The uniqueness of Vygotsky's challenge to traditional views on development resides in part in his critique of an evolutionary view of development (in which he was not, however, at all consistent), and in his recognition of revolution as normal. Recall his statement that "a revolution solves only those tasks which have been raised by history" (p.62). Here we quote the passage in full:

> To the naive mind, revolution and history seem incompatible. It believes that historical development continues as long as it follows a straight line. When a change comes, a break in the historical fabric, a leap—then this naive mind sees only catastrophe, a fall, a rupture; for the naive mind history ends until back again straight and narrow. The scientific mind, on the contrary, views revolution as the locomotive of history forging ahead at full speed; it regards the revolutionary epoch as a tangible, living embodiment of history. A revolution solves only those tasks which have been raised by history; this proposition holds true equally for revolution in general and for aspects of social and cultural life during a revolution. (Quoted in Levitan, 1982, inside front cover)

Vygotsky's eloquent formulation contrasts the positivist evolutionary perspective (the naive mind) with a dialectical historical materialist perspective (the scientific mind). He is urging that we take a historical (revolutionary) rather than a societal (evolutionary) view of development. His modernist language notwithstanding, his message anticipates postmodernism's insistence on the historical embeddedness of knowledge and worldviews.

Vygotsky would go unheeded; indeed, his work was suppressed under Stalin and remained unknown (outside a very small circle) until the 1960s. Even if his writings had been widely available, however, it is doubtful that they would have had a significant impact. By the 1930s the myth/hoax of psychology was already entrenched. Biological and behaviorist reductionism (two sides of the same coin) and philosophical rationalism were already deeply ingrained in academic and research psychology. Freudian theory was transforming the cultural landscape in many ways, including how we think about the nature not only of children but of childhood, and it was beginning to be incorporated into psychological theorizing. Meanwhile, the methodolatry we spoke of earlier was rampant; psychologists' arguments about how to interpret specific data appealed not to theoretical positions, but to variations in method, apparatus, technology, and statistics.

The dominant psychological conception of the child during this period was as an essentially passive organism that was capable of being trained, molded, socialized. The emerging popular conception of the child was more obviously moral and more conflicted, but no less passive and static. While one or another image might have dominated for a brief period, the modern child was at once naturally good and naturally sinful, innocent and untrustworthy, dependent on "the other" and ever vulnerable to the dangers of "the outer," in need of freedom and in need of control. In the social construction of the child, the popular and scientific conceptions mutually influence each other, of course, and both are also influenced by (and influence) political, economic, and cultural transformations.

Obvious and instructive illustrations are the transformation in the form of life that was urban industrialization, the concomitant rise in the standard of living, and the political activism that was a response to economic exploitation. Until the twentieth century, children were primarily of economic value, to their families and to the larger society. Their life activity (except among the aristocracy) was work—in preindustrial times, on the land; with the industrial revolution, in the mines and factories. The successful mass movement to abolish the abhorrent conditions of child labor in Western Europe and the United States in the late 1800s created the possibility of a new way of conceptualizing children. So did the economic progress that accompanied industrialization, and the steady rise in the standard of living. So did advances in medicine and public health, which significantly lowered the rate of infant mortality.

Viviana Zelizer (1985) presents a sociological analysis of this transformative period in the United States and its impact on the construction of the child. Between the 1870s and the 1930s, Zelizer argues in *Pricing the Priceless Child*, the economic and sentimental values of children under fifteen years of age reversed themselves in importance, both to parents and in the culture at large. A century ago, children were necessary sources of income (for the working class, they remained so into the 1930s). For example, to the extent that parents were compensated for the wrongful death of a child, the amount depended on the child's earning capacity. In contrast, today it costs hundreds of thousands of dollars to rear a child, who produces no income. Adoptive parents now pay tens of thousands of dollars simply to have a child to rear. Courts routinely award upwards of a million dollars for the wrongful death of a child, their decisions based on the grief, sorrow, and emotional loss sustained by the parents. The value of children is no longer economic, but sentimental.

Zelizer attributes this radical transformation in part to the increased commercialism of the society; children came to occupy a separate, *extracommercial* place: "The expulsion of children from the 'cash nexus' . . . was . . . part of a cultural process of 'sacralization' of children's lives. The term sacralization is used in the sense of objects being invested with sentimental or religious meaning" (1985, p. 11).

Zelizer provides fascinating data to show how the construction of the "economically worthless" and "sentimentally priceless" child was effected. Her data are disconcerting; they are taken from real life situations which either are no longer relevant or have been resolved in ways that are today taken for granted. Having to do with the life and death of children, they are situations in which the economic worth of a child and sentimental value intersect: the public response to children being killed by streetcars and automobiles; the struggle over child labor legislation; the insuring of children's lives; parental compensation for the wrongful death of children; and the adoption and sale of children.

Zelizer's analysis is instructive in several ways. First, its focus is on ordinary people and the mundane life issues they confronted as they participated in historical transformation/lived their lives. Zelizer nicely avoids the tendency of critics (especially critics of capitalism) to present industrial capitalism as unequivocally evil and its ideological transformations in simplistic, almost conspiratorial terms. Burman (1994), for example, falls into this trap several times in her otherwise fine book, as when she suggests that outrage over child labor in Britain had more to do with "fears of unruly and potentially undesirable activities made possible by an independent income" than with the ways in which children were being exploited (p. 35); she does it again when she describes compulsory schooling as disenfranchising children and "positioning the working-class child as in need of education and socialisation" (p. 35). We wonder what justification there could be for denying that, given the sweeping transformation in forms of life, the working-class child needed education and socialization?

Zelizer's description of the change in children's value from primarily economic to primarily sentimental also highlights the fundamentality of instrumentalism in the construction of children and childhood. Psychologists (read philosophers) use children to learn about adults or abstract laws of (human) nature or both. Practitioners are concerned to train children and their families in order to produce useful (productive, compliant, happy) adults. And parents, understandably, organize their activity so as to "bring up" their children, that is, to produce adults.

In saying this our intention is not to paint a conspiracy nor to glorify children or childhood. Rather, it is to show that the child constructed in and by Western culture has no integrity as a form of life. Childhood, seen as a phase or stage of life, is a means to an end called adulthood. Development itself is understood as a process (separate from its product) that must lead somewhere (better, higher); if it does not, it is not development proper. Development is not seen as ongoing, continuous life activity. Development (this abstraction) may "possess continuity" (another abstraction) with our animal ancestors and/or our future selves and civilization. To us, however, development—the human social, relational activity—is continuously and nonpragmatically emergent.

Development as Self-Construction

Jean Piaget changed everything. The work of this Swiss biologist–philosopher–psychologist, produced over a fifty–year period from the 1920s to the 1970s, did not have a significant impact on American psychology until the early 1960s. But when American psychology was ready for Piaget, the long love affair began.

With Piaget, developmental psychology came into its own. Knowledge claims about human development and about how we know what we know grew in sophistication and quantity. Developmental psychology had something new and creative to say, and this gained it status among the diverse fields of psychology. Piaget was proudly philosophical; that his work was embraced by so many gained a bit of long-lost legitimacy for philosophy within psychology. For one thing, the conception of the passive child would be buried. Piaget's child is active. She or he does not receive knowledge of the world but invents or constructs it. Moreover, such an active being is not ignorant—gone is the notion that the child knows less than the adult. Piaget's child knows *differently* from the adult.

We could go on for many pages listing and describing the changes brought about by Piaget's fresh insights into cognition, his meticulous and fascinating observations, and his new, antiempirical method of investigation. Yet all of these changes within developmental psychology amounted to more of the same. In fact, the Piagetian paradigm contributed mightily to the myth/hoax of psychology. Piaget did not relinquish any of the fundamental philosophical presuppositions embedded within psychology. The Piagetian paradigm simply added to psychology's contributions to the social construction of the child, cementing (and liberalizing) the nineteenth-century romanticized notion of the child as "other" (exemplified, we think, by the inappropriately named child-centered approach to education and parenting that began in the 1960s). Piaget's unique child, as we shall see, is uniquely abstract—a Cartesian–Kantian–Freudian human mentality.

By the Piagetian paradigm, we are referring not merely to Piaget's own large body of work, but to the continuation of his legacy (especially in the United States). Until recently, the stagist and structural elements of his theory dominated American research. The current shift in emphasis that focuses on his constructivism may be part of an effort to save Piagetian research from sinking into oblivion under the contemporary onslaught from two different (and opposed) forces: the post-Piagetian "infant as genius" movement, and the postmodern, social-constructionist and Vygotsky-influenced activity-theoretic movement(s).

While it may be on the decline as a research paradigm, the Piagetian perspective permeates developmental psychology, educational theory and practice, and the wider culture (although it is not nearly as influential a presence there as Freudianism). The notion of invariant and linear stages of intellectual development, for example, is as much a part of the conception and understanding of growing up as is the belief in childhood psychic trauma. Piaget's ontology is as much individuated as Freud's, and he has contributed just as significantly to the construction of the autonomous, individuated subject. Both presuppose an inner–outer duality and the primacy of the biological as structurally and ontogenetically prior. Freud's individuated subject is in constant conflict with the impinging "outside" (social world); this is the source of the individual personality. Piaget's individuated subject "assimilates" what is "outside"; this is the source of the individual knower. Piaget's active child is only instrumentally active. That is, the child's interaction with physical objects in the environment is a means to an end—it stimulates internal mental schema. The development of intelligence is, for Piaget, the development of knowing.

Kant's Grandchild: The Psychologizing of Knowledge

But what is meant by knowing? What are the criteria and standards by which the child's thinking is judged? Who is the quintessential knower? Piaget's model synthesizes Western philosophical rationalism with psychology's mentalism and biology's reductionism. He not only turned Descartes's *cogito* into a biologically determined psychological reality, he also "succeeded in transforming each of the Kantian categories of knowledge from a first principle into a subject of scientific investigation" (Gruber and Voneche, 1977, p. xxix). For example, Piaget provided remarkably detailed observations of the emergence of the infant's concept of the object and development of object permanence, and he devoted entire books to investigating other Kantian categories (see, for example, *The Child's Conception of Space, The Child's Conception of Time, The Child's Conception of Physical Causality*).

What Piaget means by thinking is logical thinking. When he describes the child as thinking differently from the adult, he has a particular adult, the modern scientist, in mind. The highest stage of intellectual development—*formal operations* (which is attained in adolescence, although not by everyone)—is reached when the child can perform a set of mental operations characteristic of the hypothetico-deductive model. The *formal operational child* who recognizes that a flattened ball of clay "is the same" or "has the same amount" as it did when it was round, Piaget asserts, has performed three mental operations on what he has perceived: identity, compensation, and inversion. The significance of this, intellectually speaking, is that only by carrying out these mental operations can the individual come to know (or self-construct knowledge of) the fact of the conservation of matter.

The resolution of contradiction plays an important role in Piaget's model of thinking and the growing ability to perform these mental operations. The *concrete operational child* first says that two balls of clay have the same amount but on seeing one ball flattened into a "snake" says it now has more (or less). Such a child—so the Piagetian story goes—denies the contradiction between what he saw before and what he sees now and/or between what he sees (they do not look equal) and what he "knows" (no one added or took away any clay). The highest form of intellect, for Piaget, is "the growth of awareness of contradiction, the will to search for ways of thinking that can eliminate contradiction, in short the growth of logic" (Gruber and Voneche, 1977, p. xxi). The philosophical presupposition that identifies logic with thinking and that relegates contradiction to a mental error has thus become woven into the fabric of psychology's myth of development— and the myth/hoax of psychology.

Freud's Grandchild: The Intellectualizing of the Ego

Our Piagetian child is also egocentric. Piaget's creative twist on Freud's concept of the ego was to transform this element of personality structure into a characteristic of early cognition. The child who cannot take the perspective of another is egocentric in both thinking and speaking. Pre-school children playing side by side, for example, talk —but not to each other. Their speech is only superficially social; it lacks features that indicate awareness of the other person's point of view. Until the age of seven, speech is egocentric; that is, it is not communicative but "for oneself."

Piaget maintained that egocentric speech was evidence of egocentric thought: "This characteristic of a large portion of childish talk points to a certain egocentrism of thought itself. . . . And these thoughts are inexpressible precisely because they lack the means which are fostered only by the desire to communicate with others, and to enter into their point of view" (Piaget, 1955, p. 206).

According to Piaget, childhood egocentrism declines in one stage and reappears in another (from which it goes through another period of decline). The egocentric thought of the young child is thought that is unanalyzed and prelogical. It arises from things being schematized "in accordance with the child's own point of view, instead of being perceived in their intrinsic relations" (Piaget, 1955, p. 249). Thus, the child's view is narrow not only because it is personal relative to other people, but also because it does not take into account general laws and properties of objects.

Take Piaget's well-known "three mountain" task. A child of a certain age is placed before a model of three mountains which vary in height and other features. A doll is placed so that it has a different "view" of the mountains. The child is asked to describe first what she or he sees and then what the doll sees. The egocentric child cannot "take the doll's point of view" (cannot perform the necessary mental operations on the objects of perception—for example, transforming the objects in space), but simply repeats the first description to describe what the doll sees.

Piaget's claims about egocentrism rest on and perpetuate the philosophical presuppositions of duality and causality—his analysis is based on the dichotomy of inner–outer/private–social worlds, and a parallelism between causal mechanisms that operate in the physical and the mental realms. Piaget's inner–outer duality is essentially psychoanalytic; to account for the transitions from egocentric to social speech and from egocentric thinking to logical thinking, he had to introduce "needs." Accordingly, the child's world is really two worlds—that of inner needs and that of objective reality. The young, egocentric child is motivated to satisfy only inner needs; development in thought is the gradual adaptation to outer reality. Here is Vygotsky's critique, as good a description of Piaget's metaphysics as we have seen:

> When Piaget borrowed Freud's concept that the pleasure principle precedes the reality principle, he adopts the whole metaphysic associated with the concept of the pleasure principle. Here the principle is transformed from an auxiliary or biologically subordinate characteristic into a kind of independent vital force, into the prime mover of the whole process of mental development. (1987, p. 77)

Vygotsky goes on to reject Piagetian/Freudian duality, pointing to the problems inherent in assuming a separation between satisfying needs and adapting to reality. In doing so, he exposes the passivity of Piaget's supposedly active child:

> Piaget has argued that things do not influence the mind of the child. But we have seen that where the child's egocentric speech is linked to his practical activity, where it is linked to his thinking, things really do operate on his mind and influence it. By the word "things" we mean reality. However, what we have in mind is *not reality as it is passively reflected in perception or abstractly cognized.* We mean reality as it is encountered in practice. (1987, p. 79, emphasis added)

Self-Construction Deconstructed

Earlier we referred in passing to alternatives to Piaget's paradigm, including neo-Piagetian constructivism and social constructionism. During the 1970s, the growing fascination of developmentalists with "the social world" coincided with emerging doubts about Piaget's asocial child. New experimental and observational technology (such as video, film, and other equipment for measuring eye movements, rates of sucking, and other physical behavior) made it possible for infants and babies to be scrutinized in ways they never could before. The importance of social interaction (usually identified or idealized as the mother–child dyad) was recognized. The assumptions of developmental psychology were modified to take into account the fact that the child lives in a "social world." We turn now to an examination of some of the knowledge claims and investigative practices of this new approach to see whether it in fact has succeeded in ridding psychology of its philosophical presuppositions.

In *Deconstructing Developmental Psychology*, Burman (1994) critically analyzes the developmental psychology of the past twenty-five years. She describes how recent research attempts to overcome the split between the biological and social but ultimately fails, in part because it cannot give up its evolutionary framework. In Burman's view, the contemporary developmental psychologist conceptualizes the infant as a biological organism "equipped with a reflexive repertoire of behaviours that function to elicit care, nurturance and attention. This is interpreted . . . as being of 'survival value' to the species as well as to the individual (since the individual is portrayed as the species' future)" (1994, p. 35). The way in which subtle differences in infants' behavior elicit a fine-tuning of their caregivers' responses to their needs is cited by developmentalists as evidence of children's readiness for adaptation to social interaction. One example is the way mothers quickly learn to respond differentially to their infants' crying patterns. The child is thus seen as "prewired" to make the gradual shift from a biological to a social being.

As Burman points out, what the researchers have accomplished is not the elimination of the biological–social/inner–outer duality, but its reinforcement. The suggestion that development takes place "from lesser to greater involvement with and awareness of the social world" conjures up "the image of a transition from isolation into sociality, with the epithet 'social' qualifying 'world' functioning retrospectively to designate the world the child had previously inhabited as pre- or non-social" (1994, p. 36).

Piaget's infant was recapitulating the universal, predetermined general laws that supposedly govern the intellectual development of the species. The "outer world" was required so that it could be manipulated by the infant, thereby making it possible for internal mental structures of thought to transform. In this way, the child's development is individually and autonomously self-constructed. Social interaction with other human beings became an important factor in development only in middle childhood.

By contrast, the neo- and post-Piagetian infant is individualistically *predisposed* to sociality. It is not only the caregiver who is attuned to the infant's mental states and behavioral subtleties; the infant too is capable of detecting and interpreting the caregiver's behavior (but see Burman, 1994, for problems identified in research design and data interpretation). The driving force of development is no longer Kantian categories or Freudian intrapsychic conflict. Now development is propelled by our inherent social-ness, the necessity of living in a social world. This new conception of development required new psychological objects such as *mutual intention-ality, intersubjectivity,* and *relatedness.* In recent years developmental psychologists have made a variety of knowledge claims about these newly constructed psychological objects. For example, all three are implicated in the positing of an innate predisposition for cooperative turn taking. Inferred from the way infants and mothers synchronize their body movements (Kaye, 1982; Trevarthen and Hubley, 1978), this primitive form of related-ness is said to lay the groundwork for later discourse.

Discourse itself has also received much attention from developmentalists. It is worth looking closely at recent attempts to account for development within social constructionist and constructivist frameworks of discourse. In much of this work, discourse is seen as the arena for or instrument of the coming together of the private and the social. Often a narrative or dialogic perspective is employed (sometimes attributed to Bakhtin, 1981) in order to show, empirically, how the adult and child must create intersubjectivity. Infants and babies who were once said to be responding verbally to stimuli, expressing meanings, or processing information are now said to be learning to "transcend" their "private world" as they verbally interact or dialogue with the significant adults in their environment.

An excellent example of this work is to be found in the writings of James Wertsch, the influential American Vygotskian. During the 1980s Wertsch conducted a series of studies employing what he called a microgenetic analysis of mother–child dyads completing a puzzle-copying task. Wertsch was interested in how the joint activity of putting the puzzle together was accomplished. He argues that entering into a certain level of intersubjectivity is required in order to carry out productive joint cognitive activity (Wertsch, 1985a, p. 175).

In his analysis of the discourse of one young child and his mother who failed to complete the task (put the puzzle together), Wertsch gave the following interpretation:

> A cursory examination of this excerpt reveals that the child was not very successful at "transcending his private world." He apparently never understood that the pieces represented wheels on a truck. It seems that throughout the interaction he viewed the pieces as circles or crackers rather than as wheels. Because of the child's constant inability to negotiate or "buy into" a situation definition that would be more appropriate for carrying out this culturally defined task, the adult was forced to adjust her communicative moves such that they could be interpreted within his alternative framework. (1985a, pp. 172–73)

This child continued to refer to the circular objects as circles and crackers in spite of the fact that his mother called them wheels. We can agree with Wertsch that mothers use various semiotic mechanisms ("the truck wheels," "yes, they're like circles," "one like that one") in creating joint cognitive activity with their children, and that wheels might be more "culturally appropriate" than circles or crackers in this experimenter-defined task. But we reject his appeal to inner–outer/private–social duality and conflict, as when he asserts that the child could not transcend his "private world," or uses expressions like "buy into," "forced," "negotiate," and "alternative framework." In his desire to establish intersubjectivity as a requirement for joint activity, Wertsch turns out to be making what is, in our opinion, the highly questionable claim that "circle" and "crackers" lie in the secret depths of the child's alienated and bifurcated inner life. What evidence is there that the child has "an alternative framework" (or, indeed, any framework at all)? Why do we need to posit the existence of a framework from which to interpret "communicative moves"? Do we, in fact, ordinarily "interpret communicative moves" when we are engaged in discourse?

Furthermore, Wertsch's mothers are characterized as relating to their babies' words or sounds as private property. He identifies their creative use of language to encourage a new situation definition for the child—as he puts it, to help the child "think differently by talking differently" (p. 176)—as a way of producing higher and higher levels of intersubjectivity by compelling the child to give up her or his "private world" in favor of the adult's world and words. We disagree. Anticipating the relational, noninstrumental, activity-theoretic, and performatory analysis we will put forward in Part III, we see Wertsch's mothers as responding not to the supposed inner meaning ("private world") of the child's words, but to the noninterpretive activity of speaking together, to the creative meaning making of their discourse/dialogue/narrative. Intersubjectivity is a requirement for joint activity only if the duality of private and social is presupposed. Without the duality, intersubjectivity *is* joint activity. Thus, even in Wertsch's (self-proclaimed) activity-theoretic, sociocultural account we discern an interpretive bias, a commitment to an individuated ontology, and an exaltation of the private.

These elements of psychology's myth of development (and the myth/hoax of psychology) are similarly present in work that fuses developmental with clinical perspectives toward the end of accounting for language development through (not surprisingly) mother–child discourse. The following illustration is taken from the work of the highly regarded developmentalist–psychoanalyst Daniel Stern.

Within psychoanalytic circles, Stern tells us, the acquisition of language has been seen as important in the child's achievement of separation and individuation. Stern, however, wants to argue that language is "potent in the service of union and togetherness" (1985, p. 172). Speaking, dialoguing, communicating, constructing shared meanings compel the asocial infant to be social (with some significant loss of a holistic sense of self and potential neurosis). Infants are motivated to talk, says Stern (supporting the arguments of Dore, 1985), in order to reestablish a "personal order" with their mothers at a time when there is increasing pressure to conform to a "social order." According to Dore, this is a time when the mother begins to require that her baby "organize his action for practical, social purposes: to act on his own (getting his own ball), to fulfill role functions (feeding himself), to behave well by social standards (not throwing his glass), and so on. This induces in the child the fear of having to perform in terms of nonpersonal standards (toward a social order) which orients him away from the personal order of infancy" (p. 15; quoted in Stern, 1985, p. 171).

Here we have gone back again to the Piagetian–Freudian egocentric child (who is, you will remember, forced to repress her or his inner needs in favor of adapting to outer reality), all dressed up in "relational" clothing.

Another psychological object constructed by developmental psychology which Stern addresses is "sense of self." As we discussed briefly in Chapter 1, there is considerable interest in how infants come to form a sense of self (and little interest in how the concept *sense of self* was formed). Stern (1985, 1990) is in the predisposition camp. He claims that subjectivity is a natural phenomenon, that infants are predisposed to be aware of self, and that there are in fact four phases in the development of the infant's sense of self over the first year and a half of life (the emergent, core, subjective, and verbal selves). With each developmental phase, the infant's subjective perspective is reorganized.

In "Ideology Obscured: The Political Uses of Daniel Stern's Infant," Cushman (1991) presents an ideological critique of Stern's position. The self is socially constructed, Cushman insists. Stern's claims about the infant's emerging sense of self are Eurocentrically biased and, as such, unwittingly perpetuate the status quo; there exist cultures which are characterized by a qualitatively different sense of self from the one defined by Stern. To our way of thinking, Cushman is right; he just doesn't go far enough. His "politically correct" critique points to the ways in which Stern's particular self serves to perpetuate the status quo through reinforcing the mythic individuated subject. But he does not raise the question of whether self itself perpetuates the same myth. The philosophical presupposition of *self* is at the heart of the socially constructed myth/hoax of psychology. In our view, the cutting edge in any critique of Stern's infant needs to be the deconstruction of the self as a socially constructed, politically biased, ideological concept.

In an attempt to avoid the scientific and philosophical dangers inherent in attributing motives and intentionality to infants and very young children (dangers into which both Stern and Dore fall), some developmental psychologists adopt the position that Burman calls "as if." That is, they argue that adults treat babies "as if they were fully initiated social partners, as if they were able to participate in a social system" (1994, p. 39). They account for development with the claim that "by treating the infant as socially competent . . . she becomes so" (p. 39).

Burman summarizes what, in her opinion, is one of the more promising versions of this view, Kenneth Kaye's (1982) *The Mental and Social Life of Babies*. Her summary and critique help us to see just how deep-rooted are the interpretive, evolutionary, dualistic, and causal biases of developmental theory. According to Burman, Kaye gets off to a good start by asserting that the infant is "born social in the sense that his [*sic*] development will depend from the beginning upon patterns of interaction with elders" (Kaye, 1982, p. 29, quoted in Burman, 1994, p. 40). When the infant comes to have expectations about these patterns of interaction (for example, expectations of what the mother will do), then it can be said that mother and infant are a social system. These expectations are not genetically programmed, but arise out of experience. The social system is thus a joint construction of mother and child.

Burman presents Kaye's discussion of one of the earliest instances of such a social system—the pattern of interaction in breast feeding. Apparently, the infant sucks in bursts and pauses, and the mother has a "tendency to jiggle the nipple of her breast (or the teat of the bottle) during the pauses." To Kaye, the combination of these patterns "constitutes the earliest form of mutual adaptation and turn-taking" (Burman, 1994, p. 41). What is happening is that the mother is treating her infant as a turn taker—creating turns to take and setting up patterns—and the infant "will start to take her own turn and assume her place in the social world" (p. 41).

Burman's issues with Kaye (aside from the obvious gender and cultural biases in his descriptions) are many. For one thing, he perpetuates the very biological–social opposition he is attempting to transcend. Mothers' jiggling and infants' sucking and pausing are biological givens which *come to function* as social. Furthermore, the interactional patterns turn out to be products of evolution "every bit as much as those features we think of as innate to the individual organism" (Kaye, 1982, p. 24, quoted in Burman, 1994, p. 42). Human sociality is thereby made understandable in terms of evolution. Burman goes on to point out that while Kaye does not posit any explicit causality between early and later developments, he nevertheless identifies a basic unit (turn taking) that "becomes the building block for everything else" (p. 42). We might add that in doing so Kaye reproduces the reductionistic form of theory building that seeks one explanatory principle for all of development; he insists that there be a pattern to patterns.

Burman has helped us to see that psychology's construction of the socially situated and socially competent infant has not gotten us very far from Darwin's son. Development is still driven by evolution. Certainly this is important to see if we are to understand the myth of development which psychology has constructed. If we want to understand the social construction of the myth/hoax of psychology, however, there are other problems with the socially competent and socially situated infant to consider.

Many critics of psychology's conception of development, including Burman, point out its ideological and political biases. As we have tried to show in telling the story of developmental psychology, its investigative practices and knowledge claims are rampant with the gender, class, and cultural biases inherent in mentalism, rationalism, causality, duality, interpretation, and explanation. Our deconstruction has focused on developmental psychology's methodological biases rather than on its ideological ones. That has not been because we regard the latter biases as unimportant. On the contrary, they have played a significant role in motivating some of the most cogent and thoroughgoing of the postmodernist critics to investigate the philosophical and methodological biases (in addition to Burman, 1994 and Morss, 1990, see Burman, 1990; Gilligan, 1982; Morss, 1993, 1995).

WHAT DEVELOPS?

In telling the story of how psychology constructed development, we must note that not one among the cast of characters, be they the fallen heroes (Lamarck, Darwin, Hall, Piaget, Freud, Stern, Wertsch, Kaye) or those who toppled them (Morss, Cushman, Burman), has asked the crucial question, *What develops?* What is the unit of analysis for a developmental psychology, or (if you prefer) a developmental approach to the human–social realm? Isn't the unit of development worthy of deconstruction?

Nowhere in the literature is the unit of analysis, presumed to be the individual, examined. In assuming that what develops is the individual (the infant, the child—even in some cases, the mother), the protagonists have kept a critical piece of psychology's philosophy hidden away. To say that the individual is socially situated, socially constituted, socially competent, social from birth, does not in any way challenge the assumption that it is the individual who develops; it only adds attribution to what is deemed essential.

What is it that weds individualism to development? To tackle this question with the seriousness it merits, we will need some new tools. Fortunately, the tools are available to us; they were invented/discovered by Vygotsky and Wittgenstein. We will make use of them in the chapters that follow.

For now, we want only to set forth two ideas for further discussion—*reality* and *boundedness*. The belief in something called reality dies hard. To debate whether reality is given, objective, utilitarian, and value-laden, or "really" socially constructed and relative, presumes its existence. As to boundedness, it is presumed to be a universal property of objects (including people); everything (and everyone) begins and ends somewhere.

We (the writers) suspect that we (members of our culture) cling for dear life to the concept of *the individual as what develops* as a consequence, in part, of our acceptance of reality, of particulars, and of boundaries. Persons understood as particulars must have boundaries. What is the boundary of "the person"? For centuries, the answer to that question has been the body. Psychology without philosophy, unscientific psychology—that is, a psychology freed from the myths of reality, truth, and explanation—is also divested of the myth of (bounded) particulars. The mythic construction of development has contributed enormously to the myth/hoax of psychology. As we said at the beginning of this chapter, the phenomenon of human development does not depend on psychology. More to the point: for nearly a century scientific psychology depended on the fact that people develop; now it is increasingly dependent on people's not developing. Perhaps, in an unscientific, unphilosophical psychology, there is no *unit* of development at all. Perhaps the problem is *unitarianism!*

Part III

The Practice of Method: A New Epistemology for an Unscientific Psychology

> What is your disease? You ask this question again and again.—How can one make you stop doing this?
> By drawing your attention to something else.
>
> —*Ludwig Wittgenstein*

The extended critiques (obituaries) of philosophy and psychology and, more generally, modernism that we and others have made mean very little—it seems to us—in the absence of a practice (a post-postmodernist practice of method) for going forward, for getting, in Wittgenstein's sense, from "here to there." Indeed, in the ecologically valid, radically activistic antilaboratory in which we have worked for almost a quarter of a century, the endless activities of creating development environments have "preceded" (often by decades, sometimes by seconds) the "learning" which we now present to you as epistemologically (not temporally) antecedent to our development. What Lev Vygotsky calls learning that leads development requires, as far as we can tell, an activity-theoretic practice (of method) to build and sustain an environment conducive to growth. Any effort, therefore, to objectify or systematize our results, to use our results to construct knowledge-theoretic environments or practices, that is, practices where knowing and learning in themselves dominate or overdetermine development (as opposed to leading it in a unified, dialectical, Vygotskian sense), is likely, we would suggest, to fail.

This is not to say that learning is possible only in our community, nor that learning is possible only in an environment structurally identical or even similar to ours. What we are saying is that any effort to evolve developmental learning which downplays the significance of environment has little chance of succeeding. Relation-based activity and its products will ultimately reduce to identity-based reified knowing if the activity is conducted in an identity-based environment (such as the compartmentalized and departmentalized university). Activity transpires in an environment much as stories are told in one. If the environment is identity-based, the activity (like the story) will ultimately be interpreted relative to it. Hence, truth will slip in the side door despite the best intentions of the therapist or storyteller. An environment which does not play the dualistic role of "other" must be constructed, continuously; only in this way will relational activity not be dependent on conceptual other but on activistic relatedness, or practical–critical, relational activity. No method, but a continuous *practice of method*, must prevail.

In the environment that we, along with many other people, have built, Vygotsky and Wittgenstein work with each other. Their work informs and is informed by our relationally activistic practice of method. Bringing them together in a development environment has helped us to create a new epistemology, a clinical practice/cultural–performatory approach to human life and, inextricably connected, its understanding.

8

The Noninterpretive Community and Its Clinical Practice

THE NONINTERPRETIVE COMMUNITY

What is the nature of this learning (leading development) environment in which, among other things, Vygotsky and Wittgenstein have been joined? It is a kind of community, not a community determined by geographical characteristics nor, for that matter, a community defined by commonality of task or ideology. It is, to paraphrase Vygotsky, a tool-*and*-(its)results. Our community is not a mediating tool designed to achieve a certain result. It is a community which at once supports development and has as its noninstrumental, nonpragmatic (tool-and-result) activity, the development it supports.

To paraphrase Marx's political metaphor, it is a community *for* itself, not *in* itself. However, this *tool-and-result community for itself* is not isolated from the world. Nor—more importantly—is it isolated from history. Quite the contrary. After all, human history is itself a community-and-(its)results. Indeed, that our community is connected to (continuous with) history is more likely than is the case for the typical societal goal-oriented communities and institutions (such as self-perpetuating academic institutions/communities and mental health treatment centers).

It is sometimes argued that such goal-directed institutions and communities are closer to the instrumentalist society in which they are located. We disagree. For one thing, society abstracted from history (or relating to society as abstracted from history) produces an increasingly superalienated comprehension of societal life which distorts society. Granting (with Marx) the key role of garden variety alienation in the accurate viewing of commodified society, more alienation, superalienation, that is, the almost total separation of society from its history, does not make matters clearer but utterly confused and confusing. Should history indeed be over, society must thereby become incomprehensible. For even alienated understanding requires an awareness of that from which a society is alienated or else such understanding will radically and quickly regress into fundamentalist society-in-itself distortion—that is, society becomes completely and reactionarily *identified* with history. Such is the case, in fact, in postmodern contemporary American and international society.

It is proximity to the history element of the history/society dialectic in which we all—and always—live that is most critical in a historical moment of societal degeneration such as ours. Hence, our tool-and-result community *for* itself evolves as a more and more embodied subculture within the broader cultural environment of postmodern times. While our purpose is not to change the world (for we have no purpose, hidden or otherwise), our commitment is to be the world: not to "take it over" but "to be taken over." If a qualitatively new understanding—a new epistemology—is to transform our species developmentally it will necessarily have, we think, this tool-and-resultish characteristic.

The extraordinary success story of Western science over nearly 350 years has to do, among other things, with its remarkable capacity to be about something (which of course required the precise ontological discovery—largely due to Galileo and Newton—of what it was to be about). The next step in species development, we suggest, demands an understanding which is about nothing or (more accurately, if negatively) is not *about about*. Aboutlessness (if you still crave abstraction) is to a qualitatively new *practice of method* and the journey we shall take with it what weightlessness—an equally geocentric conception—is to space travel.

It is remarkable to us how little attention is typically paid, even in the most cogent and insightful postmodernist, feminist, poststructuralist, and social constructionist critiques, to the environment, the community, in which those critiques are themselves developed. For if their argument that modernist institutions are, materially and ideologically, absolutely dualistic (referent-based, truth-based, and identity-based) is correct—as we wholeheartedly believe it is—then mustn't the community in which such quite proper critiques are developed be as free as possible from material and ideological overdetermination? We think so. For a quarter of a century, our "experimental" work has been devoted to creating an environment—a community—which is *ecologically valid*, not only interpretation-free but assumption-free. While many from more traditional environments have contributed substantially to our work and several have reached "conclusions" similar to our own, it is the practical–critical history and methodology of our (tool-and-)results that distinguish them. While our tool-and-results no doubt embody our own assumptions (and, thereby, the assumptions of the society at large as they are present in us), they are designed to challenge any and all assumptions; no self-conscious part of our work knowingly affirms in either thought or action these assumptions. Nor does anything in our work imply, explicitly or subtextually, that via some intellectual act we can somehow supersede the pernicious influences of the institutional modernism we are critiquing.

What, then, are the critical features of our tool-and-result community *for* itself? It is developmental, therapeutic, philosophical, and performatory.

A Development Community

A development community (a tool-and-result community *for* itself) is radically antiinstrumentalist; it is, in Marx's language, a "practical–critical, revolutionary activity." But it does not seek instrumentally to make a revolution; it is continuously, endlessly, making itself. A development community self-consciously rejects systematic philosophy and its instrumentalist tools.

In his last-gasp defense of philosophy and causality the philosopher Donald Davidson has said, "Cause is the cement of the universe; the concept of cause is what holds together our picture of the universe, a picture that would otherwise disintegrate into a diptych of the mental and the physical" (Davidson, 1980, p. xi). Our community has a postmodernist, Wittgensteinian wariness of pictures, concepts, and cement. Davidson and other analytical die-hards—philosophers in search of truth—are still seeking to solve the deadly dualistic problems they (and modernism in general) have created. By contrast, a development community finds ways to treat those problems therapeutically—in Wittgenstein's words and sense, to make them vanish.

It is not that there are no causes or causal talk in our development community. Rather, our community is not a causally cemented one. It is not connected with or by conceptual cement. It is not connected at all. Philosophers seek always to create something (including their very acts of creation) which can be appraised. But while appraising (and the complex conceptual paraphernalia necessary to do it) has undoubtedly played a critical role in the *aboutness* game that is modernism, it seems to us that a modernist, appraisalist epistemology makes continued species and personal development impossible. Truth referentiality, identity, (the logic of) particularity, and the rest of the instrumentalist tools of appraising must be abandoned in favor of a logic of subjectivity and activity, a practice of method.

For it is not only pictures that mislead us. More importantly, *picturing* misleads us. The search for (objective) truth which yielded 2500 years of development has now become the primary obstacle to continued development. "Aha!" we can almost hear the nay-sayers, the critics, the cult baiters, the enlightened appraisers, exclaiming. "When there are no objective criteria, the door is wide open to dogmatism and authoritarianism or tyrannical (patriarchal) rule. The so-called leaderless group is potentially the most undemocratic, autocratic structure of all. Modern science ushered in the Enlightenment by introducing objective criteria to replace the rule of hierarchical subjectivity. That's why America is a republic and not a democracy."

We agree. Still, there are serious problems with objective criteria. The rule of objectivity has produced a paralyzing, stultifying era of what Gergen calls *identity politics* (1995) and what we call *identity psychology* which profoundly limit social and personal growth. Is the claim (the Truth) that objectivity is more democratic and, therefore, more developmental than subjectivity a subjective or an objective claim? Is it not possible that the epochs of objectivity have produced a new meaning of subjectivity (through diverse discoveries including everything from human rights to computers) which demands a thoroughgoing reconsideration of the objective–subjective duality itself? Must we not consider the possibility that the epistemological systemization (first given shape by the Greeks) that underlay human development for 2500 years might take us no further? And if we may not even ask such questions, is it not objectivity that has become the tyrant?

Our development community is less concerned with the objective study of subjectivity than with the subjective study of objectivity. Indeed, we are actually concerned with neither. Instead, we seek to discover—in practice— a logic of development (a practice of method, a new epistemology) that is relation-based and activity-based, and to create new forms of life, new and ever-varied Vygotskian *zones of proximal development* in which all learning leads development—the only learning, Vygotsky said, worthy of the name.

A Therapeutic Community

The complex interconnected domination of knowing, believing, describing, truth (and falsity) telling, referring, denoting, "abouting" (talking about things), judging, appraising, cognizing, and so on, that began with the Greeks (following the emergence of self-conscious abstracting) reached its apex in modernism. To remark that epistemology is all about knowing is, in our Western culture, simply definitional (whatever definition is). Understanding, during the modernist period, has all but been reduced to cognitive knowing and its various instrumentalities. To understand, so the modernist story goes, is ultimately to *know* something *about* something else. As we have said, the brilliance of modern science lay in its having discovered precisely (or so it seemed) the right thing to be *about*. The hegemony of aboutness derives from the inseparable validity and technological consequences of modern physics' ontology. It is not as if aboutness is genetically, or even culturally, always and everywhere "the way." Modern physics and the related technology (or, at least, the assumption of the relationship) made it that way.

The scientific community—an earlier version of a tool-and-result community *for* itself—has dominated modernist society and culture. Hollywood portrayals of mad scientists notwithstanding, science did not take over the world; the world took over science. Socialism's ultimate failure did not lie in its inability to "take over" the world (as it foolishly aspired to do), but in the capitalist world's astounding ability to use socialism (welfare statism) without incorporating any of its essential humanism. The activity (and art) of destruction to which the scientific community has been historically connected has further shaped its antidevelopmental epistemology. For the military connection of modern science, from its earliest moments in the 1600s to the discovery of nuclear energy three hundred plus years later, has tended to overidentify *knowing* with *controlling*.

The wholesale acceptance by psychology, from its birth in the late nineteenth century to the present, of the modern scientific worldview included, of course, this militant overidentification of knowing and controlling. Yet even within the psychology constructed in the image of modern science an alternative epistemic attitude began to emerge, particularly in the area of clinical psychology. Freud himself, it seems to us, was deeply conflicted about this. On the one hand, his psychoanalytic method was self-consciously overdetermined by his commitment to the worldview and epistemology of modern science. His method of interpretation was designed to be every bit as explanatory, descriptive, truth-referential, and identity- and particularity-based as physics. While some within the scientific community viewed psychoanalysis as bordering on the metaphysical and meaningless, many (and surely Freud) viewed it as objectively scientific to its core.

That said, the *practice* of the "talking therapy" or "cure" in its original form and, even more so, in its subsequent neo-Freudian and post-Freudian forms, revealed that the *activity* of two (or more) people talking about emotional life was itself of seeming developmental value. And while there were, of course, "scientific" (objective) accountings for why this was so, the value of the talking activity itself sometimes seemed to many (mostly practitioners) to be greater than the "truths" or "insights" reached. Yet this appeared to violate the scientific paradigm to which psychotherapy ultimately appealed. Why should the mere relational activity of dialoguing (the conversation) be of more value than the discovery of cognitive truths about the patient or client? Every practitioner worth her or his salt has often had this experience of clients' or patients' "getting better" (at least a little better) from the simple, "merely" relational activity of talking about themselves with the therapist or group, of building a particular new kind of relationship/new form of life.

Surely the dialogue of physicists with matter does not yield change— positively or otherwise. The cognitive modality of scientific epistemology "does not allow it." After all, physics is not designed to make matter "feel better"; it is designed to know more and more about matter in order to control it better. Perhaps, it began to be thought, the therapeutic relational activity itself is of value because "knowing" emotionally is not so much about understanding what it is about in the process of controlling it. Perhaps therapeutic understanding is not knowing at all. Perhaps it is not cognitive. Perhaps the point is not to make therapy more scientific but to challenge the all-encompassing scientific paradigm. Perhaps the understanding involved in therapy is other than scientific.

These thoughts need not appeal to a nineteenth-century introspective theory of knowledge which attributes to the individual a privileged view of herself or himself and, thereby, special knowledge of that self. No. What we are referring to here is a relational activity that yields an understanding which is neither introspective nor cognitive. It is not knowledge about anything, an insight that uncovers a deep truth, a particular predicate, or a description of a particular individual. Rather, it is an understanding which is inseparable from the relational activity of creating understanding without having to refer to any *abstract other* for the purpose of appraising it. Even as psychology and psychotherapy become more and more officially scientized, objectified, controlling, and "successful," this clinical working tradition continues to flourish and attract skilled theoreticians interested in exploring such peculiarly nonscientific knowing. It is one significant source of postmodernist thought.

Unlike the quintessential therapeutic community of the 1960s, our therapeutic community is not a more open and humane environment for treating the "mentally ill." Rather, it is a community in which the epistemic attitude is more *therapeutically developmental* than *cognitively controlling*. Our operative question is not who or what is true or right but how we can further develop from where we are to where we collectively choose to go. How do we get from "here to there"? What we learn (knowledge) is what was necessary for such development. All learning, therefore, leads development even as community development is an environmental precondition for any learning. The human study of nature may well demand control. The human study of human life, it seems to us, "demands" development and a new epistemology rooted practically and critically in relational activity and the transformation of life.

A Philosophical Community

Philosophy (with a capital *P*) is dead—or so we believe. The activity of unsystematic philosophizing is, therefore, ever more critical. The questioning activity, not "the answer" or even the answering activity, is what dominates in our development community. Philosophizing, the asking of big questions about little matters, serves to relocate us continuously in history. The asking of such philosophical questions makes us increasingly aware of the uniquely activity-theoretic lives (history) of our species.

We do not agree with Marx that our species is distinguished (from bees and spiders) by our ability to make plans (as in architectural designs) and then, in causal fashion, to realize them. Rather, our "uniqueness" lies in the historical facticity of our making plans (a "mental" activity) and making buildings or bridges (a "physical" activity) and connecting the two (a "conceptual" activity). The historical dialectical interplay of these different sorts of activities "defines" our species as unique not in the abstract, but in life and history as lived. It is a practical "definition," not a dead one. Philosophizing without philosophy, continuously playing Wittgensteinian language-games, serves to challenge in every moment the "natural tendency" of language in the broader still-modernist culture to become reified as a thing-in-itself which is "above us" and about us. The language-game serves to remind us of the activity of language and of the continuous transformation of language as activity.

In his recent challenge to cognitive science, Searle (1992) cogently argues that mental activity and physical activity are only problematically dualized and thus unable to be spoken of in the same breath and sentence when they are linguistically reified, that is, when the activity or process of them is negated. Searle, arguing strongly on behalf of consciousness in the face of decades of behavioral and cognitive science denial, puts the matter (and the mind) this way: "One can accept the obvious facts of physics—that the world consists entirely of physical particles in fields of force—without denying that among the physical features of the world are biological phenomena such as inner qualitative states of consciousness and intrinsic intentionality" (1992, p. xii).

Philosophizing prevents us from institutionalizing our words. We need not be reminded, as some postmodernists tell us, "In the beginning was the deed" (rather than "the Word"). Development, it seems to us, requires instead that we remember there is no beginning. This is what allows us to make meaning rather than merely to discover or use it. The dictionary is of value only as a tool for result. Tool-and-result meaning making, developmental meaning, is among our species' most important tool-and-result activities. As such, the language of our development community is not more private but less private than most. For language as activity is structurally democratic. Not only the official meaning makers and truth tellers—the experts and the metaexperts, the philosophers and the scientists—but all may participate. Here the pragmatist Rorty, of whom we spoke rather harshly in Chapter 3, is helpful. He speaks of an imaginary world in which

neither the priests nor the physicists nor the poets nor the Party [would be] thought of as more "rational,"' or more "scientific" or "deeper" than one another. No particular portion of culture would be singled out as exemplifying (or signally failing to exemplify) the condition to which the rest aspired. There would be no sense that, beyond the current intradisciplinary criteria, which, for example, good priests or good physicists obeyed, there were other, transdisciplinary, transcultural, ahistorical criteria, which they also obeyed. There would still be hero-worship in such a culture, but it would not be worship of heroes as children of the gods, as marked off from the rest of mankind by closeness to the immortal. It would simply be admiration of exceptional men and women who were very good at doing the quite diverse kinds of things they did. Such people would not be those who knew a Secret, who had won through to the Truth, but simply people who were good at being human. (Rorty, 1982, p. xxxviii)

Our community seeks to be such a world. The continuous playing of language-games (philosophizing without Philosophy) helps us to do so.

A Performatory Community

The *zone of proximal development* (zpd) is to Vygotsky what *form(s) of life* is to Wittgenstein. We have sometimes characterized our community as one in which we play (in Vygotsky's sense) language-games (in Wittgenstein's sense). A zpd is, we think, simply a form of life in which people collectively and relationally create developmental learning which goes beyond what any individual in the group could learn on her or his "own." For many contemporary orthodox Vygotskians, what happens in the zpd is relatively traditional cognitive learning. In our opinion, this reformist point of view (discussed in Newman and Holzman, 1993) reduces the Vygotskian zpd to, at best, a radical technique for enhancing standardized learning. But it does not heed Vygotsky's revolutionary demand to create a new psychology and, thereby, a new unit of study for psychology—a social unit rather than an individualized unit. For Vygotsky, the revolutionary scientist, the unit which learns developmentally is not the individual-in-the-group (the particular member of the set) but the group *for* itself.

We have come to believe (and in this we probably part ways with Vygotsky) that such a relational unit as the group *for* itself is not really a unit at all. Might it turn out to be that there is no unit of development, after all? Might it be that there is "only" developmental unity? The group that develops must continuously create and recreate the form of (group) life; that is, the group activities must include the continuous making of the group. But this will not happen unless the environment (the community) in which the group exists allows it to happen. To do so it must be non-interpretive.

To paraphrase Vygotsky yet again, the group *for* itself must be "a head taller than itself." What does that mean? What must we do to recreate the zpd continuously so that the environment does not insidiously interpret its activity to death (as even the best of them are prone to do)? We must perform relationally. The per-*form*-ance *of life*—the synthesis of Vygotsky and Wittgenstein—is required to sustain a developmental learning community. For it is only in performing—a human skill which for most of us is left to atrophy after early childhood—that we can be who and what we are not (a head taller than ourselves). Thus, the *form of life* in the ever-changing zpd's that make up our community environment is filled with play—that is, it is performatory. We are, as our critics have observed with dismay, forever being who we are not. We are performing. We are shamelessly inauthentic. For from what does authenticity derive?

SOCIAL THERAPY

The unscientific, noninterpretive, relational, activity-theoretic—and in-authentic—approach we have been practicing and developing for the past twenty-five years is what we mean by social therapy (see Holzman, 1996; Holzman and Newman, 1979; Holzman and Polk, 1988; Newman, 1991a, 1994, 1996; Newman and Holzman, 1993). It is (for the moment, we are using traditional taxonomy—albeit in an untraditional way) a developmen-tal–clinical psychology. This being so, it is also accurate to say that it is an antipsychology, because a developmental–clinical practice challenges psy-chology at its mythic roots. The dominant psychological paradigm (and its institutional materialization) is profoundly antidevelopmental—even, or especially, in its conception and construction of development. The recent deconstructionist investigations of psychology's myth of development which we presented in Chapter 7—showing its obsession with origins, end points, smooth trajectories in between; its resultant hierarchical and essen-tially elitist structure; its construction of the idealized child and childhood; its focus on the "idea" of progress—suggest that development is ideological rather than a valid or useful construct of a human psychological science (Burman, 1994; Bradley, 1989, 1991; Broughton, 1987; Cushman, 1991; Morss, 1990, 1992, 1995; Walkerdine, 1984).

While we reject scientific psychology's construct/story of development, we do not reject the human activity of development. To us, human devel-opment is the activistic, relational, qualitative transformation of the given circumstances; the existing environment; the totality. Children, for example, qualitatively transform (more precisely, they participate in the process of qualitative transformation) many times in their first few years. Becoming a speaker (or a signer, as in the case of many deaf children) of language is not the mere acquisition of a skill or behavior. It is qualitatively, emotionally, intellectually, socially, totally transformative. Given the critical importance of language in our culture, new worlds of possibility, learning, social relationships, imagination, and creativity open up once the young human being is able to make meaning (in history) and use words (in society).

This is no idealization of childhood (see Bradley, 1991). We are making a methodological point here—human beings transform totalities (develop, make history). The process by which children become members of a language community is a particularly good example because it is so ordinary (and, in our opinion, so often misunderstood by modernist developmental psychologists and psycholinguists). For it is not the case that the child is admitted into the language community only after she or he is a competent language user. Mothers, fathers, and others, for example, respond to babies' babbles as discourse elements—they admit the child into the language community without requiring that she or he "have all the credentials." The child becomes a speaker by virtue of being related to as a speaker well before she or he is one!

How can we account for this seeming paradox of language development? And what are its consequences? The activity of the language community has to be transformed (from a focus on language use to a focus on the language activity) to include someone who does not speak. To respond to a two-year-old who has not yet learned the societally appropriate uses of language as a speaker requires a transformation of the linguistic environment (including its adult conventions) so that the creative process of language—the activity of language making as opposed to language using—dominates. A reshaping of the total environment from a societally determined arrangement to a form of life activity occurs in order for the child to be included. The environment of infancy and early childhood supports development/is developmental in just this sense.

Academic psychology as a whole reveals its antidevelopmental stance in the very way it has organized the discipline. Since developmental psychology (complete with its antidevelopmental biases) is a specialty or branch of scientific psychology, then presumably there is some psychology (some aspects of human beings and the study of human beings including—shockingly—so-called social psychology, the psychology of learning, and personality) that is nondevelopmental. What human sense does this make?

The long-standing separation of developmental and clinical psychology is another case in point. The theoretical study and treatment of mental illness, psychopathology, and emotional distress in our society are strikingly nondevelopmental, both in the modernist and in our and others' postmodernist senses of development. Despite the proliferation of approaches since Freud, the basic model of psychotherapy and other clinical practices rarely considers development to be an important factor in cure. To the extent that emotional development is considered at all, it is seen as a consequence or outcome of cure. According to the dominant model (which, as we saw in Chapter 6, psychology and psychiatry adopted from medicine and science and opportunistically adapted to justify their existence), the way to deal with emotional problems and pain is to focus on "the illness." Alleviating its symptoms and finding its so-called underlying causes are the two most common methods employed; perhaps then the patient can develop emotionally.

Development is, however, the centerpiece of the clinical practice/cultural–performatory approach of unscientific social therapy. It is not the instrumentalist and evolutionary process of constructing a private, individuated self that must, for better or worse, relate to "a social world" (psychology's myth of development), but the continuous and qualitative transformation of the determining circumstances, creating new emotional meaning, performing new emotional forms of life. Rather than trying to root out dysfunction or change behavior patterns (practices which might help individuals, or those around them, feel and/or function better for a time), social therapy attempts to reinitiate emotional development as a *precondition* for cure. Further development—not intrapsychic awareness, problem solving, or behavioral change—is necessary, we believe, in order to do something about emotional pain.

To our way of thinking, one characteristic of the postmodern social crisis is that human development, in the sense that we are using it, has all but come to a halt, replaced and repressed by the gathering, storage, and retrieval of information. To the extent that scientific psychology does not self-reflexively confront the cessation of development, in our opinion, it will continue to contribute mightily to it. Psychology, including pop psychology, has become the institutional guide to everyday emotional, cognitive, and "moral" life. The ideological, metaphysical, reductionistic, antidevelopmental biases of scientific psychology (both academic and professional practice) permeate the everyday thinking, speaking, and other doings of ordinary people. In our view, for a psychotherapeutic approach to be of any real help to them, it must be developmental, unscientific, cultural–performatory. It must help people to manifest the human capacity to transform totalities, to create new meaning, to be "who we are not," to develop our own development continuously.

In order to do so it must, among other things, engage the antidevelopmental assumptions and presuppositions of scientific psychology and the psychology of everyday life, and the confusions these assumptions and presuppositions create for all of us. In Vygotsky's words, it must engage "the philosophy of the fact" (Vygotsky, 1987, p. 55). In Wittgenstein's words, it must engage the fact that "a whole mythology is deposited in our language" (Wittgenstein, 1971, GB 35).

9

Wittgenstein, Vygotsky, and a Cultural–Performatory Understanding of Human Life

Lev Vygotsky and Ludwig Wittgenstein—each reflecting and contributing to the cultural, political, social, and intellectual conflicts of his respective "moment" in history, each an insider who was, ultimately, an outsider (or, some would argue, an outsider who was inside),[1] each currently being revived and revised by academia and popular culture—are worthy of study in their own right. Each of them, discontent with the existing epistemological tools, troubled by the assumptions, biases, and consequences of the available scientific paradigms, was self-consciously involved in investigating the distinctly human activities of science, methodology, and practice. Vygotsky's views on human development and Wittgenstein's views on philosophy and language are closest to our own.

WITTGENSTEIN

Thinking is sometimes easy, often difficult but at the same time thrilling. But when it's most important it's just disagreeable, that is when it threatens to rob one of one's pet notions & to leave one all bewildered & with a feeling of worthlessness. In these cases I & others shrink from thinking or can only get ourselves to think after a long sort of struggle. I believe that you too know this situation & I wish you *lots of courage!* though I haven't got it myself. We

This discussion of Wittgenstein and Vygotsky is based on ideas first presented in Newman and Holzman, "A New Method to Our Madness," which appeared in *Practice, The Magazine of Psychology and Political Economy*, 1993, 9(2), 1–21.

are all *sick* people. (Ludwig Wittgenstein, from a letter to Rush Rhees, quoted in Monk, 1990, p. 474)

I then thought, what is the use of studying philosophy if all that it does for you is enable you to talk with some plausibility about some abstruse questions of logic, and so on & if it does not improve your thinking about the important questions of everyday life, if it does not make you more conscientious than any . . . journalist in the use of DANGEROUS phrases such people use for their own ends. (Wittgenstein, from a letter to Norman Malcolm, quoted in Monk, 1990, p. 474)

It is not our aim to refine or complete the system of rules for the use of our words in unheard-of ways.

For the clarity that we are aiming at is indeed *complete* clarity. But this simply means that the philosophical problems should *completely* disappear.

The real discovery is the one that makes me capable of stopping doing philosophy when I want to. The one that gives philosophy peace, so that it is no longer tormented by questions which bring *itself* in question. Instead, we now demonstrate a method, by examples; and the series of examples can be broken off. Problems are solved (difficulties eliminated), not a *single* problem.

There is not *a* philosophical method, though there are indeed methods, like different therapies. (Wittgenstein, *Philosophical Investigations*, 1953, p. 51, §133)

Wittgenstein was perhaps the most influential philosopher of the twentieth century. His writings from 1919 until the 1950s turned Western philosophy upside down and, arguably, destroyed it. As often (and ironically) happens when ideas challenge a field at its very roots, some of his contemporaries sought to systemize Wittgenstein and insert his work into existing and newly developing philosophical movements. Various schools of thought claimed his writings as their own—if not their sole source of inspiration, at least a major influence. As we saw in Chapter 3, in the 1920s the logical positivists (the group of philosophers, mathematicians, historians of science, and scientists known as the Vienna Circle) took Wittgenstein's early masterpiece, the *Tractatus Logico-Philosophicus*, as their handbook, and the "ordinary language" philosophers (associated with J. L. Austin) regard themselves as his disciples. Wittgenstein, however, was not a system builder. His life-as-lived, including his philosophical activities, was more concerned with not leaving a system that bore his name.

Wittgenstein led, if not a wonderful life (as he is supposed to have declared just moments before his death, according to one of the many stories about him), surely a conflicted life. Born in 1889 in Vienna (a hub of Continental cultural and intellectual fervor from the 1870s until Hitler's rise to power), Wittgenstein spent most of his adult life in Cambridge, England—a place he found unbearably stuffy and "loathsome" and which he periodically left for more rural, less intellectual, less pretentious surroundings, including Ireland, Norway, the United States, and the Soviet Union. The youngest of eight children born to Karl Wittgenstein (whose grandfather, Moses Maier, took the name of his employers to comply with the Napoleonic decree of 1808 requiring Jews to adopt a Christian surname) and Leopoldine Kalmus (who was also partly Jewish), he grew up in one of the most influential Viennese families, one which possessed enormous wealth, provided a rich cultural and intellectual environment for its children, and assimilated (the children were brought up as Catholics) quite successfully into Austria's upper bourgeoisie/aristocracy.

When just a young man, Wittgenstein gave away his money to his siblings and lived the rest of his life with a minimum of material goods. Though he was attracted in his youth to the proto-Nazi, anti-Semitic, and homophobic writings of Otto Weininger, throughout his life his thoughts and writings expressed torment over his (homo)sexuality, the nature of (his) sin, his Jewishness, and the obligation to live a meaningful and moral life. He hated the pomposity and insularity of the academic community (as often as he could, he escaped to the cinema to watch American musicals), yet he could be as pompous as the next Oxford don.

Almost immediately after the publication in 1919 of the *Tractatus*, Wittgenstein acknowledged its dogmatism and errors. From then on his philosophical writings increasingly eschewed theory and centered on philosophy without theses or premises—philosophy as method, *philosophical method to do away with philosophy*. In the preface to *Philosophical Investigations*, the best known of his later writings (published after his death), Wittgenstein repudiated the *Tractatus* and his "old ways of thinking" and "grave mistakes"—within academia, a highly unusual display of intellectual honesty. Young students flocked to him, attracted by both his passion for (doing away with) philosophy and his brilliance.

Monk's (1990) fine biography is entitled—aptly, we think—*The Duty of Genius*. Wittgenstein expressed in his life-as-lived a recognition of a strongly felt obligation (some say an obsession) to produce something meaningful with his intellectual gifts. While he repeatedly advised his students to leave the university, he himself never really did. In one of the many telling anecdotes that Monk makes use of in explicating Wittgenstein's life and work, we are told of the time he advised Maurice Drury that he would be better off getting a job among the working class where the air was healthier, because there is "no oxygen in Cambridge for you." As to his own decision to remain at Cambridge, Wittgenstein is said to have remarked, "It doesn't matter for me. I manufacture my own oxygen" (Monk, 1990, p. 6).

Nearly six thousand articles and books of commentary on Wittgenstein's philosophical writings have been published (Monk, 1990). Several hundred memoirs, biographies, and recollections of Wittgenstein have been written by those who knew him intimately, as well as by people who only met him once or twice. His work and life have inspired poetry, music, paintings, and works of fiction. He has been the subject of television documentaries, plays, and performance pieces, and most recently an award-winning film

(*Wittgenstein*, by the late British filmmaker Derek Jarman). The historical moment in which Wittgenstein lived was conflicted, tormented, and momentous. One way of life was dying and another was taking its place. The eighteenth-century Enlightenment and the nineteenth-century ideal of progress, both born of the great promise held out by capitalism, would give way before the reality of its limitations; the fascism prefigured in the writings of Weininger and other German nationalists already loomed on the horizon. It was a time of some of the most barbaric and decadent human actions and beliefs as well as some of the most progressive and creative. Perhaps the ongoing fascination with Wittgenstein has something to do with how his life-as-lived was a microcosm of a changing Europe and a changing world.

That Wittgenstein's philosophical work has a therapeutic bent and that his approach was more clinical than experimental or abstractly and systematically philosophical is acknowledged by many of his interpreters and biographers (for example, Baker, 1992; Baker and Hacker, 1980; Fann, 1971; Janik and Toulmin, 1973; Monk, 1990). In their analytical commentary on the *Philosophical Investigations*, Baker and Hacker (1980) discuss several sections of this work in therapeutic terms. Concerning its opening paragraphs, in which Augustine's picture of human language is shown, they say:

> Numerous sophisticated accounts of meaning are unconsciously rooted in the Augustinian picture, and this manifests a disease of the intellect. This will have many symptoms. But a philosopher need not exhibit all of them to be diagnosed as suffering from this disease. Rather, the disease manifests itself in a syndrome of symptoms. Comparison with the normal form of the Augustinian picture facilitates identification of those exhibiting a form of this syndrome. Developing the normal form might also have a therapeutic role. (p. 34)

Some philosophers place a therapeutic goal at the center of Wittgenstein's philosophy. Peterman (1992) presents an account of Wittgenstein's later philosophy that highlights its therapeutic character. Setting up standards for philosophical therapy, he evaluates Wittgenstein's writings in relation to this general model. According to Peterman, Wittgenstein's work in its entirety was an ethical, therapeutic project, the *Tractatus* emphasizing the ethical dimension and *Philosophical Investigations* emphasizing the therapeutic. Baker (1992) also finds Wittgenstein's philosophizing to be more consistently therapeutic than is commonly recognized and, related to such an enterprise, more context-specific and person-relative, that is, focused on the dynamics of the thinking that individuals do, not on the geometry of thought. Some psychologists, too, have begun to approach Wittgenstein in a similar way and find in his writings insights into emotions, feelings, and beliefs that illuminate their views on the subjective and ethical dimensions of human development (for example, Bakhurst, 1991, 1995; Chapman and Dixon, 1987; Gergen and Kaye, 1993; Jost, 1995; Shotter, 1993a and b, 1995; Stenner, 1993; and several of the essays in Phillips-Griffiths, 1991).

Looking at Wittgenstein in this way raises questions about psychology, philosophy, and the relationship between them. Philosophy and psychology, as we have shown, were once related disciplines (parent and child). But they grew further and further apart during most of this century, as orthodox psychology severed its ties with philosophy and attached itself to the medical and natural science traditions (all the while ignoring, for the most part, the philosophical roots—and paradoxes—of natural science). In some areas of contemporary psychology—critical psychology, phenomenological psychology, feminist psychology, and social constructionism—philosophy and psychology are being drawn together again; Wittgenstein is among those philosophers whose work is being seriously studied (others are Husserl, Heidegger, and Merleau-Ponty). However, given psychology's historical myopia—and its mythic essence—is Wittgenstein's work at all elucidated by seeing or exploring its therapeutic quality? Conversely, does his "therapeutic philosophy" contribute anything to deconstructing and reconstructing psychology? What exactly is meant here by therapeutic? What is the illness that needs therapeutic treatment? Whom is he attempting to cure? What is the meaning of cure? How did Wittgenstein himself see the relationship between philosophy and psychology?

To us, such questions are both more and other than an interesting adjunct to an analysis of Wittgenstein's philosophy. To our way of thinking, it is in terms of philosophical therapy that Wittgenstein's work can be viewed true to his life-as-lived and philosophy-as-practiced. Furthermore, Wittgenstein's antiphilosophical philosophy (his antifoundationalism) provides critically important methodological tools for a new, humanistic, developmental–clinical practice/cultural–performatory approach to emotional life. His self-appointed task was to cure philosophy of its illness. (Ours, as we will try to show, is closer to curing "illness" of its philosophy.) We are all sick people, says Wittgenstein. No small part of what makes us sick is *how* we think (related in complicated ways to what we think and, even more fundamentally, to *that* we think or *whether* we think), especially how (that or whether) we think about thinking and other so-called mental processes and/or objects—something which we (the authors) think we (members of our culture) do much more than many of us like to think! It gets us into intellectual–emotional muddles, confusions, traps, narrow spaces; it torments and bewilders us; it gives us "mental cramps." We seek causes, correspondences, rules, parallels, generalities, theories, interpretations, explanations for our thoughts, words, and verbal deeds (often, even when we are not trying to or trying not to). But what if, Wittgenstein asks, there are none? Describing his method, he says:

In philosophy one feels forced to look at a concept in a certain way. What I do is suggest, or even invent, other ways of looking at it. I suggest possibilities of which you had not previously thought. You thought that there was one possibility, or only two at most. But I made you think of others. Furthermore, I made you see that it was absurd to expect the concept to conform to those narrow possibilities. Thus your mental cramp is relieved, and you are free to look around the field of use of the expression and to describe the different kinds of uses of it. (quoted in Monk, 1990, p. 502)

Why should suggesting or inventing other possibilities be curative? We think "other ways of looking at" a particular concept free us from the overdetermining representationalist societal tie between language and thought. Being free to look around the field of use, we can see and describe different kinds of uses of language (and even see and describe language in different ways). Despite the fact that the nature of the relationship between language and thought has been the subject of philosophical, psychological, and linguistic debate for hundreds of years, what have evolved, so it seems to us, are extremely narrow cognitive/analytical ways of conceptualizing the relationship between the two. There is a growing body of critical work by linguists, philosophers of language, and psychologists challenging the objectified linguistics that underlie such conceptualizations (for example, Billig, 1991; Davis and Taylor, 1990; Duranti and Goodwin, 1992; Shotter, 1993a and b).

In an earlier work examining the evolution of the relationship between thought and language in Western culture, we focused on how the dominant conceptions of language have come to overdetermine (in fetishized fashion) not only how we speak but also how we think and/or think we think (Holzman and Newman, 1987). Thoughts, beliefs, ideas, and so on—the family of concepts associated with human cognition—modeled on a fetishized conception of language are seen as rule-governed and internal (even if, for some analysts, they are externally caused or even externally constructed). But language, the activity, is neither rule-governed nor private, although it is certainly possible to describe it in these ways. When these descriptions, however, come to *define what it is*, then language, the human activity, inseparable (process and product) from its activistic, labor-producing human creators, is distorted into a commodified product of a pervasive, pernicious, sometimes bizarre (philosophically speaking) sort. Once fetishized, that is, separated and abstracted from the process/producers of its productive activity, language must then be "connected" ("reconnected") to life in some way in order for it and, therefore, life, to make sense (in a distinctly denotative, referential, representational, and extensional way). Transference, as we noted earlier, is one of the dominant techniques for doing so in contemporary culture.

At least since the advent of modern science, relating to language as primarily denotative and representational (and, by extension, relating to mental life as being fundamentally cognitive) has become the dominant way to make this language-to-life connection: the correspondence theory of truth, once again. (The sentence "It is snowing" is true if and only if it is snowing.) Indeed, that words (at least some words) name objects seems perfectly sensible—even, perhaps, natural. However, such an understanding obscures how language is used; obviously, human beings do many more things with words—not to mention with phrases and sentences—than naming objects. What is even more problematic is that this late modernist understanding of language as use obscures and distorts the activity of language, that is, the creating, developing, and learning of language. In his later work, Wittgenstein recognized that it is language seen as activity which prevents the philosophically muddled separation of thought and language, and of language and what it is, presumably, about.

> I shall in the future again and again draw your attention to what I shall call language-games. These are ways of using signs simpler than those in which we use the signs of our highly complicated everyday language. Language-games are the forms of language with which a child begins to make use of words. The study of language-games is the study of primitive forms of language or primitive languages. If we want to study the problems of truth or falsehood, of the agreement and disagreement of propositions with reality, of the nature of assertion, assumption and question, we shall with great advantage look at primitive forms of language in which these forms of thinking appear without the confusing background of highly complicated processes of thought. When we look at such simple forms of language the mental mist which seems to enshroud our ordinary use of language disappears. We see activities, reactions, which are clear-cut and transparent. (1965, BBB, p. 17)

One cannot see or show the activity of language without stripping away the abstraction and reification of denotation ("the mental mist")—that is, without exposing language as activity. We think Wittgenstein found some ways to do this. His accomplishment was in developing a method to expose the gap between so-called mentalistic activities and social activities so as to reveal the cognitive bias of Western philosophy (and, let us add, scientific psychology) as it is manifest in our thinking (and/or what is called thinking). In example after example, he shows the extent to which our thinking is overdetermined by notions, assumptions, and presuppositions about language (and ways of thinking) which derive from its fetishization and identity as fundamentally and passively mentalistic (as opposed to activistic). His method of therapeutic cure—exaggerating the normal process of assuming language to be rule-governed, consistent from situation to situation, denotative, and so on, thereby showing the absurdity of such assumptions—clears up confusions and, hopefully, prevents individuals from asking the kinds of questions or thinking the kinds of thoughts that get them into these confusions in the first place. His method is remarkably practical and therapeutic for ordinary people with everyday life problems.

While Wittgenstein is said to have fathered what is known as "ordinary language" philosophy, it seems to us that such a characterization distorts his overall methodology and obscures the therapeutic nature of his work. The writings of Baker (one of the philosophical world's foremost interpreters of Wittgenstein) on Wittgenstein and his analysts, followers, and detractors are helpful here (Baker and Hacker, 1980; Baker, 1988; Baker, 1992). They question the value of continued attempts by philosophers to label Wittgenstein, attach him to a school of thought, catalogue his remarks, and compare him to other philosophers, in other words, to systematize his thought. Baker (1992) argues persuasively against the tendency to search for uniformity and generalizability in Wittgenstein's use of particular words or phrases and to draw philosophical conclusions from his work, on the grounds that such practices are nothing less than a violation of the Wittgensteinian enterprise. Instead, Baker recommends that "scrupulous attention" be paid to Wittgenstein's "overall therapeutic conception of his philosophical investigations." Wittgenstein, he continues, neither advocated "any general positive position" nor undertook "to give any general outline of the logical geography of our language," but rather "always sought to address specific philosophical problems of definite individuals" (p. 129). We find Baker's medical analogy compelling:

> He [Wittgenstein] did not see himself in the role of a public health official whose brief was to eradicate smallpox from the face of the earth (for example to eliminate Cartesian dualism once for all by means of the Private Language Argument). Rather he operated as a general practitioner who treated the bumps that various individual patients had got by running their heads up against the limits of language. (1992, p. 129)

Wittgenstein's focus was not ordinary language, but on doing something about how language, especially language about language of the type philosophers speak and write, obscures ordinary life. Notions of how children learn to speak; of what it means to know something; of what feelings such as love, anger, and fear are; of how our experiences are "connected to" reality, are not ordinarily the self-conscious subject of everyday discourse. Nevertheless, these notions exist and play an overdetermining, constraining, and less than developmental role in our everyday life activity. Wittgenstein's principal "clientele" were philosophers, the very people whose everyday professional discourse does consist of such philosophical questioning. But as the quotations that open this chapter illustrate, he was no less concerned with how the obscuring of life through language affects ordinary people—philosophy, for him, being akin to "tidying up a room."

We view Wittgenstein's work as therapy—for philosophers, whose obsession with philosophical problems is their pathology (we sometimes say that they are psychotic in this obsession), and for ordinary people, who get into just as many intellectual–emotional muddles as philosophers, despite their lack of interest in matters philosophical (we sometimes say that they are neurotic in this lack of interest). By virtue of the complicated network of social, communicative institutions that have evolved—especially the institution of language—versions of philosophical pathologies manage to permeate everyday life. For Wittgenstein, the institution of language is a carrier of pathology. Enshrouded in a "mental mist," the activity of language is difficult to see. Moreover, it is increasingly difficult to do, as the activity of meaning making—necessary for language making and all human development—has become more and more dominated by the behavior of language using. Language using itself is, in turn, overdetermined by its fetishized relationship to thought (Newman and Holzman, 1993).

It is helpful to look at some examples of Wittgenstein's "psychotherapy for psychotics," that is, how he works to cure philosophers of their obsession with interpretation, and their need for the metaphysical (order, causality, consistency). We present somewhat lengthy excerpts from Wittgenstein's writings so as to show, to the extent possible, his method of creating the philosophical (exploratory) environment. In *Remarks on the Philosophy of Psychology, vol. I* (1980), Wittgenstein writes:

> 903. No supposition seems to me more natural than that there is no process in the brain correlated with associating or with thinking; so that it would be impossible to read off thought-processes from brain-processes. I mean this: if I talk or write there is, I assume, a system of impulses going out from my brain and correlated with my spoken or written thoughts. But why should the *system* continue further in the direction of the centre? Why should this order not proceed, so to speak, out of chaos? The case would be like the following—certain kinds of plants multiply by seed, so that a seed always produces a plant of the same kind as that from which it was produced—but *nothing* in the seed corresponds to the plant which comes from it; so that it is impossible to infer the properties or structure of the plant from those of the seed that it comes out of—this can only be done from the *history* of the seed. So an organism might come into being even out of something quite amorphous, as it were causelessly; and there is no reason why this should not really hold for our thoughts, and hence for our talking and writing. [Cf. Z 608.] (p. 159)

> 904. It is thus perfectly possible that certain psychological phenomena *cannot* be investigated physiologically, because physiologically nothing corresponds to them. [Cf. Z 609.] (p. 160)

> 905. I saw this man years ago: now I have seen him again, I recognize him, I remember his name. And why does there have to be a cause of this remembering in my nervous system? Why must something or other, whatever it may be, be stored-up there *in any form*? Why *must* a trace have been left behind? Why should there not be a psychological regularity to which *no* physiological

regularity corresponds? If this upsets our concepts of causality then it is high time they were upset. [Cf. Z 610.] (p. 160)

Here Wittgenstein is engaging the fundamentality of causality, correspondence, and essence in Western thought and philosophy. Obviously, there are neurological and cognitive processes going on as we speak and remember, but it does not follow that such processes are causally connected to (correspond to) what we are saying or remembering, or to the activity of saying or remembering. Here Wittgenstein is not so much exaggerating the normal process of making causal connections as he is showing its pervasiveness. His analogy to the seed and the plant exposes the absurdity of the deeply held belief in essences and containment. (The old religious idea that one can somehow find the tree in the acorn still holds great sway over ordinary, everyday thinking.)

In these next excerpts (also from *Remarks on the Philosophy of Psychology*), we can see Wittgenstein's therapeutic method most clearly:

912. One says: "He appears to be in frightful pain" even when one hasn't the faintest doubt, the faintest suspicion that the appearance is deceptive. Now why doesn't one say "I appear to be in frightful pain" for this too must at the very least make *sense?* I might say it at an audition; and equally "I appear to have the intention of . . . " etc. etc. Everyone will say: "Naturally I don't say that; because I *know* whether I am in pain." It doesn't ordinarily *interest* me to know whether I appear to be in pain; for the conclusions which I draw from this impression in the case of other people, are ones I don't draw in my own case. I don't say "I'm groaning dreadfully, I must see a doctor", but I may very well say "He's groaning dreadfully, he must. . . . " (p. 161)

913. If this makes no sense: "I know that I am in pain"—and neither does "I feel my pains,"—then neither does it make sense to say: "I don't bother about my own groaning because I *know* that I am in pain"—or—"because I *feel* my pains."

So much, however, is true: I don't bother about my groaning. (p. 162)

914. I infer from observation of his behaviour that he must go to the doctor; but I do *not* make this inference for myself from observation of my behaviour. Or rather: I do that too sometimes, but *not* in analogous cases. [Cf. Z 539.] (p. 162)

915. Here it is a help to remember that it is a primitive reaction to take care of, to treat, the place that hurts when someone else is in pain, and not merely when one is so oneself—hence it is a primitive reaction to attend to the pain-behaviour of another, as, also, *not* to attend to one's own pain-behaviour. [Cf. Z 540.] (p. 162)

916. What, however, is the word "primitive" meant to say here? Presumably, that the mode of behaviour is *pre-linguistic*: that a language-game is based *on* it: that it is the prototype of a mode of thought and not the result of thought. [Cf. Z 541.] (p. 162)

917. It can be called "putting the cart before the horse" to give an explanation like the following: we took care of the other man, because going by analogy with our own case, we believed that he too had the experience of pain—Instead of saying: Learn from this particular chapter of our behaviour—from this language-game—what are the functions of "analogy" and of "believing" in it. [Cf. Z 542.] (p. 162)

Here Wittgenstein is showing what happens when language is fetishized; when a "foolish" consistency from one structure to another is insisted on; when an attempt is made to extrapolate from one linguistic situation to another, for example, from how one talks about the pain of others to how one talks about one's own pain. The assumption of a uniformity or a consistency to language, in this case, that what is involved here is merely the substitution of one pronoun for another, leads to absurd notions and statements. It is not that grammars inform or shape in a Chomskian sense what is said; rather, they are fetishized extrapolations from life activities and are misleading in precisely the way Wittgenstein shows. As he states clearly, these are different language-games, different parts of social–cultural life, different forms of life (activities). The perfectly normal process of assuming that language is consistent from situation to situation, from the "he" to the "I" relative to pain, for example, is laughable, absurd. The therapeutic usefulness of showing this is that the absurdity exposes analytically the extent to which we are overdetermined by these systematically reified linguistic suppositions.

Our goal is to delineate the Wittgensteinian elements of the cultural–performatory therapy we practice, social therapy, and the social–therapeutic quality of Wittgenstein's philosophical therapy. Our deconstructionist/reconstructionist aim is twofold: to see more clearly how exposing the activity of language reveals the activity of meaning making and to show the practical–critical potential of this exposing (itself an activity) for reinitiating human development in a postmodern historical period permeated by superalienation, the near-elimination of meaning making and, consequently, of human development.

VYGOTSKY

In the years immediately following the first socialist revolution Vygotsky, a leading Marxist theoretician of his time, played a key role in the restructuring of psychology and education, and in the formation of what we now call special education. As the acknowledged leader of a group of Soviet scholars who passionately pursued the building of a new psychology in the service of what it was hoped would be a new kind of society, Vygotsky constantly engaged the methodological underpinnings of the two philosophical–scientific paradigms to which he was heir—the dualistic and categorical Western scientific tradition and the newly emerging, but almost immediately idealized and dualized, Marxism.

Tragically, Stalin would all too soon put an end to this brief period of experimentation not only in science, but in culture, education, social relations—all forms of life (Friedman, 1990; Newman and Holzman, 1993; van der Veer and Valsiner, 1991). Although Vygotsky died of tuberculosis at the age of thirty-eight, he was nonetheless a victim of Stalinist repression; his work came under attack from academicians/ideologues while he was alive and was suppressed after his death. The lively debate he conducted in the 1920s with Jean Piaget about the speaking and thinking of very young children was virtually forgotten until the English-language publication in 1962 of Vygotsky's *Thought and Language*. Most of the nearly two hundred papers, articles, and speeches he wrote on language, learning and development, school instruction, poetry, literature, theater, artistic creativity and imagination, children's play and drawing, written language, memory, emotions, mental retardation, deafness, and blindness remained unpublished in any language until recently. Over the past ten years there has been a revival of interest in his work (which is often referred to as social–cultural or cultural–historical psychology) among developmental, social, and educational psychologists; sociolinguists; and scholars of communication and discourse.[2] And since the collapse of the Soviet Union, there has been increased interest in the intellectual and political history of Vygotsky and Soviet psychology (for example, Joravsky, 1989; Kozulin, 1990; van der Veer and Valsiner, 1991).

Vygotsky made significant substantive discoveries about human development. As we see it, these were made possible by critical methodological breakthroughs concerning the development of human psychological science. His work was both foundational and antifoundational (it was similar to Wittgenstein's in this respect). He subjected virtually all of existing psychological thought and much of Western and Marxian philosophical thought to intense scrutiny in his effort to build a new science—and in what he built planted the seeds of a new psychology (what we sometimes call an antipsychology). Vygotsky's writings contain many statements of concern with methodology as inseparable from science. We see his struggle to avoid the pitfalls of old paradigms and new dogmas, and to create something new:

> I don't want to discover the nature of mind by patching together a lot of quotations. I want to find out how science has to be built, to approach the study of mind having learned the whole of Marx's *method*. (1978, p. 8)

and

> Practice belongs to the deepest roots of scientific operation and restructures it from beginning to end. It is practice that poses the task and is the supreme

judge of theory; practice is the criterion of truth; it is practice which dictates how to build concepts and how to formulate laws. (1982, pp. 388–89)

The relationship between "Vygotsky's psychology" and "Vygotsky's methodology" has been the subject of much debate among his interpreters and followers (for example, Bakhurst, 1991; Davydov and Radzikhovskii, 1985; Kozulin, 1986, 1990; Newman and Holzman, 1993; van der Veer and Valsiner, 1991). Included in these discussions are varying opinions regarding Vygotsky's debt to Marx's philosophical writings.

To us, Vygotsky was first and foremost a Marxist activity theorist: he took activity, not behavior, to be the critical feature of uniquely human development. As we understand it, the ontological difference between activity and behavior is the difference between actually changing totalities and "changing" particulars (using pseudoscientific general laws), between qualitative transformation and quantitative accumulation (Newman and Holzman, 1993). We believe Vygotsky followed Marx in this; human beings do not merely respond to stimuli, acquire societally determined and useful skills, and adapt to the determining environment. The uniqueness of human social life is that we ourselves transform the determining circumstances. As Marx puts it, "The coincidence of the changing of circumstances and of human activity or self-changing can be conceived and rationally understood only as *revolutionary practice*" (Marx, 1973, p. 121). Revolutionary practice, what Marx elsewhere refers to as "revolutionary, practical–critical activity," is changing that which is changing which is changing that which is changing; it is the "practical overthrow of the actual social relations" (Marx and Engels, 1973, p. 58).

Vygotsky's contribution, in our opinion, lay in his recognition that a new unit of study (activity) requires (indeed, is not separate from) a new methodology for studying it. His lifelong task was the investigation of the very nature of psychology as a science. The *science activity*, like all human activity, embodies its own paradox—it must create (not fictionalize) its object of investigation:

> The search for method becomes one of the most important problems of the entire enterprise of understanding the uniquely human forms of psychological activity. In this case, the method is simultaneously prerequisite and product, the tool and the result of the study. (Vygotsky, 1978, p. 65)

This new conception of methodology as tool-and-result—what we call the practice of method (Newman and Holzman, 1993)—is monumentally radical. As we see it, Vygotsky is challenging nothing less than the Western scientific–philosophical paradigm, including theories of knowledge from Plato to Kant (and beyond). In traditional terms, method is something separate from experimental contents and results, that is, from that for which it is the method. It is something to be applied, a functional means to an end, basically pragmatic or instrumental in character. This dualistic conception of method (tool *for* result, not tool-*and*-result) presupposes a theory of knowledge that requires objects of knowledge and tools (a method) for attaining knowledge about the objects.

For Vygotsky, as for Marx, method is not something to be applied—it is to be practiced. It is neither a means to an end nor a tool for achieving results. There is no object of knowledge and no knowledge separate from the activity of practicing method; the result (product, object) is inseparable from (undefinable, unnamable, and, perhaps, unknowable apart from) the tool (process of production). They come into existence together, in a relationship of dialectical unity (like Wittgenstein's language-games, where the rules of playing come into existence, if they do, through the playing of the game). The dominant scientific paradigm in Vygotsky's day and ours is not monistic, dialectical tool-and-result. It is a pragmatic, instrumental tool for result methodology. (See Newman and Holzman, 1993, for further discussion of the distinction between tool-and-result and tool for result methodologies.)

This methodological break with the dominant dualistic–instrumental–reductionistic scientific paradigm has been consistently and unfortunately (however unconsciously) overlooked by most contemporary Vygotskians whose work—identified more as *mediation theory* than as *activity theory*—focuses on the appropriation of already existing tools (for results). Indeed, so deep-rooted are the dualism and overdetermining cognitive bias of tool for result methodology that Vygotsky himself—despite his self-conscious goal of overthrowing it—sometimes overlooked it! But to miss Vygotsky's method is to lose his revolutionariness, which to our way of thinking is to render him useless as a practical–critical psychologist (an antipsychologist).

Vygotsky's best known work concerns the speech of very young children and its relationship to the development of thinking. Much of his most incisive and poignant analysis is contained in a devastating critique of Piaget's findings on childhood egocentric speech and thought and, not surprisingly, of Piaget's methodology. The orthodox view, as presented in most developmental psychology textbooks, pits Vygotsky's position directly against Piaget's. However, there are also attempts to show that the two positions are compatible and capable of being integrated (for example, Bearison, 1991). We think that both of these interpretations are methodologically misguided.

Ever mindful of the task he has set for himself—the search for method and, with it, a new psychology—Vygotsky described how he was going to approach Piaget's work:

> We must attempt a critique of the theory and the methodological systems that provide the foundation for Piaget's studies. Within this framework, the

empirical data will concern us only to the extent that they are basic to theory or concretize methodology. (Vygotsky, 1987, pp. 55–56)

Just how did he characterize Piaget's methodology? As ahistorical, acultural, abstract, and metaphysical—a study, if you will, of the universal, the idealized, "the eternal child." Says Vygotsky: "The task of psychology, however, is not the discovery of the eternal child. The task of psychology is the discovery of the historical child" (Vygotsky, 1987, p. 91).

Piaget's eternal child is egocentric (on the way from being autistic to becoming rational and social) until the age of seven or eight. Her or his speech is asocial, "for oneself," not communicative, and in fact serves no function but is a mere reflection of egocentric thinking. Her or his earliest thinking is private, personal, and autistic; it expresses "inner needs" as opposed to (as well as dualistically separated from and prior to) "outer reality." Vygotsky's child is *historical*—learning to speak is a social historical human activity. Learning to speak, the child's development, the child—*is* history. The child's speech is always social; egocentric speech is a form of social speech that "develops through a movement of social forms of collaboration into the sphere of individual mental functions" (Vygotsky, 1987, p. 74). Her or his earliest thinking is as much intellectual as emotional—there is no separation between "inner needs" and "outer reality." Furthermore, autistic thinking is not prior to realistic thinking—its development is in fact dependent on the development of realistic thinking.

Vygotsky shows the Freudian (metaphysical) framework within which Piaget operates, as when Piaget posits that the child is first motivated to satisfy inner needs and only later forced to adapt to objective reality. Such a separation of the child's world(s) is a psychoanalytic manifestation of the fundamental dualism between the individual (the private) and the social. Essentially, Piaget has adopted "the whole metaphysic associated with the concept of the pleasure principle. Here the principle is transformed from an auxiliary or biologically subordinate characteristic into a kind of independent vital force, into the prime mover of the whole process of mental development" (Vygotsky, 1987, p. 77).

In Newman and Holzman (1993), we continued Vygotsky's critique in this way:

Piaget is then forced by logical necessity into yet another abstraction—pure thought. Having divorced needs and satisfaction from the process of adaptation to reality, he is left with realistic thinking dangling in air, completely cut off from the needs and desires of the child. But Vygotsky holds fast to Marx's historical monism and to the historical child. Need and adaptation must be considered in their unity. "In the child, there exists no form of thinking that operates for the sake of pure truth, no form of thinking divorced from the earth, from needs, wishes, and interests." [Vygotsky, 1987, p. 77] (Newman and Holzman, 1993, p. 124)

Piaget's argument is weakened considerably by Vygotsky's analysis, for neither the child's thinking nor speaking is egocentric in Piaget's sense, that is, nonsocial. The remaining (deconstructive/reconstructive) task is to sever the presupposed link between speaking and thinking. For Piaget (followed by most writers who compare Piagetian and Vygotskian perspectives on speech and thought) assumes that thinking is reflected in speaking. However, Vygotsky (like Wittgenstein) rejects the bifurcation of individual and society that necessitates some kind of causal and/or linear connection between thought and language. (How else could a person develop? The "inner" has to be outwardly expressed, doesn't it? The "outer"—culture, norms, values, and so on—must become "inner," mustn't it?) For Vygotsky, speaking and thinking are not two separate processes, but a unity reflected in word meaning:

> The structure of speech is not simply the mirror image of the structure of thought. It cannot, therefore, be placed on thought like clothes off a rack. Speech does not merely serve as the expression of developed thought. Thought is restructured as it is transformed into speech. It is not expressed but completed in the word. (Vygotsky, 1987, p. 251)

The implications of *language completing thought* ("thought completed in the word"), of course, go well beyond the polemic with Piaget. The dominant Western philosophical–linguistic–psychological paradigm ("the confusing background of highly complicated processes of thought," as Wittgenstein calls it) rests on the assumption that language expresses thought. So deep-rooted is the paradigm that even the varied social and constructionist views of language which hold that people, not words, create meanings rarely acknowledge this presupposition. Vygotsky does not reverse the order of the "relationship"; he rejects the bifurcated and static view of language and thought and, thereby, does away with the necessity of "reconnecting" them: that is, he rejects the overdetermined and overdetermining conception that language, at its root, denotes, names, represents, expresses. Language completing thought (the unity speaking/thinking) identifies language as sociocultural relational activity.

Wittgenstein's later work supports Vygotsky's view. It challenges in practice the dominant paradigm of language as expressing thought and the dualism, parallelism, and correspondence theory such a paradigm embodies and/or implies. Recall, for example, Wittgenstein's comments on the metaphysicality and absurdity of causal connection and physiological–psychological parallelism: "Why must something or other, whatever it may be, be stored-up there *in any form*?" His language-games—a means of exposing the activity of language and the form(s) of life—consider language as the completion of thought. They are one way that Wittgenstein helps shape Vygotsky's developmental (anti)psychology into a noninterpretive clinical practice/cultural–performatory approach.

Vygotsky's goal was to create a science that could do two things: shed light on the historical development of human beings/human culture ("What new forms of activity were responsible for establishing labor as the fundamental means of relating humans to nature and what are the psychological consequences of these forms of activity?" [Vygotsky, 1978, p. 19]) and address the myriad challenges presented by a new socialist state. It was this ambition which led to his lifelong concern with the relationship between learning/instruction and development. The empirical work of Vygotsky and his colleagues focused on education and remediation, and dealt with illiteracy, cultural differences among the hundreds of ethnic groups that formed the new nation, the problem of millions of abandoned and homeless children who roamed the country, and the absence of services for those unable to participate fully in the formation of the new society. With his (noninstrumentalist) tool-and-result methodology, Vygotsky made several discoveries about child development and learning that are the (anti)foundation for a developmental, cultural–performatory psychology. Interestingly compatible with Wittgenstein's path of inquiry, they reveal the tool-and-result, relational character of human life activity.

Reviewing the educational theory and practice of his day, Vygotsky found it wanting. He rejected the dominant views of the relationship between learning and development: the separatist perspective, the identity perspective, and an unspecified interactionist perspective (Newman and Holzman, 1993; Vygotsky, 1987). To him, learning and development were neither a single process nor independent processes. Rather, he identified *the unity learning-and-development* and made the provocative assertion that learning *leads* development. Commenting on the pedagogical practice (still in effect seventy years later) that creates an abstraction—developmental level—and bases teaching and learning on it, he says, "Instruction would be completely unnecessary if it merely utilized what had already matured in the developmental process, if it were not itself a source of development" (1987, p. 212). The discovery of the dialectical unity learning–leading–development does away with the dualistically biased bifurcation of learning and development and the idealization of "pure development" (as generality and abstraction) on which how much and what a person can learn are based.

The revolutionariness of learning–leading–development is incomplete (in Vygotsky's sense of completion) without his extraordinary discovery of the zone of proximal development (zpd). The person, the mind, development, learning, psychological processes such as thinking, speaking, remembering, problem solving, and so on, are created or produced through participation in and internalization of social–cultural–historical forms of activity:

> Every function in the child's cultural development appears twice: first on the social level and later, on the individual level; first *between* people *(interpsychological)*, and then *inside* the child *(intrapsychological)*. This applies equally to all voluntary attention, to logical memory, and to the formation of concepts. All the higher mental functions originate as actual relations between people. (Vygotsky, 1978, p. 57)

The zpd is the difference between what one can do "with others" and what one can do "by oneself." Vygotsky was neither the first nor the last to notice that children (and adults) can "do more" in collaboration with others. But it was he who specified the social–cultural–historical process by which this occurs. Learning–leading–development, a social activity, both creates and occurs in the zpd. In our view, the zpd is not a traditional psychological unit to be fit into the existing antidevelopmental paradigm or substituted for other psychological units. Surely this can be done, and has been, with it. But we think that doing so violates Vygotsky's overall project and disguises the tremendous creativity inherent in it. We see the zpd as nothing less than a critical element of a new relational epistemology, one not grounded in an overdetermining and individualized mentalism, dualism, and functionalism. It does away with the philosophically overdetermined distinction between individual and society, inner and outer. The zpd suggests that human beings do not "come to know the world," nor "act upon it" or "construct" it, for such statements subtextually embody a separation of human beings and the world (resulting in the necessity of employing an abstract explanatory mode in order to understand how "in the world" an individual develops).

In our exploration of Vygotsky's methodology and findings, we describe the zpd as the life space in which and how we all live—inseparable from the we who produce it. It is the socially–historically–culturally produced environment in which and how human beings organize and reorganize their relationships to each other and to nature, that is, the elements of social life. It is where and how human beings—determined, to be sure, by sometimes empirically observable circumstances—totally transform these very circumstances (making something new); it is the "location" of human (revolutionary) activity. The zpd, then, is simultaneously the production of revolutionary activity and the environment that makes revolutionary activity possible (Newman and Holzman, 1993).

As a principal activity of childhood, play is of enormous interest to Vygotsky; he examines its developmental course and role in overall development. For him, it is no mere idle or frivolous behavior. It is a *leading* factor in development; it creates a zpd—"a child's greatest achievements are possible in play" (1978, p. 100). Both play and nonplay situations, then, can create zpd's in which revolutionary activity (learning–leading–development) occurs. The difference is that in nonplay, action dominates meaning; in play, meaning dominates action. This is so because the unique feature of play is the creation of an imaginary situation which frees the child from situational constraints. In analyzing the course of play's development (and its role in overall development), Vygotsky shows a transition from early (free) play, when the imaginary situation is dominant, to game play, when the rules of the game dominate (Vygotsky, 1978).

Even the earliest forms of play (free play) contain rules within their creation: "Whenever there is an imaginary situation in play, there are rules—not rules that are formulated in advance and change during the course of the game but ones that stem from an imaginary situation" (Vygotsky, 1978, p. 95). Such rules—coming into existence in the actual creation of the imaginary situation, unknown and unnamed (Vygotsky calls them *covert*)—can only be understood in relation to their productive activity. The rules of game play (which come later developmentally) are more like rules as we usually think of them, for example, directions, instructions, means to an end, that is, the game (Vygotsky calls these rules *overt*). The "for"–"and" distinction we applied to methodology (tool for result versus. tool-and-result) is helpful in appreciating Vygotsky's discoveries concerning play and development. We propose that rules are to the imagination what tools are to reality; there are rules for results, and rules-and-results.

The significance of this distinction for development is that "early play is characterized by rules-and-results—the imaginary result informs the mode of performance (playing) as much as the performance informs the imaginary result. It is only later . . . that the transformation from rules-and-result to rules for result occurs—in game play where rules are the how-to's, the instrumentation to an end result separate from, yet determined by, the mode of performance of the game " (Newman and Holzman, 1993, p. 101). Further, what Vygotsky identified as action dominating meaning in real life is the revolutionary activity of creating tools-and-results, while what he identified as meaning dominating action in the imaginary sphere is the revolutionary activity of creating rules-and-results (Newman and Holzman, 1993).

Vygotsky's entire enterprise continuously interweaves the relationship between learning and development with the relationship between language and thought. The activities of speech and language (cleared of mental mist) are the psychological tools-and-results created by human beings that make human learning and development possible. The synthesis of Vygotsky's method and his empirical findings concerning early child development tells us that human beings are not just tool users/language users but tool makers/language makers. Children learn to talk and to use language by engaging in the revolutionary activity of making meaning (taking the elements of their life space and reorganizing them to make something new). Our reading of Vygotsky suggests that meaning making leads language making (which leads language using). In early childhood, the *activity* of language dominates. Playing with language—using the predetermined tools of language to create something other than what is predetermined, disrupting the existing organization of sound, syntax, and meaning—is the joint activity that occurs in the zpd of infancy and early childhood (Newman and Holzman, 1993). Many psychologists miss this aspect of Vygotsky's work; they blur the critical distinction between activity and use, and even identify meaning *with* use (for example, Bruner, 1983, 1985; Wertsch, 1991).

Very young children—unencumbered by knowing what (or even that) language is, ignorant of the rules by which one is judged a societally correct speaker, not yet possessing the culturally produced and commodified need to "express oneself" nor the craving for generality—are marvelous meaning makers. Year-old toddlers do not say, "Give me a dictionary and a grammar book. I'll be back in a couple of years." No. They say things—they babble, use words, make meaning—as an inseparable part of the process of participating in social life. They participate in the social process (relational activity) before they know the rules of how to participate. They "rise above themselves" and perform "a head taller" than they are (Vygotsky, 1978; 1987); they "perform ahead of themselves" and engage in the "being ahead of yourself" activity (Newman and Holzman, 1993).

For children, games (in Wittgenstein's sense) are virtually the full time activity of life. However, it seems to us that while games are well and good, without play, they cannot account for the existence or development of language (or anything else). The same, of course, holds true for play. Human play is not trivial because and as it is related to games. A synthesis of Vygotsky's play and Wittgenstein's games enriches each of them and, in our opinion, further involves them in the building of a new developmental–clinical practice/cultural–performatory approach to understanding human life.

It is only by playing the game that children learn the rules. In this sense, children are far better learners than adults; they learn much more and much better than we do. They learn in the Vygotskian sense of learning—"The only 'good learning' is that which is in advance of development" (Vygotsky, 1978, p. 89). As adults, we have learned the official language (and facts) so well and are governed so completely by the rules of language placed "out there" that we have forgotten how to engage in—or have precious few existing environments which support—making meaning, babbling, playing new language-games, performing. The better we know the correct way to play language-games (which includes, interestingly, having little or no knowledge that they are games), the worse we are at playing in the way children play, that is, as relational activity. The better we are at *using* language, the more distant language *activity* becomes. The better we know language societally, the more confusion (metaphysics) it creates for us.

To our way of thinking, the first language-game is "Making Meaning (Jointly) in the ZPD." The joint activity (in and of the zpd) of playing this game in its infinite variations is what makes using language in societally appropriate ways possible at all. Language as denotative is a rather late development. This approach eliminates the "logical need" for the age-old bifurcation of language and what it is "about." Meaning making, a revolutionary activity, is what makes both language making and language using possible.

CULTURAL NOT COGNITIONAL

While both Wittgenstein, in his later writings, and Vygotsky show the metaphysical presuppositions and assumptions of Western philosophy and science, Wittgenstein is more consistently antifoundational and antifunctionalist and more explicit in identifying metaphysicality as an illness.

In exposing how we are overdetermined by all manner of metaphysical presuppositions, Wittgenstein points to the obstacles that stand in the way of carrying out the type of investigation necessary for seeing and showing language as activity. One such obstacle is "our craving for generality,... the resultant of a number of tendencies connected with particular philosophical confusions" (1965, *BBB*, p. 17) that leads philosophers into metaphysical traps. Wittgenstein describes four such tendencies: (1) the tendency to look for something in common to all the entities which we commonly subsume under a general term; (2) the tendency to assume that in order to understand a general term one must possess a kind of general picture (as opposed to pictures of particulars); (3) the tendency to confuse two meanings/uses of "mental state"—a state of consciousness and a state of hypothetical mental mechanism; and (4) the tendency to be preoccupied with the method of science (1965, *BBB*, pp. 17–18). The first three reflect the centuries-old philosophical search for essences from above, outside, extra, or beyond (metaphysical); the fourth represents the influence on philosophy of modern science's search for essences from inside or below—that is, its reductionism.

Philosophers, Wittgenstein says, are on the one hand confused by language—by our usual forms of expression and by simplistic ideas about the structure of language—and on the other tempted by the scientific method of reducing the explanation of natural phenomena to the smallest possible number of primitive natural laws. To Wittgenstein, the latter is "the real source of metaphysics" (Wittgenstein, 1965, *BBB*, p. 18).

Recall our discussion of the positivistic paradigm of explanation associated with Western physical and social science and with so-called common sense. This deductive–nomological model (as proposed, for example, by Hempel, 1965), consists in generalization(s) or general law(s) as first premise(s), and descriptions of empirically verifiable states of affairs (best if *reduced* as close to perceptual experiences as possible) as second premise(s). Finally, a description of the event being explained is logically derived (by either deductive or inductive logic) from the two premises. Curing philosophy, for Wittgenstein, surely had to include getting rid of this logical positivist paradigm of explanation: "I want to say here that it can never be our job to reduce anything to anything, or to explain anything. Philosophy really *is* 'purely descriptive'" (Wittgenstein, 1965, *BBB*, p. 18).

What Wittgenstein means by *descriptive* is best understood relative to and by contrast with the traditional positivistic/deductive model of explanation. He is offering a radical alternative to the orthodox (and abstract) scientific conception of explanation, an alternative to a pseudoscientific, metaphysical accounting for life activities which is completely separated from life activities (and is itself not seen as a life activity). He seeks to find a way of showing, of "pointing-to" (noninterpretively, nondeductively), that makes social processes more comprehensible (comprehension also being an activity, not an abstract explanation or interpretation).

A neo-Wittgensteinian challenge to the traditional positivistic/deductive model of explanation, a critique most associated with philosophers loosely identified with the so-called ordinary language school, flourished during the two decades following Wittgenstein's death in 1951. These philosophers of social science and history (among them, Dray, 1957; Scriven, 1959; and Winch, 1958) argued that explanation cannot be comprehended by a structural explication of it, but rather only through the study of how explanatory language is used. Pointing to Wittgenstein's observations on description, they tried to show various ways in which mere descriptions could be explanatory in appropriate contexts. Their exploration of explanation was typically a critique of the logical positivists by way of showing the subtle ways in which explanatory language could be *used*, thereby "proving" that it was not necessary to satisfy the abstract criteria of the structural model in order for something to be explanatory.

This procedure—making some sort of use/meaning equation and then focusing on linguistic or ordinary language analysis—characterized the work of many of the post-Wittgensteinian philosophers (for example, Austin, 1962; Searle, 1969; and Strawson, 1964). It may have helped to bury logical positivism. It surely provided a deeper understanding of linguistic subtleties. And no doubt it contributed to the subsequent revolution in the study of language. Yet it also served to obscure the critical distinction between *use* and *activity* which, from our point of view, is fundamental to understanding both Wittgenstein and Vygotsky.

A discussion of Wittgenstein's tool imagery by the contemporary American Vygotskian Wertsch provides us with an instructive illustration of the blurring of the distinction between use and activity (and the instrumentalization of Vygotsky). Wertsch (1991) quotes one of Wittgenstein's best known statements about words:

Think of the tools in a tool-box: there is a hammer, pliers, a saw, a screwdriver, a rule, a glue-pot, nails and screws.—The functions of words are as diverse as the functions of these objects. (And in both cases there are similarities.)

Of course, what confuses us is the uniform appearance of words when we hear them spoken or meet them in script and print. For their *application* is not presented to us so clearly. (Wittgenstein, 1953, p. 6; quoted in Wertsch, 1991, p. 105)

Wertsch prefaces this quote this way: "In *Philosophical Investigations*, Wittgenstein addressed the difficulty of distinguishing one language game from another and the issue of how language games could be conceptualized as being organized in a tool kit" (1991, p. 105).

But is it not words—not, as Wertsch says, language-games—that are organized (as Wittgenstein says, can be thought of as being organized) in a toolbox? Tools in a toolbox (thinking of them) helps us to understand the use of language (for example, words) in society. But language-games help us to see the activity, not the societal use, of language. We think that Wittgenstein, Vygotsky, and Marx understand, in varying ways and to varying degrees, the activity/use dialectic of activity leading use (although Wittgenstein would be most unhappy, we suspect, with the word *dialectic*).

A language-game is not to be found in a toolbox (analogically or any other way) any more than an activity in alienated society can be found in its product. It is not in the toolbox but in the contradictory unity of history/society that language activity and other forms of life are to be found. Meaning derives from the social activity of language making (language-games), even as it is expressed or used (taken from the toolbox) in society in ways that are meaningful. Conflating use and activity leads to strange formulations like Wertsch's "language games . . . organized in a tool kit."

Views on the Vocabulary of the Mind

Clarifying the use–activity distinction helps us to create and to explicate further a new cultural therapy (an unscientific psychology) rooted in an unphilosophical epistemology—the practice of method.[3] Let us summarize and "clinicize" what we have said so far by distinguishing and contrasting between "two views on the vocabulary of mind," the *pictorial* and the *pragmatic* (Gergen, 1994) (prefigured in Chapter 6 in our discussion of two theories of meaning). The pictorial view, which we would argue remains dominant in practice in our culture (for language in general and for mental language in particular), identifies mental vocabulary as fundamentally referential. Its primary function is to give accurate (truthful) descriptions of *states of mind* in ordinary emotive, attitudinal, and cognitive terms; in physiological terms; in phenomenological terms; in intrapsychic terms; in behavioral terms (by those who believe that the discrete and discernible events of mental life are the behaviors associated with it); and otherwise. These descriptions correspond, on the pictorial view, to objective states of inner (and sometimes of outer) "reality."

The utterance of such descriptions in therapy is typically either a first-person effort (by the clinical client) to express and/or communicate a mental state, or a second-person or third-person attempt to attribute such a state to the first person (variously called the patient, the client, or the member of the group). Accordingly, the clinical client is typically urged by the therapist to say "what's going on." That is, the therapist asks the client or patient to describe with as much detail, honesty, and depth as she or he can the "inner realities" to which she or he has a special, although presumably by no means omniscient, observational relationship. The therapist is, characteristically, skilled at supporting the client in doing this and, moreover, is qualified to offer alternative descriptions of the client's state of mind which challenge the truthfulness, the meaningfulness, the coherence, the clarity, and the value of the client's first-person descriptions.

Diagnosing, so it seems to us, is but one element of this describing and redescribing (defining) process. While the diagnosis per se may or may not be conveyed to the client directly (in more liberal therapeutic settings it typically is, although in the most liberal–radical environments it may be "officially" renounced or relabeled as a "story"), it at least informs the therapist's nondiagnostic redescriptions. Indeed, as we and others (for example, Deleuze and Guattari, 1977; Gergen, 1994) have pointed out, such redescription in medical or pseudomedical pictorial-based language often receives a very positive response from the client, since it may normalize her or his subjective state of mind. In effect, "the vocabulary of the mental health professions does serve to render the alien familiar, and thus less fearsome. Rather than being seen as 'the work of the devil' or as 'frighteningly strange,' for example, nonnormative activities are given standardized labels, signifying that they are indeed natural, fully anticipated, and long familiar to the sciences" (Gergen, 1994, p. 148). The preceding characterization of talk therapy (which also aptly characterizes, to a significant degree, mental talk in ordinary life) is, obviously, simplistic by virtue of being so narrow in its focus. Yet it is not inaccurate as far as it goes.

In recent years Thomas Szasz, along with others more or less influenced by him, has given us severe critiques of the pictorial view of mental vocabulary and/or the validity of some or all diagnostics or mental descriptions. Still, it is this view of mental/emotional language which continues to dominate clinical practice. For evidence we need only note, with Gergen (1994), the exponential growth in the number of psychological practitioners, as well as in the number of diagnostic descriptions (see, for example, DSM-IV). At the present moment there are more therapists, using many more scientific and pseudoscientific medicalized or quasi-medicalized, pictorially based descriptions of many more clients than at any previous time in history. Psychological diagnostic description has permeated the broader culture—with, in our opinion, pernicious consequences.

The pictorial view of mental language has also been the object of the most thoroughgoing critiques during this past half century by a good number of philosophers whose field of study is philosophical psychology.[4] Much of this criticism is associated with Wittgenstein, and in particular with the *Philosophical Investigations*. Psychologists (and others with expertise in related practical fields) have discovered his later writings in their efforts to explore nonpictorial approaches to psychological concerns and paradoxes in carving out "psychological philosophy" as a subject of investigation (for example, Chapman and Dixon, 1987; Gergen, 1994; Hyman, 1991; Jost, 1995; Morss, 1992; Shotter, 1991, 1993a and b, 1995; and Stenner, 1993). As van der Merwe and Voestermans (1995) put it, "The present resurgence of interest in Ludwig Wittgenstein is related to the growing concern in the philosophy and methodology of the behavioural sciences with the role played by conceptual frameworks, models and metaphors in the mediation of our experience of the world" (p. 27). Wittgenstein's influence on the varied areas of psychology is growing by leaps and bounds.

Accordingly, it seems to us increasingly important to ask how (and, indeed, whether) he is being understood. Van der Merwe and Voestermans, among others, think he has been rather seriously misunderstood. Wittgenstein's "message" to psychologists, they note, "is to move about around things and events in the world instead of trying to delineate essential features" (1995, p. 38). They are convinced that psychologists have not gotten that message clearly:

> Wittgenstein himself provided an opportunity for escape from what he deemed as the prime task not just of philosophy but of all efforts at understanding, including psychological understanding. He has outlined two main routes. On the one hand, he introduces the notion of language-game. This notion "brings into prominence the fact that the speaking of language is part of an activity or a form of life" (*PI*: §23). On the other hand, he remained preoccupied, one could say, with purifying strategies, that is, with attempts to employ philosophical analysis for clarification of concepts. Along this latter strategic line the language-game approach has become an end in itself without much reference to or participation in the activity or the form of life of which language-use is a part. . . . Psychologists in general have favoured this second route at the expense of really taking up the challenge of what it means "to move around about things," that is to say, to come to grips with the role forms of life actually play. (1995, p. 39)

In an important sense this means going beyond the pragmatic view of language with which Wittgenstein is frequently associated. Surely, words are *used* within society in the manner of tools for results. And certainly Wittgenstein is susceptible to being classified (if classification is your game) as a pragmatist or as an instrumentalist in light of such remarks as "Look at the word or the sentence as an instrument and its meaning as its employment" (*PI*: § 421). Perhaps even more damning is his oft-quoted remark "For a large class of cases—though not for all—in which we employ the word 'meaning' it can be defined thus: The meaning of a word is its use in the language" (*PI*: §43). Moreover, he is frequently classified as a pragmatist by other philosophers. Yet such classification can (and does) obscure Wittgenstein's "form-of-lifeism." For while he uses the notion and language of language-games in various ways, central to his understanding, we believe, are such provocative formulations as the following: "The term 'language-*game*' is meant to bring into prominence the fact that the *speaking* of language is part of an activity, or of a form of life" (*PI*: §23) and "Only in the stream of thought and life do words have meaning" (*Z*: §173).

The common overidentification of *words* and *language-games* derives, we believe, from a deeper and commonplace confusion as to what language-games are. Not surprisingly, given Wittgenstein's antiessentialism and antidefinitionalism, nowhere in his writings does he define precisely what a language-game is. Different language-games, like everything else, simply bear a "family resemblance" to one another. But many psychologists (interested particularly in issues of analytical metapsychology) have taken the meaning–use equation as a pragmatic frame of reference for understanding the language-game as a philosophical/psychological technique for the analysis of mental vocabulary. This is surely one way in which Wittgenstein himself uses the term.

We agree with Baker (1992), however, that the meaning–use equation is not to be identified with understanding. Neither an equation (an identification) nor, indeed, any analysis, *performs* the activity moving "about around things and events" associated with the form of life and theory of meaning. In our opinion, therefore, an understanding of the language-game as a mere pragmatic tool of analysis is a serious misunderstanding. Understanding does not lie in "delineating essential features" of facts in the world (as in Wittgenstein's earlier *Tractatus*). Nor does it entail describing the uses of concepts and language in society. It is, rather, a social activity, a performance, a moving "about around things and events in the world." To understand and change meaning we must be historically active, that is, revolutionarily active, practically–critically active. We must change "the aspect" (the totality of things) by our activity—moving about around things, changing our location—not by means of philosophical or psychological analysis. For, as van der Merwe and Voestermans put it, "Language and naming do not come out of the blue. Both originate in the forms of life to which practice, precisely in its bodily and emotionally structured form, belongs" (1995, p. 42).

Indeed, it is Wittgenstein's form of life along with his form of thought (and not just what he had to say *about* them) which are, in our opinion, critical to the creation of a new, unscientific psychology in general and a new clinical practice/cultural–performatory approach in particular. For while a *pragmatic* understanding of the vocabulary of mental language, in contradistinction to a *pictorial* understanding of mental language, may be of substantial value from the critical deconstructionist and social constructionist metapsychological points of view, we suggest that it is "form of lifeism" which proves most vital in creating a new social psychology (Jost, 1995), a new developmental phenomenology (van der Merwe and Voestermans, 1995), and a new domain of clinical practice (Gergen and Kaye, 1993; Newman and Holzman, 1993).

In the development of the social therapeutic group practice over the past two decades, we have sought to make use of the therapeutic Wittgenstein's practical–critical (unsystematic) form of life, activity-theoretic understanding. In what does this consist? It must first be said that for practical purposes both the pictorial and the pragmatic "metaviews on the vocabulary of mind" must be abandoned. For while the pragmatic view is surely both closer to life and closer to Wittgenstein, it is plainly not close enough. Why? Because like the pictorial view it is, at heart, identity-theoretic; the pictorial, relative to reality so-called; the pragmatic, relative to specific societal uses. The quite particular piece of space–time reality (the fact) named in the pictorial description, and the equally particular societal use (the instrumental tool) named in the pragmatic description, obscure the prominence of relational activity: "The *speaking* of language is part of an activity, or of a form of life."

Both pictorial and pragmatic theories of mental meaning give way to relational activity as the basis for social therapeutic approaches. For only in the activity of life as it is lived, relationally, do words have meaning. To alter the form of life is to alter the meaning of words and discourse. But what of the nagging practical/theoretic concern that this activity-theoretic approach somehow leaves out the "something" in "the mind" (or, in phenomenological terms, "the body") crying out for expression or inclusion? Recall what Vygotsky (1987) has to say about the "relationship" between thought/thinking and language/speaking: "Thought is not expressed but completed in the word."

So it is, we would argue, with all "mental states" or acts, not just thought or thinking. Vygotsky's assertion is, it seems to us, a brilliant and most useful critique of the concept of "expression," the companion-piece to every and any dualistic, identity-based theory of mind, mental vocabulary, and/or mental acts. The move to relational activity requires a full-blown reontologizing away from the stuff of the mind and the stuff outside the mind (a Cartesian mind/body, man/nature dualism) to a self–other unity. Only such an activity-theoretic ontology, it seems to us, can further mix with other elements of life and history to produce the forms of life which, on the one hand, make meaning itself possible and, on the other, make possible—

through the transformation of meaning—the transformation of life and its form. Plainly, this Vygotskian–Wittgensteinian activity-theoretic, relational, radically monistic view of mental language and meaning is a horse of a very different color from the identity-theoretic, dualistic, Cartesian viewpoint.

Performing Diagnostics

We may now be more able to approach the issue of classification and diagnostics in clinical work from a fresh (and less dualistic) point of view. Moreover, a more concrete discussion of how social therapy performs diagnosing can, we hope, inform our "abstract" theoretical formulations.

Perhaps we of a critical persuasion, following Szasz (1961), have been much too easily taken in by the endless (relentlessly humorous, characteristically trivial) critiques of diagnostic descriptions (a form of psychological liberalism) without paying sufficient attention to the diagnostic form(s) of life. For all that he has contributed to our thinking about such matters in the last quarter of a century, perhaps Szasz has actually done us a disservice. By focusing our attention so much on the myth of mental illness he has diverted our critical eye from the myth/hoax of psychology. Perhaps our selves have become "sufficiently saturated" (Gergen, 1991) so that mental illness is painfully real. But psychology, misshaped by its identity-theoretic, antirelational, pseudoscientific paradigm, has become a haven (and a proselytizer) for forms of alienation which are recognizably nondevelopmental. One such traditional therapeutic form of alienation is *diagnosing*, clinical psychology's mode of classification.

The social therapeutic process, as we have said, is a collective moving about around things and events in the world. It is, more particularly, a moving about around emotional things and events in the world: "depression," "anxiety," "three painful days," "I'm angry at you," and so on. How do we move about around them? Surely not by analytically seeking to discover their essences. Definitely not by determining the truth value of judgments in which they are contained. And not even by cognitively uncovering the complex societal uses of such language. We do it by changing the form of relational life. In a word, we collectively and creatively *perform* (not act) our lives without the identity-based presuppositions of the existing alienated form(s) of (our) society. For only as we create new forms of relational life can we understand the existing forms of action. Only as we perform our lives together can we understand our lives as performance.

In social therapy, the (first-person, second-person, or third-person) descriptions uttered by clients and therapists, whether in individual or group sessions, are not treated as referential; that is, they are not related to as true or false judgments but as lines in a play (better still, a poem) that we are at once collectively creating and performing. The social therapist, as performer/director, helps to keep the activity performatory by continually reminding the clients that they are in a play and not in "real life," where their descriptions and/or judgments *are* true or false.

It is not an easy thing to create such an environment. This is despite the fact that, as Vygotsky teaches us, imitation and group performance are critical to growth, development, and cultural adaptation (for example, in how we acquire language) during our earliest years. By the time we reach early adolescence, most of us have learned that the use of our performatory skills, our capacity to be who we are not, to be "a head taller" than we are, to do what we don't know how to do, is inappropriate except in "special" circumstances. Performing is denigrated as "acting out" or, for a few, the expression of an extraordinary gift or talent for "acting." In social therapy, our ordinary childhood ability to perform is reawakened and nurtured.

In such a radically performatory environment, the group members and especially the therapist are not, of course, knowers. This is not merely because they do not know some or even most answers, but because there are no answers to be known. Yet the collective performance can grow and develop. Can we know whether that is happening? No. Nor do we need to know for it to happen. The group plays language-games in all their infinite variety. It performs its own relational life. Indeed, it performs therapy and thereby creates psychology anew and continuously. In such an environment descriptions (or seeming descriptions, if you prefer) are like lines in a play or a poem in that they are, in a most important sense, not about anything at all. Poetic meaning, in many cases, self-consciously derives from the poem itself and not from what it is about. If in a play (perhaps a Sunday matinee) a performer says the words "It is a dark and dreary day," it is unlikely that either other players or audience members will quarrel with her or him on the grounds that it is really seventy-five degrees outside and the sky a perfectly cloudless blue.

In such a moving around about emotional things and events—changing the form of relational life, creating a performatory environment—diagnoses themselves can be harmless and sometimes even valuable. Despite all our facetious observations about the more absurd characterizations in *DSM-IV*, it ain't funny. Why? Because in everyday pictorial, identity-theoretic therapy these descriptions (diagnoses) are frequently used to stigmatize, constrain, and punish those to whom they are applied. We do not change that by using any kind of analysis. We change it only by changing the diagnostic form of alienation: opening up diagnosing to everyone, continuously, although nonreferentially and nonjudgmentally. We can all perform diagnosing together. Not to get it right. Not to give everyone a chance to do it. But to create/perform jointly a zone of relational development (if we may take poetic license with Vygotsky's formulation) in which we can together create new forms of life, new meanings, new lives. For the task of social therapy is to make the fog disappear, the mental mist vanish, to create an environment which does not require neurosis.

Why, after all, must we accept the process of definition as a primary feature of therapy or consultation? Why must we join what is in place? The problem is not diagnosis but "joining what's in place," that is, the diagnostic form of alienation, the definitional form of description, the identificational form of discourse, the analytical form of therapy and emotive dialogue. If "diagnosing" is a problem (and indeed it is), let everyone do it in a radically democratic, performatory environment and it will no longer be a problem. For it is not the diagnosis but the alienated, authoritarian, patriarchal, and private "truth" of such classification that does harm. People performing their emotional lives together includes the client or patient in history at least as much as an authoritarian pseudomedical, pseudoscientific diagnostic description includes her or him in alienated society.

FORMS OF LIFE AND FORMS OF ALIENATION

Scientific psychology is, to put it most broadly, the *commodification of human subjectivity*—cognitive and emotional. Commodification, in general, is the ultimate philosophical particularization of economically overdetermined Western ontology, even as alienation (and transference) is the eventual emergent epistemology necessary to know anything about a commodified world. It is a processless individuated world (object) understood (known) by a lifeless individuated subject.

The modernist paradigm, with the scientific model as its perfect abstraction and high technology as its most pragmatic accomplishment, does not, of course, long remain pristine (if it ever was!) in the context of capitalism's overwhelming political, economic, and ideological takeover. Commodification, well under way even before capitalism's total victory, becomes ubiquitous in the nineteenth century. Scientific psychology is probably the most expensive (to human society) and extensive product of the sickening synthesis of pseudoscience and pseudoeconomics. (Economics, as much a myth and hoax as psychology, also serves to rationalize or interpret human activity rather than to account for it, still less to change it. If its principal owners—the state—did not so completely control the laboratory—the society—in which it is carried out, we believe that, like psychology, it would receive no "scientific" validation whatsoever.)

The scientific argumentation to justify mental states as hidden deep (or not so deep) inside the individual and, therefore, subject to discovery (like molecular structures and amoebas) by various investigatory means is, in and of itself, methodologically weak even by hard science standards. But the cash value of being able to commodify subjective life in capitalist culture is substantial. And so the dirty deeds are done, as we showed in some detail in Part II. The result, scientific psychology, is little more than capitalistic "magic" with pseudomeasurements and pseudolaws playing the contemporary role of incantation and exhortation in what is nothing more than modernist witchdoctory. In the clinical area, the presence of real people and, therefore, real relationships (in contrast, for example, to research psychology, where people are turned into "experimental subjects") makes commodified psychological science (modernist magic) more difficult.

How does clinical psychology deal with this obstacle? The so-called scientific approaches to therapy tend to dehumanize the client by conceptually transforming her or him into either a biophysical chemical repository or a behavioral subject. Insofar as these ontic tricks are not played, silly and obviously unscientific *DSM-IV*–like generalities are utilized for pure cash-value purposes. (They resemble the shockingly simple-minded "laws of history" formulated by Hempel [1965], which, as noted earlier, have no conceivable function except to justify the a priori claim that there are such laws.) The overriding imperative? *It must look like science*. With commodified knowledge bought and sold freely in the late capitalist marketplace, "scientific" or "objective" is the trademark required for foolishness to be construed as knowledge. And so the person coming for help with her or his emotional pain is typically offered (explicitly or subtextually) explanations, truths, interpretations, accountings, objective appraisals, and so on—not because there is much evidence (scientific or otherwise) to suggest that such findings are helpful (hence the rapid resort to drugs), but because only "scientific" responses are commodifiable and, therefore, ontologically/economically comprehensible enough to have cash value.

Alienation, of course, is not a homogeneous property of life in general in capitalist society. It is, rather, manifest as varied and evolving forms of knowing (and known), that is, forms of nonlife, or forms of epistemic alienation. Traditional therapy, in its varied approaches, is merely the name or description given to the alienated interventions of alienated therapists into the emotional lives of their alienated clients in our alienated culture. It all makes "good sense," of course, because alienated forms of life (forms of alienation) are precisely the "sense-making" arrangement of late capitalist culture. Freudianism's momentary popularity within psychology and its long-standing pervasiveness in modified form within the broader culture have little to do with its usefulness or helpfulness and everything to do with how well it transferentially "makes sense" of mental life. It is a marvelous, although as many have argued, utterly useless, story or approach for analyzing fiction(s), both psychoanalytic and literary.

To understand the Wittgensteinian notion of *form of life* as it is practically employed in social therapy in the performatory moving about around the events of the world, it is useful to view it in its paradoxical and dialectical unity with *forms of alienation*. Our "emotional states of mind" in late capitalist culture are thoroughly alienated, individuated, and truth-referential commodifications. The being of them and the understanding of them are, through commodification, inextricably connected, not dialectically, but by fast-drying (calcified) ideological cement. Whereas knowledge of physical truths (also alienated) employs an aboutness that at a minimum captures a scintilla of the "real" relationship between an observer and a distantly observed inanimate star, the crude application of this physicalistic scientific–epistemic model to human-to-human activity fundamentally distorts the particular, self-referential, (paradoxical) relational, activistic dimension of life-as-lived. It is these cemented, truth-referential, alienated, and individuated so-called expressions of so-called inner life (emotional, cognitive, and attitudinal states of mind) that we must move about around in creating a new, socially completed form of emotive relational life.

The performance *of life* is that creatively varied and continuous movement about around the rigid, alienated events (states) of emotional life in our scientifically psychologized culture. Analysis and/or storytelling will not do, because each, in its own way, appeals to a significant other instead of being practically–critically relational. What is needed, instead, is the performatory, relational activity-based practice of method. In philosophically performing (moving practically–critically about around cemented alienated mental events) we dealienate (to the extent possible, given the overall societal environment) our individuated selves and reestablish our social relationality *in practice*, that is, in *revolutionary, practical–critical, socially completed activity*.

We do not negate our alienated consciousness and emotionality; we do not repress it; we do not analyze it or "storify" it out of existence. Rather we revolutionarily engage it; we perform (move) about around it. We thereby rekindle our capacity as social makers of meaning by performing ahead of ourselves—performance, not prediction, after all, being the human "ahead of ourselves" capacity. We collectively create the diagnoses and, indeed, the therapy in its entirety as a new relational, practical-critical, revolutionary psychology which is, in the final (not analysis, but) *practice of method* (of course, there is no finality, merely Vygotskian completion), a continuously developmental (though thoroughly pointless) relational activity.

The therapist's role? To remind group members to be wary of the "alienates" Reality and Truth; to support the continuous organization and reorganization of relational activity; to encourage every manner of performance consistent with radically democratic, noncoercive, and nonabusive group-determined criteria; to persist in urging the *forming of life* as opposed to the passive acceptance of *forms of alienation*. The social therapy group typically begins (week after week) with group members' placing before us the varied forms of alienation (themselves) that is our emotional life in capitalist culture. Then we must begin to move about around them by creating a new meaning, a new world, a new relational activity. This is sometimes called (in the codified and reified language of social therapy talk) "building the group."

Our performance grows, develops, and our disease(s) eventually vanishes. We have collectively drawn our attention to something else. We are performing the revolutionary activity. Next week we will do it again. For unlike the famous tree in the (philosophical) forest which makes a noise when it falls whether someone hears it or not, or the star in the heavens which shines brightly whether we see it or not, our so-called emotional states—alienated forms of life, Wittgenstein teaches us—simply no longer exist when our attention is drawn to something else. Our alienated emotional states, despite all of scientific psychology's efforts (fully supported by the rest of modernist/capitalist ideology), are simply not trees in the forest or stars in the sky; they are not anything like these things. Our psychopathology lies, to a large extent, in relating to them as such. Social therapy is simply the cultural–performatory, practical–critical, revolutionary, philosophical, relational, and developmental activity of "drawing your attention" to something else, of forming a new life not once and for all but continuously, of making the revolution every moment of our relational lives.

Emotional states as emotional states are a form of alienation unlike some other alienated, commodified processes in our culture. The story of science and the story of psychology are very different stories. One is a progressive tale about our species' relationship to nature, the other a dreadfully simplistic and ultimately reactionary and useless narrative which is supposedly about our relationships to each other. Creating new forms of life by performing does not make the alienated states of mind go away. But it radically alters our relationship to them and, thereby, to the world in which they exist. They vanish as truths even as they become more and more recognizable as "alienates," less the states of our mind and more the minds of our omnipresent, ideologically transmitted state. Regaining "mental health" through engaging in such relational activity is, indeed, a political act. For as Lotringer pointed out, "One does not cure neurosis, one changes a society which cannot do without it" (1977, p. 7). In continuously creating new forms of life, in moving about around our alienated mental states, we are trying to do just that.

And what becomes of *self-conscious abstracting*, that most remarkable species development which Jaynes speculates emerged somewhere between the *Iliad* and the *Odyssey* and which, in the shape of philosophy and its epic progeny, has ideologically ruled the world for more than 2500 years? It is liberated in the complex process of our going forward. Philosophy gives way to philosophizing, knowing gives way to activity, and the forming of alienation gives way to the forming of life.

NOTES

1. Vygotsky had no formal training in psychology prior to delivering a major address on the crisis in psychology at the Second Neurological Congress in Lenin-

grad in 1924. By the 1930s his writings were subjected to political/ideological scrutiny and found unacceptable to Stalin's totalitarian bureaucracy. Wittgenstein (with virtually no formal training in philosophy) constantly advised students to steer clear of philosophy and do "something useful." He often spoke of his disdain for academia and periodically spent long periods away from the university.

2. The proliferation of books, articles, and journals devoted to activity-theoretic, cultural–historical, and/or sociocultural approaches influenced by Vygotsky continues exponentially. This listing, in addition to being selective, will, no doubt, be out of date by the time of reading: the collection of essays in Chaiklin and Lave (1993); Daniels (1993); Moll (1990); Wertsch (1985b); and the following texts and articles: Cole (1995); Holzman (1993, 1995); Lave and Wenger (1991); D. Newman, Griffin and Cole (1989); Newman and Holzman, 1993; Rogoff (1990); Tharp and Gallimore (1988); Wertsch (1985a, 1991).

3. The ideas in this section were first put forth at the 103rd Annual Convention of the American Psychological Association in August 1995 in a presentation entitled, "Diagnostics: The Human Cost of the Rage to Order," by Fred Newman and Kenneth Gergen.

4. Some of the earliest thinkers on these matters include Gilbert Ryle, *The Concept of Mind* (1949); G. E. M. Anscombe, *Intention* (1959); Stuart Hampshire, *Thought and Action* (1959); H. L. A. Hart and A. M. Honoré, *Causation in the Law* (1959); William A. Dray, *Laws and Explanation in History* (1957), and most of the books in the series edited by R. F. Holland, *Studies in Philosophical Psychology*, including Anthony Kenny, *Action, Emotion and Will* (1963) and A. I. Melden, *Free Action* (1961).

Bibliography

Albee, G. W. (1981). Politics, power, prevention and social change. In J. M. Joffe and G. W. Albee (Eds.), *Prevention through political action and social change.* Hanover, NH: University Press of New England, pp. 3–24.

Albee, G. W. (1986). Toward a just society: Lessons from observations on the primary prevention of psychopathology. *American Psychologist, 41,* 891–898.

Albee, G. W., Joffe, J. M., and Dusenbury, L. A. (Eds.) (1988). *Prevention, powerlessness and politics: Readings on social change.* Beverly Hills, CA: Sage.

Albino, J.E.N. (1995). Five-year report of the policy and planning board, 1994. *American Psychologist, 50,* 620–632.

American Psychiatric Association (1994). *Diagnostic and statistical manual of mental disorders, 4th ed.* Washington, DC: American Psychiatric Association.

American Psychological Association (1995, July). *APA Monitor, 26,* 7.

Anderson, H. and Goolishian, H. (1993). The client is the expert: A not-knowing approach to therapy. In S. McNamee and K. J. Gergen (Eds.) *Therapy as social construction.* London: Sage, pp. 25–39.

Anscombe, G.E.M. (1959). *Intention.* Oxford: Blackwell.

Ariès, P. (1962). *Centuries of childhood: A social history of family life.* New York: Vintage Books.

Ash, M. G. and Woodward, W. R. (Eds.) (1987). *Psychology in twentieth century thought and society.* Cambridge: Cambridge University Press.

Austin, J. (1962). *How to do things with words.* Oxford: Oxford University Press.

Baker, G. P. (1988). *Wittgenstein, Frege and the Vienna Circle.* Oxford: Blackwell.

Baker, G. P. (1992). Some remarks on "language" and "grammar." *Grazer Philosophische Studien, 42,* 107–131.

Baker, G. P. and Hacker, P.M.S. (1980). *Wittgenstein: Understanding and meaning.* Oxford: Blackwell.

Bakhtin, M. M. (1981). *The dialogic imagination: Four essays by M. M. Bakhtin*. Austin: University of Texas Press.

Bakhurst, D. (1991). *Consciousness and revolution in Soviet philosophy*. Cambridge: Cambridge University Press.

Bakhurst, D. and Sypnowich, C. (Eds.) (1995). *The social self*. London: Sage.

Baritz, L. (1960). *The servants of power: A history of the use of social science in American industry*. Westport, CT: Greenwood Press.

Bearison, D. J. (1991). Interactional contexts of cognitive development: Piagetian approaches to sociogenesis. In L. Tolchinsky Landsmann (Ed.) *Culture, schooling and psychological development*. Norwood, NJ: Ablex, pp. 56–70.

Benjamin, W. (1969). The work of art in the age of mechanical reproduction. In *Illuminations*. New York: Schocken Books, pp. 217–251.

Berger, J. (1966). *The success and failure of Picasso*. Baltimore: Penguin Books.

Billig, M. (1982). *Ideology and social psychology*. Oxford: Blackwell.

Billig, M. (1991). *Ideology and opinions: Studies in rhetorical psychology*. London: Sage.

Bradley, B. S. (1989). *Visions of infancy: A critical introduction to child psychology*. Cambridge: Polity.

Bradley, B. S. (1991). Infancy as paradise. *Human Development, 34*, 35–54.

Brandt, L. W. (1979). Behaviorism—the psychological buttress of late capitalism. In A. R. Buss (Ed.) *Psychology in social context*. New York: Irvington, pp. 77–100.

Brecht, B. (1994). The modern theatre is the epic theatre. In J. Willett (Trans. and Ed.) *Brecht on theatre*. New York: Hill and Wong.

Broughton, J. M. (Ed.) (1987). *Critical theories of psychological development*. New York: Plenum.

Brown, R. E. (1979). *Rockefeller medicine men: Medicine and capitalism in America*. Berkeley: University of California Press.

Bruner, J. S. (1983). *Child's talk: Learning to use language*. New York: W. W. Norton.

Bruner, J. S. (1984). Narrative and paradigmatic modes of thought. Invited address, American Psychological Association, Toronto.

Bruner, J. S. (1985). Vygotsky: A historical and conceptual perspective. In J. V. Wertsch (Ed.) *Culture, communication and cognition: Vygotskian perspectives*. Cambridge: Cambridge University Press, pp. 21–34.

Bruner, J. (1993). Explaining and interpreting: Two ways of using mind. In G. Harman (Ed.) *Conceptions of the human mind: Essays in honor of George Miller*. Hillsdale, NJ: Lawrence Erlbaum.

Bulhan, H. A. (1985). *Frantz Fanon and the psychology of oppression*. New York: Plenum.

Burman, E. (Ed.) (1990). *Feminists and psychological practice*. London: Sage.

Burman, E. (1994). *Deconstructing developmental psychology*. London: Routledge.

Burtt, E. A. (1954). *The metaphysical foundations of modern science*. Garden City, NY: Doubleday Anchor Books.

Buss, A. R. (1975). The emerging field of the sociology of psychological knowledge. *American Psychologist, 30*, 988–1002.

Buss, A. R. (Ed.) (1979). *Psychology in social context*. New York: Irvington.

Buss, D. M. (1995). Evolutionary psychology: A new paradigm for psychological science. *Psychological Inquiry, 6(1)*, 1–30.

Butterfield, H. (1962). *Origins of modern science*. New York: Collier Books.

Cassell, E. J. (1991). *The nature of suffering and the goals of medicine.* New York: Oxford University Press.

Chaiklin, S. and Lave, J. (Eds.) (1993). *Understanding practice: Perspectives on activity and context.* Cambridge: Cambridge University Press.

Chapman, M. and Dixon, R. A. (Eds.) (1987). *Meaning and the growth of understanding: Wittgenstein's significance for developmental psychology.* Berlin: Springer.

Chomsky, N. (1959). A review of B. F. Skinner's *Verbal Behavior. Language, 35,* 1.

Cole, M. (1995). Culture and cognitive development: From cross-cultural research to creating systems of cultural mediation. *Culture and Psychology, 1,* 25–54.

Cole, M., Hood, L., and McDermott, R. P. (1978). *Ecological niche-picking: Ecological validity as an axiom of experimental cognitive psychology.* (Monograph). New York: Rockefeller University, Laboratory of Comparative Human Cognition. [Reprinted in *Practice, 4(1),* 117–129].

Cooper, D. (1970). *The cubist epoch.* London: Phaidon Press.

Cushman, P. (1990). Why the self is empty: Toward a historically situated psychology. *American Psychologist, 45,* 599–611.

Cushman, P. (1991). Ideology obscured: Political uses of the self in Daniel Stern's infant. *American Psychologist, 46,* 206–219.

Cushman, P. (1995). *Constructing the self, constructing America: A cultural history of psychotherapy.* Reading, MA: Addison-Wesley.

Daniels, H. (1993). *Charting the agenda: Educational activity after Vygotsky.* London: Routledge.

Danziger, K. (1979). The social origins of modern psychology. In A. R. Buss (Ed.). *Psychology in social context.* New York: Irvington, pp. 27–46.

Danziger, K. (1987). Social context and investigative practice in early twentieth century psychology. In M. G. Ash and W. R. Woodward (Eds.) *Psychology in twentieth century thought and society.* Cambridge: Cambridge University Press, pp. 13–34.

Danziger, K. (1994). *Constructing the subject: Historical origins of psychological research.* Cambridge: Cambridge University Press.

Davidson, D. (1980). Actions, reasons and causes. In D. Davidson, *Essays on actions and events.* Oxford: Oxford University Press, pp. 3–19.

Davis, H. and Taylor, T. (1990). *Redefining linguistics.* London: Routledge.

Davydov, V. V. and Radzikhovskii, L. A. (1985). Vygotsky's theory and the activity-oriented approach in psychology. In J. V. Wertsch (Ed.) *Culture, communication and cognition: Vygotskian perspectives.* Cambridge: Cambridge University Press, pp. 35–65.

Dawes, R. M. (1994). *House of cards: Psychology and psychotherapy built on myth.* New York: The Free Press.

DeBerry, S. T. (1991). *The externalization of consciousness and the psychopathology of everyday life.* Westport, CT: Greenwood Press.

Deleuze, G. and Guattari, F. (1977). *Anti-Oedipus: Capitalism and schizophrenia.* New York: Viking Press.

Dore, J. (1985). Holophrases revisited, dialogically. In M. Barrett (Ed.) *Children's single word speech.* London: Wiley.

Dray, W. (1957). *Laws and explanation in history.* Oxford: Oxford University Press.

Duranti, A. and Goodwin, C. (Eds.) (1992). *Rethinking context: Language as an interactive phenomenon.* Cambridge: Cambridge University Press.

Ewen, S. (1976). *Captains of consciousness: Advertising and the social roots of the consumer culture.* New York: McGraw-Hill.

Fann, K. T. (1971). *Wittgenstein's conception of philosophy.* Berkeley: University of California Press.

Fanon, F. (1963). *The wretched of the earth.* New York: Grove Press.

Fanon, F. (1967). *Black skin, white masks.* New York: Grove Press.

Faulconer, J. E. and Williams, R. N. (Eds.) (1990). *Reconsidering psychology: Perspectives from continental philosophy.* Pittsburgh: Duquesne University Press.

Feinstein, A. R. (1967). *Clinical judgment.* Baltimore: Williams & Wilkins.

Feyerabend, P. (1978). *Against method: Outline of an anarchistic theory of knowledge.* London: Verso.

Foucault, M. (1965). *Madness and civilization: A history of insanity in the age of reason.* New York: Pantheon.

Foucault, M. (1975). *The birth of the clinic: An archaeology of medical perception.* New York: Vintage Books.

Fowler, R. D. (1995). 1994 report of the chief executive officer: The winds of change. *American Psychologist, 50,* 600–611.

Freedheim, D. D. (Ed.) (1992). *The history of psychotherapy: A century of change.* Washington, DC: American Psychological Association.

Friedman, D. (1990). The Soviet Union in the 1920s: An historical laboratory. *Practice, The Magazine of Psychology and Political Economy, 7,* 5–9.

Fry, S. L. (1991). A conversation with Edward L. Bernays, Fellow, PRSA. *Public Relations Journal,* 31–33.

Fukuyama, F. (1989). The end of history? *The National Interest, 16,* 3–18.

Fulani, L. (Ed.) (1988). *The psychopathology of everyday racism and sexism.* New York: Harrington Park Press.

Furumoto. L. (1987). On the margins: Women and the professionalization of psychology in the United States, 1890–1940. In M. G. Ash and W. R. Woodward (Eds.) *Psychology in twentieth century thought and society.* Cambridge: Cambridge University Press, pp. 93–114.

Garfinkel, H. (1967). *Studies in ethnomethodology.* New York: Prentice-Hall.

Gergen, K. J. (1982). *Toward transformation in social knowledge.* London: Sage.

Gergen, K. J. (1991). *The saturated self: Dilemmas of identity in contemporary life.* New York: Basic Books.

Gergen, K. J. (1994). *Realities and relationships: Soundings in social construction.* Cambridge, MA: Harvard University Press.

Gergen, K. J. (1995). Social construction and the transformation of identity politics. Presented at the New School for Social Research, New York City.

Gergen, K. J. and Kaye, J. (1993). Beyond narrative in the negotiation of therapeutic meaning. In S. McNamee and K. J. Gergen (Eds.) *Therapy as social construction.* London: Sage, pp. 166–187.

Gergen, M. M. (Ed.) (1988). *Feminist structure of knowledge.* New York: New York University Press.

Gergen, M. M. (1995). Postmodern, post-Cartesian positionings on the subject of psychology. *Theory and Psychology, 5(3),* 361–368.

Gilgen, A. R. (1982). *American psychology since W.W.II: A profile of the discipline.* Westport, CT: Greenwood.

Gilligan, C. (1982). *In a different voice: Psychological theory and women's development.* Cambridge, MA: Harvard University Press.

Gödel, K. (1962). *On formally undecidable propositions of Principia Mathematica and related systems.* London: Oliver and Boyd.

Goffman, E. (1961). *Asylums.* Chicago: Aldine.

Golding, J. (1968). *Cubism: A history and an analysis.* London: Faber and Faber.

Golub, E. S. (1994). *The limits of medicine: How science shapes our hope for the cure.* New York: Times Books.

Greer, C. (1972). *The great school legend: A revisionist interpretation of American public education.* New York: Basic Books.

Gross, P. R. and Levitt, N. (1994). *Higher superstition: The academic left and its quarrels with science.* Baltimore: Johns Hopkins University Press.

Gruber, H. E. and Voneche, J. J. (1977). *The essential Piaget.* New York: Basic Books.

Hampshire, S. (1959). *Thought and action.* London: Chatto and Windus.

Harding, S. (1986). *The science question in feminism.* Ithaca, NY: Cornell University Press.

Harding, S. (Ed.) (1987). *Feminism and methodology.* Milton Keynes: Open University.

Harding, S. and Hintikka, M. B. (Eds.) (1983). *Discovering reality: Feminist perspectives on epistemology, metaphysics, methodology and philosophy of science.* Dordrecht, Holland: D. Reidel.

Hare-Mustin, R. T. and Marecek, J. (Eds.) (1990). *Making a difference: Psychology and the construction of gender.* New Haven, CT: Yale University Press.

Harré, R. and Gillett, G. (1994). *The discursive mind.* London: Sage.

Hart, H.L.A. and Honoré, A. M. (1959). *Causation in the law.* Oxford: Clarendon Press.

Hempel, C. (1965). *Aspects of scientific explanation and other essays in the philosophy of science.* New York: The Free Press.

Henriques, J., Holloway, W., Urwin, C., Venn, C., and Walkerdine, V. (1984). *Changing the subject.* London: Methuen.

Herman, E. (1995). *The romance of American psychology: Political culture in the age of experts.* Berkeley: University of California Press.

Herrnstein, R. J. and Murray, C. (1994). *The bell curve: The reshaping of American life by differences in intelligence.* New York: The Free Press.

Hilgard, E. R. (Ed.) (1978). *American psychology in historical perspective: Addresses of the APA, 1892–1977.* Washington, DC: American Psychological Association.

Hoffman, L. (1993). A reflexive stance for family therapy. In S. McNamee and K. J. Gergen (Eds.) *Therapy as social construction.* London: Sage, pp. 7–24.

Holzman, L. (1993) Notes from the laboratory: A work-in-progress report from the Barbara Taylor School. *Practice, the Magazine of Psychology and Political Economy, 9(1),* 25–37.

Holzman, L. (1995). Creating developmental learning environments: A Vygotskian practice. *School Psychology International, 16,* 199–212.

Holzman, L. (1996). Newman's practice of method completes Vygotsky. In I. Parker and R. Spears (Eds.) *Psychology and society: Radical theory and practice.* London: Pluto. pp. 128–138.

Holzman, L. and Newman, F. (1979). *The practice of method: An introduction to the foundations of social therapy.* New York: New York Institute for Social Therapy and Research.

Holzman, L. and Newman, F. (1987). Language and thought about history. In M. Hickmann (Ed.) *Social and functional approaches to language and thought.* London: Academic Press, pp. 109–121.

Holzman, L. and Polk, H. (Eds.) (1988). *History is the cure: A social therapy reader.* New York: Practice Press.

Hood, L., McDermott, R. P. and Cole, M. (1980). "Let's try to make it a good day"—Some not so simple ways. *Discourse Processes, 3,* 155–168.

Hunt, M. (1993). *The story of psychology.* New York: Doubleday.

Hyman, J. (Ed.) (1991). *Investigating psychology: Sciences of the mind after Wittgenstein.* London: Routledge.

Ingleby, D. (Ed.) (1980a). *Critical psychiatry: The politics of mental health.* New York: Pantheon Books.

Ingleby, D. (1980b). Understanding mental illness. In D. Ingleby (Ed.) *Critical psychiatry: The politics of mental health.* New York: Pantheon Books, pp. 23–71.

Janik, A., and Toulmin, S. (1973). *Wittgenstein's Vienna.* New York: Simon and Schuster.

Jaynes, J. (1976). *The origin of consciousness in the breakdown of the bicameral mind.* Boston: Houghton Mifflin.

Joravsky, D. (1989). *Russian psychology: A critical history.* Oxford: Blackwell.

Jost, J. T. (1995). Toward a Wittgensteinian social psychology of human development. *Theory & Psychology, 5(1),* 5–25.

Kamin, L. J. (1974). *The science and politics of I.Q.* Potomac, MD: Lawrence Erlbaum.

Kant, I. (1965). *Critique of Pure Reason.* New York: St. Martin's Press.

Kaye, K. (1982). *The mental and social life of babies.* Chicago: University of Chicago Press.

Keller, E. F. (1985). *Reflections on gender and science.* New Haven, CT: Yale University Press.

Keller, E. F. and Grontkowski, C. R. (1983). The mind's eye. In S. Harding and M. B. Hintikka (Eds.) *Discovering reality: Feminist perspectives on epistemology, metaphysics, methodology and philosophy of science.* Dordrecht, Holland: D. Reidel, pp. 207–224.

Kenny, A. J. P. (1963). *Action, emotion and will.* London: Routledge and Kegan Paul.

Koch, S. (Ed.) (1959). *Psychology: A study of a science.* New York: McGraw-Hill.

Koch, S. and Leary, D. E. (Eds.) (1992). *A century of psychology as science.* Washington, DC: American Psychological Association.

Kovel, J. (1980). The American mental health industry. In D. Ingleby (Ed.) *Critical psychiatry: The politics of mental health.* New York: Pantheon Books, pp. 72–101.

Kozulin, A. (1986). Vygotsky in context. In L. S. Vygotsky, *Thought and language.* Cambridge, MA: MIT Press, pp. xi–xvi.

Kozulin, A. (1990). *Vygotsky's psychology: A biography of ideas.* Cambridge, MA: Harvard University Press.

Kuhn, T. (1962). *The structure of scientific revolutions.* Chicago: University of Chicago Press.

Kvale, S. (Ed.) (1992). *Psychology and postmodernism*. London: Sage.

Lave, J. and Wenger, E. (1991). *Situated learning: Legitimate peripheral participation*. Cambridge: Cambridge University Press.

Lawler, J. (1978). *IQ, heritability and racism*. New York: International.

Lerner, E. (1991). *The big bang never happened*. New York: Times Books.

Levitan, K. (1982). *One is not born a personality: Profiles of Soviet education psychologists*. Moscow: Progress.

Lotringer, S. (1977). Libido unbound: The politics of "schizophrenia." *semiotexte, 2(3)*, 5–10.

Lovejoy, A. O. (1960). *The revolt against dualism: An inquiry concerning the existence of ideas*. 2nd ed. LaSalle, IL: Open Court.

Magaro, P., Gripp, R., and McDowell, D. J. (1978). *The mental health industry: A cultural phenomenon*. New York: John Wiley & Sons.

Marx, K. (1973). Theses on Feuerbach. In K. Marx and F. Engels, *The German ideology*. New York: International, pp. 121–123.

Marx, K. and Engels, F. (1973). *The German ideology*. New York: International.

McNamee, S. (1993). Reconstructing identity: The communal construction of crisis. In S. McNamee and K. J. Gergen (Eds.) *Therapy as social construction*. London: Sage, pp. 186–199.

McNamee, S. and Gergen, K. J. (Eds.) (1993). *Therapy as social constuction*. London: Sage.

Melden, A. I. (1961). *Free action*. London: Routledge and Kegan Paul.

Moll, L. C. (Ed.) (1990). *Vygotsky and education: Instructional implications and applications of sociocultural psychology*. Cambridge: Cambridge University Press.

Monk, R. (1990). *Ludwig Wittgenstein: The duty of genius*. New York: Penguin.

Morawski, J. G. (Ed.) (1988). *The rise of experimentation in American psychology*. New Haven, CT: Yale University Press.

Morss, J. (1990). *The biologising of childhood: Developmental psychology and the Darwinian myth*. East Sussex: Lawrence Erlbaum Associates.

Morss, J. (1992). Making waves: Deconstruction and developmental psychology. *Theory and Psychology, 2(4)*, 445–465.

Morss, J. (1993). Spirited away: A consideration of the anti-developmental Zeitgeist. *Practice, the Magazine of Psychology and Political Economy, 9(2)*, 22–28.

Morss, J. (1995). *Going critical: Alternatives to developmental psychology*. London: Routledge.

Muhlhäuser, P. and Harré, R. (1990). *Pronouns and people: The linguistic construction of social and personal identity*. Oxford: Blackwell.

Napoli, D. S. (1981). *Architects of adjustment: The history of the psychological profession in the United States*. Port Washington, NY: Kennikat Press.

Newman, D., Griffin, P. and Cole, M. (1989). *The construction zone: Working for cognitive change in school*. Cambridge: Cambridge University Press.

Newman, F. (1965). Two analyses of prediction. *Theorie*.

Newman, F. (1978). *Practical–critical activities*. New York: Institute for Social Therapy and Research. Reprinted in *Practice, the Journal of Politics, Economics, Psychology, Sociology and Culture, 1983, 1(2–3)*, 52–101.

Newman, F. (1983). Talkin' transference. *Practice, The Journal of Politics, Economics, Psychology, Sociology and Culture, 1(1)*. Reprinted in F. Newman (1991a), *The myth of psychology*. New York: Castillo International, pp. 16–44.

Newman, F. (1991a). *The myth of psychology*. New York: Castillo International.

Newman, F. (1991b). The myth of addiction. In F. Newman, *The myth of psychology*. New York: Castillo International, pp. 111–139.

Newman, F. (1994). *Let's develop! A guide to continuous personal growth*. New York: Castillo International.

Newman, F. (1996). *Performance of a lifetime: A practical–philosophical guide to the joyous life*. New York: Castillo International.

Newman, F. and Holzman, L. (1993). *Lev Vygotsky: Revolutionary scientist*. London: Routledge.

Parker, I. (1989). *The crisis in modern social psychology and how to end it*. London: Routledge.

Parker, I. (1992). *Discourse dynamics*. London: Routledge.

Parker, I. and Shotter, J. (1990). *Deconstructing social psychology*. London: Routledge.

Peterman, J. F. (1992). *Philosophy as therapy: An interpretation and defense of Wittgenstein's later philosophical project*. Albany: SUNY Press.

Phillips-Griffiths, A. (Ed.) (1991). *Wittgenstein: Centenary essays*. Cambridge: Cambridge University Press.

Piaget, J. (1955). *The language and thought of the child*. London: Kegan Paul.

Polkinghorne, D. (1983). *Methodology for the human sciences: Systems of inquiry*. Albany: SUNY Press.

Poster, M. (1978). *Critical theory of the family*. New York: Seabury.

Prilleltensky, I. (1994). *The morals and politics of psychology: Psychological discourse and the status quo*. Albany: SUNY Press.

Quine, W.V.O. (1963). *From a logical point of view*. New York: Harper & Row.

Rivlin, L. G. and Wolfe, M. (1985). *Institutional settings in children's lives*. New York: John Wiley & Sons.

Rogoff, B. (1990). *Apprenticeship in thinking: Cognitive development in social context*. New York: Oxford University Press.

Rogoff, B. and Lave, J. (Eds.) (1984). *Everyday cognition: Its development in social contexts*. Cambridge, MA: Harvard University Press.

Rorty, R. (1982). *Consequences of pragmatism*. Minneapolis: University of Minnesota Press.

Rose, N. (1990). *Governing the soul: The shaping of the private self*. London: Routledge.

Rothstein, S. W. (1994). *Schooling the poor: A social inquiry into the American educational experience*. Westport, CT: Bergin & Garvey.

Ryle, G. (1949). *The concept of mind*. New York: Barnes and Noble.

Samelson, F. (1979). Putting psychology on the map: Ideology and intelligence testing. In A. R. Buss (Ed.) *Psychology in social context*. New York: Irvington, pp. 103–168.

Sampson, E. E. (1991). The democratization of psychology. *Theory and Psychology*, *1*, 275–298.

Sampson, E. E. (1993). *Celebrating the other: A dialogic account of human nature*. Boulder, CO: Westview Press.

Santayana, G. (1911). The genteel tradition in American philosophy. *University of California Chronicle, XII*, 4. Reprinted in D. L. Wilson (Ed.) (1967) *The genteel tradition: Nine essays by George Santayana*. Cambridge, MA: Harvard University Press, pp. 37–64.

Sarason, S. B. (1981). *Psychology misdirected*. New York: The Free Press.

Schacht, T. E. (1985). DSM-III and the politics of truth. *American Psychologist, 40*, 513–521.

Schwartz, P. W. (1971). *The cubists*. London: Thames and Hudson.

Scriven, M. (1959). Truisms as the grounds for historical explanation. In Gardiner (Ed.) *Theories of History*. Glencoe, IL: The Free Press.

Searle, J. R. (1969). *Speech acts: An essay in the philosophy of language*. Cambridge: Cambridge University Press.

Searle, J. R. (1992). *The rediscovery of mind*. Cambridge, MA: The MIT Press.

Shotter, J. (1990). *Knowing of the third kind*. Utrecht: ISOR.

Shotter, J. (1991). Wittgenstein and psychology: On our "hook up" to reality. In A. Phillips-Griffiths (Ed.) *Wittgenstein: Centenary essays*. Cambridge: Cambridge University Press, pp.193–208.

Shotter, J. (1993a). *Conversational realities: Studies in social constructionism*. London: Sage.

Shotter, J. (1993b). *Cultural politics of everyday life: Social constructionism, rhetoric and knowing of the third kind*. Toronto: University of Toronto Press.

Shotter, J. (1995) In conversation: Joint action, shared intentionality and ethics. *Theory and Psychology, 5(1)*, 49–73.

Shotter, J. and Gergen, K. J. (Eds.) (1989). *Texts of identity*. London: Sage.

Shotter, J. and Newman, F. (1995). Understanding practice in practice (rather than in theory). Presented at the East Side Institute for Short Term Psychotherapy, New York. [manuscript available]

Sinha, D. (1986). *Psychology in a third world country: The Indian experience*. Beverly Hills, CA: Sage.

Skinner, B. F. (1957). *Verbal behavior*. New York: Appleton-Century-Crofts.

Soldz, S. (1988). The deficiencies of deficiency theories: A critique of ideology in contemporary psychology. *Practice, the Magazine of Psychology and Political Economy, 6(1)*, 50–63.

Stenner, P. (1993). Wittgenstein and the textuality of emotional experience. *Practice, the Magazine of Psychology and Political Economy, 9(2)*, 29–35.

Stern, D. N. (1985). *The interpersonal world of the infant*. New York: Basic Books.

Stern, D. N. (1990). *Diary of a baby*. New York: Basic Books.

Strawson, P. F. (1964). *Individuals*. London: Routledge.

Suvin, D. (1972). The mirror and the dynamo. In E. Munk (Ed.) *Brecht*. New York: Bantam Books.

Szasz, T. (1961). *The myth of mental illness: Foundations of a theory of personal conduct*. New York: Harper & Row.

Tharp, R. G. and Gallimore, R. (1988). *Rousing minds to life: Teaching, learning and schooling in social context*. Cambridge: Cambridge University Press.

Timpanaro, S. (1976). *The Freudian slip: Psychoanalysis and textual criticism*. London: Verso.

Tolman, C. W. and Maiers, W. (1991). *Critical psychology: Contributions to an historical science of the subject*. Cambridge: Cambridge University Press.

Torrey, E. F. (1992). *Freudian fraud*. New York: HarperCollins.

Trevarthen, C. and Hubley, P. (1978). Secondary intersubjectivity: Confidence, confiding and acts of meaning in the first year. In A. Lock (Ed.) *Action, gesture and symbol: The emergence of language.* New York: Academic Press, pp. 183–229.

Tuana, N. (1992). *Woman and the history of philosophy.* New York: Paragon House.

Turkle, S. (1980). French anti-psychiatry. In D. Ingleby (Ed.) *Critical psychiatry: The politics of mental health.* New York: Pantheon Books, pp. 150–183.

Ussher, J. and Nicholson, P. (Eds.) (1992). *Gender issues in clinical psychology.* London: Routledge.

van der Merwe, W. L. and Voestermans, P. P. (1995). Wittgenstein's legacy and the challenge to psychology. *Theory & Psychology, 5(1)* 27–48.

van der Veer, R. and Valsiner, J. (1991). *Understanding Vygotsky: A quest for synthesis.* Oxford: Blackwell.

Venn, C. (1984). The subject of psychology. In J. Henriques, W. Holloway, C. Urwin, C. Vensn, and V. Walkerdine (Eds.) *Changing the subject: Psychology, social regulation and subjectivity.* London: Methuen, pp. 119–152.

Vygotsky, L. S. (1978). *Mind in society.* Cambridge, MA: Harvard University Press.

Vygotsky, L. S. (1982). The historical meaning of the crisis in psychology. In A. R. Luria and M. G. Iaroshevski (Eds.) *L. S. Vygotsky: Collected works.* Vol. 1. Moscow: Pedagogika. [In Russian.]

Vygotsky, L. S. (1987). *The collected works of L. S. Vygotsky,* Vol. 1. New York: Plenum.

Vygotsky, L. S. (1993). *The collected works of L. S. Vygotsky,* Vol. 2. New York: Plenum.

Walkerdine, V. (1984). Developmental psychology and the child-centered pedagogy: The insertion of Piaget into early education. In J. Henriques, W. Holloway, C. Urwin, C. Venn, and V. Walkerdine (Eds.), *Changing the subject: Psychology, social regulation and subjectivity.* London: Methuen, pp. 153–202.

Walkerdine, V. (1988). *The mastery of reason.* London: Routledge.

Wertsch, J. V. (1985a). *Vygotsky and the social formation of mind.* Cambridge, MA: Harvard University Press.

Wertsch, J. V. (Ed.) (1985b). *Culture, communication and cognition: Vygotskian perspectives.* Cambridge: Cambridge University Press.

Wertsch, J. V. (1991). *Voices of the mind: A sociocultural approach to mediated action.* Cambridge, MA: Harvard University Press.

Wilkinson, S. and Kitzinger, C. (Eds.) (1993). *Heterosexuality: A feminism and psychology reader.* London: Sage.

Winch, P. (1958). *The idea of a social science.* New York: Routledge and Kegan Paul.

Wittgenstein, L. (1953). *Philosophical investigations.* Oxford: Blackwell.

Wittgenstein, L. (1961). *Tractatus logico-philosophicus.* London: Routledge.

Wittgenstein, L. (1965). *The blue and brown books.* New York: Harper Torchbooks.

Wittgenstein, L. (1967). *Zettel.* Oxford: Blackwell.

Wittgenstein, L. (1971). Remarks on Frazer's *Golden Bough. The Human World, 3,* 28–41.

Wittgenstein, L. (1974). *Philosophical grammar.* Oxford: Blackwell.

Wittgenstein, L. (1975). *Philosophical remarks.* Oxford: Blackwell.

Wittgenstein, L. (1980). *Remarks on the philosophy of psychology,* Vol. I. Oxford: Blackwell.

Zelizer, V. A. (1985). *Pricing the priceless child: The changing value of children.* New York: Basic Books.

Index

NATIONAL UNIVERSITY
LIBRARY LOS ANGELES

About the Authors

FRED NEWMAN received his Ph.D. in analytic philosophy and philosophy of science from Stanford University in 1963. He has been a practicing psychotherapist for twenty-five years and a playwright and theater director for the last ten. Dr. Newman is currently director of training at the East Side Institute for Short Term Psychotherapy and artistic director of the Castillo Theater, both in New York City. He also has a private practice. His most recent writings in psychology include *Lev Vygotsky: Revolutionary Scientist* (coauthored with Lois Holzman), *Let's Develop! A Guide to Continuous Personal Growth*, and *Performance of a Lifetime: A Practical–Philosophical Guide to the Joyous Life*. His playwriting credits include *Outing Wittgenstein, Lenin's Breakdown*, and *Billie and Malcolm (A Demonstration)*, which was nominated for five AUDELCO Awards for excellence in Black theater in 1993.

LOIS HOLZMAN received her Ph.D. in developmental psychology from Columbia University in 1977. She has worked as researcher and program consultant for child, youth, and higher education projects for the Community Literacy Research Project, Eureka University of Moscow, and various U.S. universities. Dr. Holzman is currently an associate professor at Empire State College, State University of New York; director of the experimental Vygotskian elementary school, the Barbara Taylor School; and on the faculty of the East Side Institute for Short Term Psychotherapy, all in New York City. She is the author (with Fred Newman) of *Lev Vygotsky: Revolutionary Scientist* and the forthcoming *Schooling for Development: Some Postmodern Possibilities*.